MW00794865

Praise for *The Art of Principled Entrepreneurship*

"In *The Art of Principled Entrepreneurship*, Andreas Widmer shows how business creators benefit society. Successful organizations create immense value by improving our lives. I always say we should measure success by how much you do to benefit others. Doing well by doing good is the right path. Professor Widmer's book can inspire, motivate, and educate future entrepreneurs. And it will help veteran business creators recall why they chose their journey in the first place."

—Armando Christian Pérez (Pitbull)

"Many people today argue that in business, we have to choose: creative expression, good values, or strong profits. This is a false choice, as Andreas Widmer shows masterfully in *The Art of Principled Entrepreneurship*. We can and should aspire to all three. This is the most encouraging business book I have read in years."

—Arthur C. Brooks, Professor, Harvard Kennedy School and Harvard Business School, and *New York Times* Bestselling Author

"*The Art of Principled Entrepreneurship* is a practical guide for how to do well by doing good. Through inspiring stories and actionable advice, Widmer shows how the principles of human progress provide a compass for business leaders looking to build a company that succeeds by helping people improve their lives. He illuminates an insight that must guide personal and business success: mutual benefit. If profit is generated by Principled Entrepreneurship—by creating value for others—then your success is in harmony with the success of your customers, employees, suppliers, communities, and society at large."

—Charles Koch, Chairman and CEO, Koch Industries

"This is a great book about becoming and being a Principled Entrepreneur, but it's so much more. It's about creating a movement, having a positive impact on people's lives, and creating long-term value for customers. If you want to create a great company and a great team, then *The Art of Principled Entrepreneurship* is your recipe book."

—Dina Dwyer-Owens, Franchise Business Leader, Author, and Motivational Speaker

The Art of
Principled
Entrepreneurship

Also by Andreas Widmer

The Pope and the CEO

The Art of
Principled
Entrepreneurship

Creating Enduring Value

ANDREAS WIDMER

Matt Holt Books
An Imprint of BenBella Books, Inc.
Dallas, TX

This book is designed to provide accurate and authoritative information about entrepreneurship. Neither the author nor the publisher is engaged in rendering legal, accounting, or other professional services by publishing this book. If any such assistance is required, the services of a qualified financial professional should be sought. The author and publisher will not be responsible for any liability, loss, or risk incurred as a result of the use and application of any information contained in this book.

The Art of Principled Entrepreneurship copyright © 2022 by Andreas Widmer

All rights reserved. No part of this book may be used or reproduced in any manner whatsoever without written permission of the publisher, except in the case of brief quotations embodied in critical articles or reviews.

BenBella Books, Inc.
10440 N. Central Expressway
Suite 800
Dallas, TX 75231
benbellabooks.com
Send feedback to feedback@benbellabooks.com

BenBella and *Matt Holt* are federally registered trademarks.

Printed in the United States of America
10 9 8 7 6 5 4 3 2 1

Library of Congress Control Number: 2021050582
ISBN 9781637740699
eISBN 9781637740705

Editing by Katie Dickman
Copyediting by Michael Fedison
Proofreading by Denise Pangia and Greg Teague
Indexing by Debra Bowman
Text design and composition by Aaron Edmiston
Cover design by Brigid Pearson
Cover image © Shutterstock / art_of_sun
Printed by Lake Book Manufacturing

Special discounts for bulk sales are available.
Please contact bulkorders@benbellabooks.com.

For Carlyse & Art

Contents

Principled Entrepreneurship: A Definition. xi

1 A Model for Principled Entrepreneurship:
  Meet Art Ciocca 1
2 Principled Entrepreneurship and the
  Story of the American Dream 17
3 Pillar 1: The Economy Exists for People,
  Not People for the Economy. 33
4 Pillar 2: To Work Is to Create;
  To Create Is to Be Human 57
5 Pillar 3: Culture Eats Strategy for Breakfast. 95
6 Pillar 4: Principled Entrepreneurs Always
  Seek to Create Win-Win Solutions 119
7 Pillar 5: Always Think Like an Entrepreneur. 145
8 Inspiring and Motivating the Next Generation 163
9 Start Today!. 187

Acknowledgments. 193
Recommended Reading. 195
Endnotes. 203
Bibliography 225
Index. 235

Principled Entrepreneurship: A Definition

Principled Entrepreneurship™ maximizes the long-term profitability of the business by creating superior value for customers while consuming fewer resources and always acting lawfully and with integrity.[1]

Principled Entrepreneurship had its origins in the 1960s, when Charles Koch first began instilling it in his approach to business. Over the years, the idea was formalized and eventually included as part of a larger Koch Industries managerial philosophy—one of the Market-Based Management (MBM) Guiding Principles. Charles trademarked the term and described Principled Entrepreneurship as continuously improving your ability to create value for others in "a philosophy of mutual benefit."[2] He encouraged its practitioners to "demonstrate to people of all backgrounds and perspectives that this philosophy will improve people's lives. Attract, motivate and empower as many people as possible to become social-change entrepreneurs dedicated to advancing a society of mutual benefit."[3]

I had the opportunity to meet Charles several times and to bring him to The Catholic University of America's campus to interview him about MBM and Principled Entrepreneurship in front of students. I believe his vision of Principled Entrepreneurship is aligned with the principles articulated, but only narrowly practiced, in the founding of the United States of America. It is a vision of an entrepreneurial, values-based society that flourishes and prospers through mutually beneficial commerce.

In that spirit of entrepreneurship, I humbly offer this contribution to further explore the idea of Principled Entrepreneurship and its potential to truly serve the pursuit of happiness and fulfillment in the United States and throughout the world.

A Model for Principled Entrepreneurship: Meet Art Ciocca

"He's the CEO you never heard of but should have!" my friend Bob Allard told me. "He changed an entire industry—you know all his products, but you do not know him. That's because he does what business leaders should do: He focuses on creating a great team and enabling them to create great products for their customers."

Bob introduced me to Art Ciocca over dinner. Art is a very proper looking, slim, and well-groomed gentleman of average height (though, because I'm 6'9", I'm not a good judge of height). It was the spark in his eyes that stuck out to me. They gave him a kind of a cat-that-ate-the-canary look. Not mischievous, but expectant and excited.

We hit it off immediately. He asked me all sorts of questions. I told him about my background and the various companies of which I've been a part, and that I am originally from Switzerland and started my career in the Swiss Guards. It took a while until I could ask my own questions of him. But when I did, he told me that he, too, had started in the military—the Navy—and how as a midshipman in college he had sailed into San Francisco Bay, standing on the deck of an aircraft carrier as they passed under the Golden Gate Bridge. He was immediately struck with the beauty of the city, finding it to be an "open frontier," which, in the words of his grandfather, meant anything was possible.

A stint as an entry-level salesperson at General Foods gave him the opportunity to move from New York to San Francisco, where he eventually changed jobs and worked for the Gallo Wine Company. Shortly after that, he was hired by the Coca-Cola Bottling Company of New York to run one of their newly acquired wine companies—Franzia. I must confess that I had not heard of his company when we first met. Its unremarkable name, "The Wine Group," didn't ring a bell. Art didn't linger on his company, though. Instead, he told me about his endeavors and his ups and downs in the business world. He told me the story of how he had bought the company with a very risky leveraged management buyout from Coke New York in the early '80s and how the situation had been touch-and-go for quite a while after that. Neither he nor his partners had many assets other than their homes, so they had put their entire livelihood on the line to buy this company, and faced miserable failure more than a couple of times. Early on, they had a debt-to-asset ratio of 26 to 1. If those were betting odds, the company would have had a 96 percent chance of failure.

But against the odds, Art and his team went on to help reshape the California wine industry during its formative years. They played a critical role in introducing Americans to wine and worked to develop strong brands with a loyal consumer following. The Franzia 5-liter WineTap, a boxed wine, went on to become the number one selling wine in the US with sales logging approximately one out of every seven glasses of wine consumed in the country.

And they did all that with a team that both managed and eventually owned the company. There was no infighting. No blowups. No politics. Just a great company that was fun to work for. Art talked about the company as a venue to pursue excellence. He wanted to create products that customers valued. And he wanted the team—everyone involved at The Wine Group—to be the company's competitive advantage. What Art practiced, I figured out later, is the art of Principled Entrepreneurship.

As he told me his story, he spoke as if it were someone else who'd achieved all these great feats. He hardly ever said "I" when he spoke of how his company became the second-largest wine producer in the world. He always said "we." You see, to Art Ciocca, his work is not only about himself. His work is about his team creating value for his customers. Success depends on happy customers and excellent employees. That's why you've never heard of Art Ciocca, but it is also the reason why you should get to know him.

I found Art's story compelling in part because of my own experience as an entrepreneur. We both had the privilege to live the American Dream even though we took a very different path to it.

I came to the US at the age of twenty-two after my stint in the Swiss Guards. I was accepted to college on scholarship without speaking proper English, then eventually worked as an unpaid intern in an early internet startup without knowing the first thing about computer software. I felt the swell of the internet bubble and witnessed the pop. I made and lost millions of dollars in business and experienced firsthand the ups and downs, the good and the bad of the business world. Through a process of soul searching, study, and analysis, I reconciled myself with the market economy. Although it has lots of room for improvement—primarily among its participants—I found it to be the system that best supports human flourishing and freedom. It's the system that to me represents the highest achievement of Western civilization: a system of personal freedom and responsibility that can bring about the common good. It is an approach to entrepreneurship that adheres to a set of universal principles that create economic win-win solutions. It is the way that private business acts as a force for good. It is the way to social mobility and equal access to opportunity. It is the way of the American Dream.

Once I had found my answers to how the market economy could coexist with doing good in the world, I started to write about it in articles and eventually my first book, *The Pope & the CEO*, in which I proposed my findings and showed how most of the answers were in front of me all along.

I met Art Ciocca right around the time my first book was published, and we talked about our frustration that business is often cast in such a negative light. We both had experiences of having to defend the free market economy. Art told me how he had recently been trying to convince a group of liberal arts professor friends of his that business is a force for good, and not the selfish, Dickensian, money-grabbing boogeyman they thought it to be. He had failed.

Over that dinner, Bob and I made a proposal to Art: Let's turn things upside down! Instead of arguing with the professors, let's get them to catch the entrepreneurial bug to give them a view of the business world from a new angle. Art loved the idea.

We devised a three-day experience where the professors would meet various entrepreneurs and learn about their vision, motivation, and companies. We then presented them with a game, where they'd first come up with some issue facing the local economy or environment around their university and then think of ways a simple phone app could help solve it. To their amazement, we had some developers on hand who immediately created a user interface and mock version of the app for the professors to see. You should have seen their reactions. They caught the entrepreneurship bug in two seconds; immediately, they were spewing out ideas, visions, and plans to make this product just right. We talked about how to finance the development: what we'd charge for the app, how to charge for it, alternative revenue models, the lot. It was difficult to end the class—the enthusiasm and desire ran so high. We asked for final observations. "Best experience in a long time," "What a thrill," "I love the product idea we came up with," "This would be so helpful to people," and "This opens so many possibilities" were the comments that came in. Not one about "We'll get rich!" or "Let's scheme to cheat our customers by giving them a product that does less than what we say." We pointed that out, explaining that what they verbalized about what they experienced during those three days is the same true motivation of the vast majority of entrepreneurs and businesspersons. It's the rule rather than the exception that the underlying principle of doing business is to help others solve problems at a profit. Ultimately, this means creating win-win solutions.

We hosted this experience for two years with more than twenty professors. They mostly reacted the same way: "This is what *I* would do, but I'm not sure the majority of businesspeople act as I do." They did catch the entrepreneurship bug, but it did not change their minds about business.

That part of the experience was a failure. The benefits of those seminars were perhaps greatest for me: I became friends with Art Ciocca.

A few months later, I received an email from a business professor who said that he loved *The Pope & the CEO* so much that he was using it in the classroom and now wanted to invite me to give a lecture to his students. Yay! I told him that a meeting would have to wait since I was at a seminar in Rome. The email came back in less than an hour: he was also in Rome.

When we met, he told me about his vision to build a business school at The Catholic University of America in Washington, DC. When he read my book, he felt that I verbalized much of what he envisioned as the guiding principles of the new business school. Our meeting was in May, and in August, I began teaching at The Catholic University of America.

I found it exhilarating to teach. Having the opportunity to introduce students to business is a privilege. I wanted to pass on what I had learned through experience, so I didn't want to use a textbook. Instead, I created a course from scratch. I used all of my past experiences to put together the course that *I wished I had taken* to introduce me to the business world. I would also use the Harvard case method to make the more salient points.

After trying a few cases, I realized that they didn't quite fit my vision for the points I wanted to bring across. The cases I could find focused too much on the theory of business. They were too cold and lifeless to my taste. Most decisions I had to make in business involved much more feeling than theory. There's a German word that describes good business decisions perfectly—it's *Fingerspitzengefühl*, or the feeling at the tip of your fingers. Making decisions in business is more of an art than a science. It's like noticing the texture of fabrics with the pads of your fingers and then following your gut. I exhausted my search for perfect case studies after a couple of semesters and resorted to simply telling the students about my own and other friends' experiences to illustrate key points. One person's stories kept coming up—those of Art Ciocca.

All these years, I had been trying to explain the abstraction of what Art Ciocca's story embodies. A thoughtful discussion with friends brought the solution into clear sight: Why didn't I just tell Art's story? His story represents the potential of the American Dream and exemplifies all the key pillars of Principled Entrepreneurship. He lived it. This is Art's story, and I'm proud to share it with you.

The Five Pillars of Principled Entrepreneurship That Nourish the American Dream

The American Dream has been the unofficial vision statement of the United States since its founding: the undying belief that anyone can succeed, regardless of where they began in life, geographically or economically. It is the ultimate statement of hope that the future can be better than the past, no matter who you are. It is a vision that brings together freedom and aspiration.

Principled Entrepreneurship is the mindset that, among other things, enables and empowers the American Dream. Principled Entrepreneurs connect people to their purpose and passion by forming teams that create value for customers.[1] I believe there are five pillars that describe the framework upon which the American Dream rests. These are not new ideas, but we sometimes need reminders. I think this is especially the case in our current work and economic environment. These pillars are basic building blocks. They must be reinterpreted, repositioned, and adapted to the current situation by every generation. The five pillars of Principled Entrepreneurship I define in this book are:

1. The Economy Exists for People, Not People for the Economy
2. To Work Is to Create; To Create Is to Be Human
3. Culture Eats Strategy for Breakfast
4. Principled Entrepreneurs Always Seek to Create Win-Win Solutions
5. Always Think Like an Entrepreneur

Pillar 1: The Economy Exists for People, Not People for the Economy

The essence of business is captured in the phrase "How may I help you?" Business is fundamentally other-directed. By asking customers this critical, classic business question, a good business puts the human person at its center; it adds value for its customers and does so profitably through the work of its team. That is its primary objective, its reason for existence.

Before money and sophisticated trading became part of human economic history, people bartered for goods and services to survive as well as find purpose. Business is an extension of that process. Today, we use money to objectively measure the value of each product or service. But the exchange of goods and services should still aim to improve people's lives. That is, we ought to create and buy goods that are truly good, and provide or contract services that truly serve.[2] Through products and services, practical value is created for consumers as an outcome of someone else's work.

Some in our economy put money exclusively at the center of their work. Others put pure innovation or progress at the center. Both are wrong. In a person-centered business approach, money and innovation are valid, even necessary, objectives to pursue as long as they are not hurting the human person. The challenge is not to pursue one or the other but to pursue all of these in tandem. This is the art of Principled Entrepreneurship, and it always starts with and ends with a human person—the customer on the one hand and the worker on the other. This describes the first pillar of Principled Entrepreneurship: the economy exists for the people, not people for the economy.

Pillar 2: To Work Is to Create; To Create Is to Be Human

What's commonly known as "Corporate Social Responsibility" (CSR) seems to judge business as an activity that is bad and irredeemable and therefore must do additional work—often making donations—to balance the negative effects of doing business. In this way, CSR often focuses mostly on the financial effects of business rather than the actual work involved and the people doing that work. That, in my estimation, is a big mistake, because work—and by extension business—is not an evil action, and it is not primarily about money.

We humans were made for work. It's what distinguishes us from animals. When we work, we can actually create something from "nothing"—we have the power to make our imagination into physical reality. Being made in the image and likeness of God, who created all, we, too, are creators.[3] And we call this ability to create "work." When we work, when we make something, we participate in God's creative power.

In fact, to be creative—to create profitable solutions to customer needs—is the primary objective of our work and, therefore, business. The entire process makes us more human. When we hone our skills, or focus our expertise through work, we flourish as people. That's why when we work, we don't just *make* more, but we *become* more. That excellence is one of the key objectives of work. When through our excellence we satisfy an important customer need, we benefit not only the consumer but also ourselves. If we work well, we ultimately benefit the common good of our society. That is why the economy exists for people and not the other way around.

A second objective of work is that we get great satisfaction from helping and enabling others to pursue their own excellence. Be it our coworkers or the customer, the other-directed process of helping someone else in the pursuit of their excellence is a logical follow-up to the first objective. If good, creative work and business is making me flourish, I ought to in turn promote that flourishing for everyone else involved in my work. This kind of collaboration within our company with members of our team creates great joy and goodwill. It makes us flourish not just as individuals but as a team in the pursuit of the true, the good, and the beautiful. In effect, flourishing is another word for becoming the full person God created me to be. That is the ultimate reward for and reason for our work, both individually and collectively.

And finally, as the third objective, there is a material reward for work well done. Satisfied customers who find that our products add value create more profit, and more profit provides the company with the ability to pay high and rising wages, continuously improve the work and company environment, and generate above-average return on investment for the owners and investors.

Nourishing others and ourselves plus being rewarded for that person-centered work adds up to what we call "the American Dream." It is an opportunity made possible by the free market—that anyone, no matter their background, can, through hard work and dedication to satisfying his or her customers, become prosperous.

Based on this understanding of our being creators at work—our ability to pursue personal excellence through our work while also generating financial and other rewards—business has three fundamental objectives:

1. To use human creativity to create goods that are truly good and provide services that truly serve by adding value to society
2. To support and promote human flourishing
3. To reward the company's constituents[4] financially

Pillar 3: Culture Eats Strategy for Breakfast

There is nothing more important to the long-term success of a company than a strong, sustainable culture. Cultural values identify the qualities and actions that are and are not acceptable behavior in an organization. Establishing and communicating these values is the first step in empowering individuals to use their own God-given talents to identify and solve problems on their own—to bring forth solutions instead of problems. Establishing these cultural values is the easy part. The most important part is to "sell" them to the organization and incentivize individuals to adopt the values as their own. Principled Entrepreneurs look for models to showcase and successes to celebrate to further instill these values in their organization. This is one of a leader's most important and leverageable opportunities, regardless of the size of her team.

The advantages of having strong cultural values are overwhelming. There is no one happier and more effective than an empowered employee. A company with clear values requires far fewer people and has less need for manuals, procedures, and other cumbersome paperwork. And there is no need for the proverbial "cop on every corner." A strong culture makes for a happier, more effective, and more efficient organization.

Whether you lead a small team in a large company or start or run a company, your key contribution as a leader is not the idea of the business, the product, or the service, but the culture you create and the virtues your company embraces.

Culture eats strategy for breakfast, as the saying goes.

Strategy[5] is the creation of unique and valuable positions, involving a different set of activities. It requires us to make trade-offs in competing, by choosing where to compete and where not to. Strategy is about creating a "fit" for all of the company's activities.[6] Strategy is clearly visible.

Culture is what we do when no one is looking. It shows what's of ultimate importance to us. It's what's left when push comes to shove—when virtue signaling is over and the "real" work begins.

Broken values are what ail our economy. Other-directedness, service, a willingness to defer gratification, friendliness, teamwork, transparency, long-term value creation—these are all values that are necessary not only to appeal to consumers, but also to attract and retain happy employees. Unfortunately, they are sorely lacking in many companies today, and that has serious consequences. According to recent Gallup research,[7] 51 percent of US employees don't care about the success of their company. These employees have "checked out." What's worse, 16 percent of them are actively disengaged. They are beyond checked out; they are actively trying to hurt their employers. Can you imagine? Over two-thirds (67 percent) of our workforce can't wait to go home. They hate their jobs and their employers.

It's easy to blame the individual for this. Too easy. I think the cause of this malady is bad corporate leadership. We construct lofty mission and vision statements and then violate them. We release extensive ethics manuals and behave like they don't apply to us. We pronounce virtue but practice vice. It is not our pronouncements that create corporate culture. It is our behavior. And it is no wonder that our teams don't like the corporate culture we built when we behave in ways that contradict what we say we care about.

Pillar 4: Principled Entrepreneurs Always Seek to Create Win-Win Solutions

Principled Entrepreneurs thrive on fair and open competition and win-win relationships, giving everyone access to opportunity and allowing for differences in outcome. I would call this the common good of society. The opposite of this behavior would be the crony capitalist who rigs the system to win at all costs.

Free, fair, and open competition is what drives the American economy and creates prosperity. There is no other sustainable way to overcome poverty. Fair competition sharpens our wit, disrupts stale and tired ideas, challenges new thinking, and, frequently, results in new and better products or ways of doing things. Competition is fundamental to capitalism, our freedom, and our American way of life. It is the reason for the enormous accomplishments of this great country. Free, fair, and open competition must be protected and promoted. Our American lifestyle and the American Dream depend upon it.

While competition drives improved performance, there are still numerous ways businesspeople can and do work together for the greater good and cultivate win-win relationships. Art offers the wine industry as a great example. The wine industry is brutally competitive in the area of sales and marketing. But it is exactly that kind of tough competition that has enabled enormous growth in that industry—compounded at about 3 percent per year for the last forty years.

It's difficult to imagine that an industry so intensely competitive in sales and marketing could cooperate when it comes to winemaking and production. Nevertheless, that is exactly what the wine industry has done for the last forty years. The thinking is simple but profound. If some wineries produce substandard wine, it is a bad reflection on all wine. That is why it is a common practice for winemakers from one company to exchange ideas with competitors. It is a common practice for highly trained enologists at universities to publish papers and invite outside companies to learn how to improve their winemaking practices. This behavior creates true win-win relationships, the kind that are indicative of Principled Entrepreneurship.

There is another form of capitalism, often called crony capitalism. This is the exact opposite of Principled Entrepreneurship. Crony capitalists are usually people or organizations with broken values who are driven to win at any cost. They consort with others to rig the system in their favor and to the detriment of others. They try to avoid, even preempt, fair and open competition. This is typically done by business people who move into government and then help their industry friends (their "cronies") create regulations that make it difficult for newcomers to enter the market. The loss of competition not only destroys innovation and creativity, it hinders the young and the poor from rising, because that market sector is now anything but free. Crony capitalism is detrimental to society because it destroys innovation and creativity, resulting in inferior products and services getting to market. Crony capitalism is a win-lose proposition, with society on the losing end.

Unfortunately, this kind of behavior by a few has become the leading narrative about business and the market economy. If you watch the top ten movies about businesspeople, you'll find that not one of them portrays business as a benevolent activity. In *The Wolf of Wall Street*, *The Founder*, *The Social Network*, and all the way back to Scrooge in *A Christmas Carol*, businesspeople are portrayed as nasty, self-absorbed, greedy people who *take* something away from society. This portrayal is fundamentally flawed. There are greedy businesspeople but not necessarily more than there are greedy politicians, lawyers, nonprofit founders, or religious leaders.

Ever since the '70s, the image of business as war has become very popular. Winning-at-all-cost strategies became all the rage. That war-like view of business is the antithesis of Principled Entrepreneurship. The economy is not a zero-sum game.

Sports offer a better analogy for business competition. As in business, the ultimate objective of sports is human excellence. Everyone in a particular sports competition measures their excellence against others, and there is at the end one person or team who wins. But it's not winning as in war. When I participate in a sports event and don't come in first, I still benefit. I have excelled, I have learned, and I have prepared myself for the next competition. And I've had fun!

The way I see it, while free market competition creates winners and losers in terms of companies, it ideally creates only winners in terms of us as individuals.[8] If the goal of work is to flourish, then this flourishing needs to be seen beyond the company I currently work for. My flourishing needs to be seen in terms of me as a person. Companies in themselves are not the ultimate goal of the economy, as Pillar 1 states. The development of each person on the team is the goal. So the question is not whether to compete or not. The question is rather: "Who do I compete against?" Ultimately, the answer should be: "Myself."

The competitors around me are doing their part to beat their best previous performance and "run" faster than me. It's like the Olympics: competition helps us run faster. Like a good race, it helps my performance if I surround myself with good competitors. Runners at the Olympics consider themselves lucky to compete on a world-class level. Like them, we get to compete in business on a world-class level through globalization. Unlike the Olympics, in economic competition, there are many, many more opportunities to win. But like the Olympics, those we measure ourselves against are not simply competitors; they are also collaborators in our mutual perfection. They are our co-opetition.

Ever since Marx, the popular way to see the world has been in adversarial terms. It's his famous great struggle of capital versus labor. An existential fight to the end. A classic either/or struggle. I have always found that to be a fundamental mischaracterization and a highly static view of the world. Besides, in my experience, what at first appears adversarial is more often a complementary relationship. It's not either/or, but both/and! The two "sides" need each other. In terms of labor and capital, history has shown that they can and should seek win-win solutions.

Pillar 5: Always Think Like an Entrepreneur

Principled Entrepreneurs are creators, not harvesters.[9] They create successful product portfolios and brands that stand for superior value. They build organizations that focus on long-term value creation, where employees are always part of the competitive advantage. Nothing will serve you better than a creator mindset, whether you run a startup or work for a large company.

Harvesters, on the other hand, are short-term thinkers, frequently focused on the balance sheet or anything else that will make them look good in the short term. All other aspects of the business, be it customers or employees, are means to an end: looking good in the short term. The trouble with this mindset is that harvesting eventually depletes the source and prevents long-term success.

Principled Entrepreneurs think long term and see the balance sheet as a means to the end—the creation of customer value—and not the end in itself. As long as the focus is on "creating" that value, the source of success will never be depleted. This is why it's important to always think like an entrepreneur.

Constantly seeking the next solution to our customers' problems or needs is what makes for a great business. This means putting the customer's needs so far ahead of our own that we destroy our current product or solution by innovating a superior one. This is the concept of creative destruction,[10] and it is one of the cornerstones of PE. Creative destruction ensures that the company we build and the team we work with is sustainable and focuses on long-term success.

It is not an attitude that only the founder or leader of a company ought to adopt. Everyone should be incentivized to do so. Approaching every issue that we face at work with the perspective of an owner or an entrepreneur means that we seek solutions that we can personally impact. We take on the responsibility and try to create a solution that is in our domain. It's a Principled Entrepreneurship mindset of always approaching problems as opportunities.

This entails taking personal responsibility to act and change things for the better, and the solutions thus found usually do more with less. They are innovative and efficient because they are borne out of an entrepreneurial spirit, focused on remaining creators at all times.

Managing where a company or a brand is on the continuum between creating at the one end and harvesting at the other is an art. Imagine a large company with several diverse divisions or a company with thirty different brands. In either case it is unrealistic to imagine all the divisions or all the brands in the same place on the continuum. The reason is that each of these brands is at a different stage in their life cycle. Some experience dynamic growth and have a lot of potential while others may be in the opposite position. In addition, it is not realistic to think that a company has the financial wherewithal to spend aggressively in all areas. A Principled Entrepreneur will carefully select the product or brand with which to drive growth and get these funds from some of the brands or products that are in a harvest mode. Making these decisions is a carefully honed art that takes years to develop. There are no formulas, books, or other guidelines to go by. That is the art of Principled Entrepreneurship.

2

Principled Entrepreneurship
and the Story of the
American Dream

It is hard to imagine the United States without the freedom of entre-preneurship. The activity of starting and growing a company, invent-ing a new product or service, or finding ways to renew an existing company—offering this opportunity to the poor and the rich alike—is so intertwined with the unprecedented social mobility of this country that the goal bears its name: the American Dream.

In this chapter, I make a case for why entrepreneurship is so impor-tant to prosperity and how I believe it is the cornerstone of the American Dream. Unfortunately it is not a well-known fact that entrepreneurship has greatly diminished during the past thirty years. Today's most com-mon image of the entrepreneur is the high-tech startup founder, and since we hear so much about them, we think they make up the bulk of entre-preneurial activity. But they are by no means the mainstay of entrepre-neurship in the United States or any other country. Most entrepreneurs are active in the brick-and-mortar sector of the economy and end up as small- and medium-sized companies (SME). It is they who are the engine of our economic growth. They are the proverbial goose that laid the golden egg—the foundation of our prosperity. In a book that explains Principled Entrepreneurship, it is fundamental to understand first why the freedom of entrepreneurship is so valuable for society and the economy, what its history is and how that sector of the economy is faring today. Therefore, I will explore both issues—their value to the economy and the fact that they are a "threatened species"—in this chapter.

I realize that this makes the chapter a bit more academic than the rest of this book, but I feel there's a lot of misinformation and misconception about the free market, competition, and entrepreneurship, and I'd like to focus on dispelling that in this way and show how important that environment is for entrepreneurs and SMEs to flourish. If you are not interested in this data and argument, or you'd like to focus right away on learning about Principled Entrepreneurship, feel free to skip this chapter and start reading chapter three.

I am not claiming that the free market economy and entrepreneurship is the end all and be all, or that we even achieved a truly free market with equal access for all in our economy. What I'm trying to show is that economic freedom is essential not only to our individual flourishing but to society as a whole. It is the foundation of any kind of sustainable prosperity. Therefore, it is important to recognize and give that free market approach credit for what it has helped us achieve to date, and then to recommit to it in our pursuit of further prosperity in our country and around the globe.

I believe that equality and freedom are central to human flourishing and progress. It is also the only known way to create lasting and peaceful prosperity for everyone. It offers all the right incentives to promote innovation and rewards wholesome values that are critical for society.[1] One cannot overemphasize how important this is for our country and the world. This kind of entrepreneurship—I call it Principled

Entrepreneurship—is responsible for the success story of the American economy. In this chapter, I would like to show you why I think that is the case and explain why the level of Principled Entrepreneurship in this country—and any country, really—is the canary in the coal mine of the economy and one that needs urgent attention. In short, I would like to convince you that there is a great opportunity and need for a surge of Principled Entrepreneurship to save the American Dream.

The Long and Ongoing Quest for Human Dignity and Freedom

The quest for human prosperity and flourishing has evolved in the past and will continue to do so in the future. Economic development over the past five hundred years has been tremendous. Prosperity was once based on land, which few owned. In much of the world, nobles owned the land and everything and everyone in and on it contributed to the owners' prosperity. Mercantilism expanded on that system and allowed a further class of people to pursue wealth.

Eventually, capital rather than land became the key ingredient to creating more well-being. The ring of prosperity widened further, allowing many more people to flourish, bringing an unprecedented number of people out of abject poverty. Life expectancy increased, disease steadily declined, and trade interests generally engendered a more peaceful world. But true prosperity still eluded many.

We can enlarge our economic system yet more, and make it even more inclusive. But to do so will require what economic expansion has always historically required: a leap forward in our respect for the human person. Historically we see that as long as people were dispensable and disposable, there could be no general prosperity and human flourishing.

The large pattern we can see emerge over hundreds, even thousands, of years is that humanity has increasingly discovered and asserted the dignity and self-determination of the individual person, and that has led to ever greater prosperity. Recognizing the centrality of the human person—the meaningfulness and immeasurable potential of every life—has inspired us to fight against slavery, despotism, and dictatorship and for self-determination and the rights to the fruits of one's labor as well as property. In short, the free and democratic market economy has emerged.

This has not been an easily achieved development, and resistance to it—economically or politically—is often fierce, resulting in uneven progress due to taking one or two steps forward and sometimes two or three steps back. But this drive toward liberty is palpable in our history.

We are now on the cusp of another stage of development in our understanding of the centrality of the individual person: prosperity is no longer found primarily in land or money but instead in human ingenuity. The past logic of wealth creation is still around, but its days are numbered. I have no illusions that we will ever have a morally "pure" economy in which all strife and injustices will be overcome. But the person-centered economy is trying to emerge. The question now is: Will we allow it? If we do, we all win.

Over the past thirty years I have witnessed many signs of this evolution. I say evolution because the emerging economy builds upon what we now have; it is not a wholesale rejection, not a revolution, but an evolution that builds on what came before it.

The US and a History of Principled Entrepreneurship

Much of this entrepreneurial opportunity in the United States was not created by chance. The US founders were very well aware of the drawbacks of the class system and the oligarchies that ran the economies in their countries of origin. Thus the "American Experiment" was to create a country not built on tribe, nationality, military might, or class, but on opportunity for everyone. The US was founded intentionally as a commercial republic.

As noted in the Federalist Papers (#10), which for all intents and purposes were a thorough explanation of the US Constitution published at the time it was being debated, the founders clearly thought it critically important for the well-being of the new nation to enshrine the protection of private (and intellectual) property[2] as well as economic, political, and religious freedom in the Constitution. These were to be the top virtues of the new country. The self-evident truths that were pointed to in the Declaration of Independence were enshrined in the Constitution as the ideal the new nation would pursue. It took it a very long time to properly understand and actually grant these rights to everyone—after all, the implementation of good principles requires people who properly understand them, and that came only gradually—but these truths remain the blueprint of the American Dream to this day, and they are well reflected in the five pillars of Principled Entrepreneurship presented in this book.

These five pillars feed off the self-evident truths described in the Declaration of Independence, though there are many Principled Entrepreneurs who are not American. This dream of a society of freedom is not a national or geographically limited opportunity. It is the dream born out of the achievements of Western civilization, which is a multi-cultural and centuries-long achievement. It does not belong to the few or to one nation, but to everyone who embraces it. That is one of the reasons why the United States of America is, and has been from the beginning, a nation of immigrants and entrepreneurs.

The draw of the American Dream was and is very strong throughout the world. It was not just the Graham Bells and Levi Strausses of the early days of the US economy who sought to have their own business in the "land of opportunity." Sixty percent of the most highly valued tech companies today were cofounded by first- or second-generation immigrants.[3]

The "soil" in which Principled Entrepreneurs thrive is an environment that nourishes freedom, a society that has the following:

- Balance of power in government and society with accountability for action and performance
- Principled democracy based on common, transcendent moral virtues, not "mob rule"
- Basic written law, applied equally to all
- Independent, informed, and participatory population
- Freedom of economic initiative for everyone in a free and competitive marketplace that enables social mobility

The American Dream is essentially a dream of entrepreneurship—entrepreneurship with specific virtues defined in the pillars of Principled Entrepreneurship. I believe that the fifth pillar—to always think like an entrepreneur in mind and deed—is the lifeblood of the American Dream, wherever that dream is being lived out in the world. It keeps a nation and society young and ensures social mobility because it is a constant renewal and reshuffling of economic actors.

That is—as long as the competition and economy remain truly free. In that case, it's like in sports—there'll always be someone who will eventually run faster or jump higher than the previous champion. And in terms of business, that means that ever newer and better products and services will come to market for a better price with higher value.

That is why we should always think like an entrepreneur, so that as a society we can move forward toward life, liberty, and the pursuit of happiness.

Why Principled Entrepreneurship Is Good for Progress and Prosperity

The key contributor to that progress has been the prevalence of small and medium-sized companies (SMEs), which includes startup companies. Traditionally, SMEs make up 99.7 percent of our total number of companies. Very large companies, or Multinational Corporations (MNCs) as they're often called, account for only 0.03 percent.[4] Since 1990, MNCs have eliminated roughly 4 million jobs, while SMEs have added 8 million new jobs.[5] Over 50 percent of the working population in the US (120 million individuals) works in a small business.[6] SMEs are responsible for 44 percent of our GDP and have filed 16 times more patents per year than large firms.[7]

Growth is one of the key benefits entrepreneurs generate. They are often called pioneers of prosperity not just because they create innovative goods and services but also because they create new jobs. And this is very logical: SMEs—due to their size—can often not compete on price and thus need employees to differentiate themselves. These have to go "above and beyond" to create happy customers willing to pay the relatively higher prices. Larger companies and MNCs, on the other hand, use economies of scale[8] and efficiency to differentiate themselves—in other words, they need to *reduce* the number of employees to stay competitive. Both play an important role and are critical to maintaining a healthy economy.

Entrepreneurs create immense benefits and rewards not just for themselves, but for society in general by simply doing their work. It is often assumed that entrepreneurs garner the lion's share of the value they create and thus their wealth is regarded with suspicion if not envy. However, research by Nobel prize–winning economist William D. Nordhaus in 2004 revealed that on average, innovator-entrepreneurs capture only 2 percent of the value they create for themselves through company ownership and salary.[9]

That means that 98 percent of the value entrepreneurs create is garnered by the employees and the general society through wages, jobs, cost savings, efficiency, comfort, and living standards. Given that fact, it is counter-productive, even absurd, to call for these entrepreneurs to "give back" or "pay their fair share" through especially high tax rates that apply only to them, or to create laws that curb their freedom of economic initiative and in essence predetermine winners and losers by preempting the competitive free market. Andy Kessler reasoned in a *Wall Street Journal* opinion piece that for every dollar of government taxation and anti-competitive regulations of companies, "[the government] theoretically take[s] 25 times that amount from compound social wealth." What that means is that we should be very careful in diverting money away from the economy. It's not that we ought not to do it at all, there are absolutely legitimate needs that we need to cover through government expenditure and regulation, but Kessler argues that we need to be aware that every time we do so—through taxation or regulation—we have to collectively work 25 times as much as the tax or regulation is valued to make up for the actual cost. Even if it were only half of that, unnecessary policies are a value-destruction scheme for society.[10] And I would add that it's those in the private sector who have most to lose from more or new competition who cheer on or even instigate the government or politicians to promote such anti-competitive action. As Kessler points out in his article, the ones who lose most from such "schemes" are the general public.[11]

Other research[12] shows that one dollar of an investment in an SME on average generates $13 of economic value in the local economy. For us, as a society seeking to create prosperity for all, there is simply no better investment than that.

Countries that invest in this way, as the US has largely done since its founding, inevitably prosper, and we will continue to prosper to the degree that we manage to remain entrepreneurial.

A Trend Toward Fewer Startups

Many people say that, since the '70s, "big money" is no longer made in *actual* entrepreneurship.

Young business school students are told that the real money today is made in the financial market through speculation and trading. This may very well be one of the reasons why the number of entrepreneurs and startup companies has diminished over that same period of time.

Others say that this could not be the case given the great tech-entrepreneurship boom of the '90s thanks to the internet. Surely the great innovators of the last forty years such as Gates, Jobs, Bezos, Brin, Grove, and Zuckerberg are indicative of a great boom of entrepreneurship.

Again, others insist that entrepreneurship numbers are down because big companies like Apple, Amazon, and Microsoft are preempting businesses startups by innovating more internally, in addition to the fact that the scale needed to deliver many of the things society needs today may no longer be within reach of a small startup. The fact is that entrepreneurship numbers have steadily declined during the past thirty years and the trend may be the result of a combination of all three of these reasons.

I, and many others, were privileged to participate in the tech boom of the '90s. This sector was the frontier for entrepreneurs at the time because it gave prime opportunity for innovation and risk taking. But when you have a gold rush, there are few long-term survivors.

Still, if you won during the tech boom, you won big. But those wins are far-and-few between. Of all the venture-backed startups since 1985, just 6 percent of them created 60 percent of the return.[13] For the winners, that's a pretty small investment with a very large return. This was justified: imagine the value that innovations like the internet, data management systems, and the smartphone added to buyers' lives. These entrepreneurs brought products to market that generated huge gains in productivity and comfort.

But these success stories should not distract us from the fact that other enterprises,[14] such as small businesses and new startups, drastically shrank during that same time frame. In 1980, new companies made up half of all US businesses. From 1978 to 2012, this declined by 44 percent as you can see in Figure 1.[15]

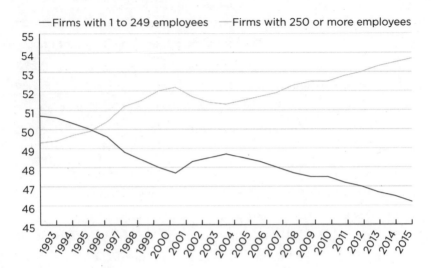

Figure 1: The Decline of Small & Medium-Sized (SME) Firms 1993–2015

The share of new firms as a percentage of total firms today hovers around 8 percent. That's much lower than the average "business birth rate" of 11 percent between 1980 and 2010.[16] This relationship between new companies being created and old ones going out of business is a natural and even healthy process, as long as the total number increases. Since the economic crisis in the early 2000s, the economy had trouble creating more new companies and after a strong performance during the teens, the early 2020s returned to a deficit of new companies being founded. There is some indication that the recent COVID-19 crisis will actually represent a boon for the starting of new companies (Figure 2), but whether that will be a temporary spike or result in an actual increase in numbers remains to be seen. I believe that the general trend in the context of the last twenty years remains tenuous and is greatly worrisome.

Many reasons could explain this decline. The internet's great benefit was that it "disintermediated"—it took out a lot of middlemen businesses that were previously needed to bring a product successfully from the producer to the consumer. In other words, the internet eliminated many small business opportunities in a wide field of distribution, retail,

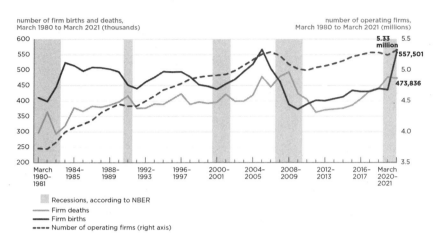

number of firm births and deaths,
March 1980 to March 2021 (thousands)

number of operating firms,
March 1980 to March 2021 (millions)

Recessions, according to NBER
—— Firm deaths
—— Firm births
==== Number of operating firms (right axis)

NBER = National Bureau of Economic Research
Note: Firm deaths and births are for years beginning March 12 (in order to match the data timing of the US Census Bureau's Business Dynamic Statistics [BDS]). BDS data cover firms with paid employees. NBER recession dates are matched to the months of peak to trough.
Source: Data before April 2018 are from US Census Bureau's Business Dynamic Statistics (BDS). Data for March 2018–March 2021 are based on the authors' estimates.

Figure 2: US Firm Births and Deaths Since 1980

and service areas. Some analysts, however, point to the financial industry's change in focus from lending to speculation as the real reason for the decrease of SMEs and startups. A *Time* magazine article[17] claimed that only a fraction of all the money washing around the financial markets these days actually makes it to "brick and mortar" business. "Around 15% of capital coming from financial institutions today is used to fund business investments, whereas it [investment in brick-and-mortar businesses] would have been the majority of what banks did earlier in the twentieth century."

Whatever the case, the consensus is that the number of entrepreneurs and startups is down. Since such activity is and has been the path out of poverty since the founding of our country, this decline of lower entrepreneurship coincides with a general decrease in social mobility. If you out-earn your parents at the same age, usually between thirty-two and forty years, you display social, or income, mobility. In the 1940s, 92 percent of people out-earned their parents; that number has dropped to

50 percent today.[18] I believe that the decrease of entrepreneurship and social mobility are highly correlated.

We would do well to reverse this decline, because everyone should have access to the American Dream; to be able to use their wisdom and creativity to excel and prosper.

We, of course, don't enjoy a perfectly competitive market economy. No society short of the kingdom of God will offer equal opportunity for everyone. Yet there is still widespread opportunity in the US. The danger is that the decline in entrepreneurship and startups is a sign that we're slowly moving in the wrong direction, and suggests that fewer are enjoying the chance to flourish. It does not have to be this way.

A decline in entrepreneurship is the antithesis of the American Dream. I came to America thirty years ago for many reasons, but a key was the economic opportunity; and many others do the same. Social mobility, "making it"—it's the quintessential promise of America. A society that is not afraid of competition, that roots for the underdog, a system that gives everyone a chance and celebrates success.[19]

I have been immensely blessed with a career in entrepreneurship, and I love this country and what it has given me. But I'm afraid we won't be able to live up to that same promise for the next generation. We're well on the way to betraying the promise that is at the core of who we are. We stand to lose our entrepreneurial spirit that this country was built on. I am confident that Principled Entrepreneurship is the way to reinvigorate this noble goal and put it in the reach of everyone.

The Principled Entrepreneur Is in Our Midst

The Principled Entrepreneur is not motivated primarily by the *what* or *how* as much as the *why* of what they do.[20] As such, Principled Entrepreneurs are not focused on any specific stage of a company or any particular role or job title. They are always active in any job inside and out of companies. Once they become entrepreneurs, they are always entrepreneurs.

Entrepreneurship is not a job description; it's an attitude. Art likes to express it as an "ownership attitude." In this book I call it "always think like an entrepreneur," because thinking like an entrepreneur works. It's the way you see and approach the world and how you take responsibility for what's in front of you, take a proprietary interest in what's going on, and become the protagonist rather than the victim or the disinterested bystander.

Principled Entrepreneurs are creative problem solvers at any level and growth stage of companies or organizations, non-governmental organizations (NGOs), universities, churches, and society in general. What their solutions have in common is that they are creative, and they make human excellence the path as much as the end goal of the undertaking.

Are you a Principled Entrepreneur? In the following pages, I identify four types of entrepreneurs. I hope that you will recognize yourself in one of them, or maybe one of these types inspires you into action. It pays off to start practicing Principled Entrepreneurship as early in your life and career as possible. Your probability for success in any given entrepreneurial project you lead increases greatly depending on the kind of effort you put in.

But it's not only about success in the business or economic sense. Entrepreneurship, and entrepreneurial thinking, also makes you happier because you take and are given initiative to pursue your excellence. We spend one-third of our life at work; most of our waking hours. If we don't excel at work, then where will we do so? A mediocre job is depressing. A job that's simply a way to pay the bills is dreadful. A job where a person is a number, an easily replaceable means to an end, is unfulfilling. Eighty-six percent of Americans say they're not happy[21]—a trend that has been progressing for a long time.[22] Sixty-five percent of

Americans are disengaged at work.[23] This is why we need more entrepreneurial jobs, why we need to think more like entrepreneurs.

Let's look at four types of Principled Entrepreneurs. I list them in descending order, based on my estimated probability of success, measured in return on investment of money as well as time and effort for each approach.

1. The "employee" entrepreneur is perhaps the most important entrepreneur of all because more aspiring young people can start practicing it at any time. Thinking like an entrepreneur as an employee within a company enables you to see issues more clearly and from a broader perspective.[24] An employee entrepreneur is attentive, notices patterns, solves problems, and takes initiative. This results in better decision making and more value creation. More importantly, it is a perfect way to prepare for increasing responsibility either within the company or in the event you discover an exciting new concept you would like to pursue independently. I believe your odds of success with this approach are close to 100 percent because there is no downside.

2. The "acquisition" entrepreneur has, according to some, a 95 percent success rate.[25] I presume that the number is probably closer to 80 percent because if you buy and start to lead an up-and-running company, it's not a given that you will be a fit with the team or culture of the company. Ideally, you will have done your research on the company you acquire so that you can confidently build your vision on a solid basis. The downside is that in most cases this costs some up-front cash. But there are lots of business owners who want to retire and sell you a company at terms that draw out the payments so it benefits both them and you. This is a super exciting area of Principled Entrepreneurship.

3. The "franchise" entrepreneur, I'm told, has about a 60 percent or better success rate than a startup,[26] but from my observations, I'd put that number closer to 40 percent. Franchises most certainly have an above average success rate with regard to all other entrepreneurial activity. This is largely due to the fact that you buy into a ready-made and proven product and marketing efforts. The downside is that the entrepreneur has to pay for this up front through the franchise fee.

4. The "pure" startup entrepreneur is sometimes said to have a 50 percent probability of success over five years.[27] My gut feeling is that it's probably more like 5 percent in the long run. Founding your own business is a lot of fun, but you have to do it at the right moment in your life. Whenever you do have that opportunity, it will pay off immeasurably if you have behaved like a Principled Entrepreneur all along in your career. Most people don't have a switch that they turn on. It's a behavior that is acquired like a virtue: through practice and commitment.

These types of entrepreneurial opportunities are just the general categories I can think of. I am sure there are many more. An often-overlooked aspect of entrepreneurship is age. "In 2019, Kauffman Foundation research found that more than 25% of new entrepreneurs were between 55–64—up from about 15% in 1996. Unrelated research from Guidant Financial and the Small Business Trends Alliance said individuals 55 or older own 43% of the country's small businesses in 2020."[28] It seems that, to some extent, age has a role to play in terms of when one "takes the plunge" and starts a company. The bottom line is that there is a Principled Entrepreneurship opportunity for everyone. Maybe it's best not to begin your career with the highest-risk engagement of starting your own company. It might make sense for a young entrepreneur to do their learning while working in the company or on the team of a more experienced mentor. This could be the most consequential learning opportunity—a veritable apprenticeship in Principled Entrepreneurship. There is a time for everything. It's certainly the case that not everyone is in a position to start or buy a company, but again, everyone can behave as a Principled Entrepreneur.

In this respect, I think of how Art developed his career. He never really had the funds or the opportunity to start his own company. "In my case, I always took a proprietary interest in most things I did from the beginning thanks to my father's example. I really got serious about being an 'employee' entrepreneur at Gallo and it helped me develop a new product that sold 3 million cases in the first year. That approach continued as president of a division of Oroweat just before moving to The Wine Group and then during the five years as president before actually becoming an owner. That adds up to about twelve years in total before actually becoming an owner-entrepreneur."

The point here is very simple: think like an entrepreneur at all levels and stages of your career. Take ownership of the challenges and opportunities you encounter at work. See it as a critical part of your entrepreneurship education. The results will impress others and amaze you.

As a society, we depend on continuing value creation to create and sustain prosperity. The more entrepreneurial everyone is, the better off we all are for it. That is why you should become and remain a Principled Entrepreneur at any of the levels I just mentioned—because any one of them will promote prosperity for all.

3

Pillar 1: The Economy Exists for People, Not People for the Economy

The ultimate resource in economic development is people.
It is people, not capital or raw material that develop an economy.
—*Peter Drucker*

Any business ought to start by looking at its customers and asking the critical and classical business question: "How may I help you?" A Principled Entrepreneur focuses on that "I" and "You." I work to add value for you profitably. Doing so allows us both to flourish. That is the core purpose of business and the economy.

How does Pillar 1—that the economy and businesses should exist for people, instead of the other way around—live up to the demands of the modern business world? The answer is that business—and by extension the economy—measures value created. The only way to create real value depends on two factors: the customer and the creator of the value. This is because without the customer we would not know what value to create, and without the worker or employee we could not create or deliver it. This chapter shows how a good business begins with a person's need and ends with another person's work, creating a profitable solution to satisfy that need. Providing such solutions for the needs of others not only promotes prosperity, it also advances human excellence and flourishing. That is why Principled Entrepreneurs create person-centered companies.

How Art Ciocca Created the Largest Brand in the Wine Industry by Focusing on the Consumer

Italy is synonymous with wine. Most Italians wouldn't think of eating a good meal without it: for them, wine isn't the "extra" or a "nice-to-have" accompaniment to their meals. For centuries, Italians have enjoyed an everyday wine called *vino da tavola*, meaning "table wine"—good, affordable wine for every home.

When Italians immigrated to the United States in the nineteenth and twentieth centuries, they missed their wine. Wine simply was not an accepted part of the American diet and, as a result, little wine was available and there were few well-regarded brands.

During Prohibition in the 1930s, every self-respecting Italian immigrant who could access grapes made their own wine. Guarino Di Giacinto was no different. He started making homemade wine during Prohibition and kept on doing so well after it ended. An immigrant from Italy, he was a blacksmith with an eighth-grade education and a three-acre farm outside of New York City. He spent every free minute working with his eight-year-old grandson Art on that little plot of land.

He taught Art to garden, to harvest, and to preserve all the vegetables and fruits they had. They also cared for chickens and goats. But Guarino's favorite part of that small acreage was the grapes he used to make wine. He saw to it that young Art also learned about winemaking.

"You and I, Art. We are winemakers!" he'd say proudly after a long day's work, pouring himself a generous glass and his grandson a thimbleful to toast to their excellent workmanship. Art loved spending time with his grandfather and enjoyed the tradition of clinking glasses, toasting one another, and celebrating their winemaking prowess. He even enjoyed drinking his modest allocation of wine they made together during the autumn months.

Art's grandfather was the quintessential Italian immigrant entrepreneur. He worked as a blacksmith for a company in downtown Manhattan and he had a shop in his garage twenty miles or so north of the city. It was backbreaking work, but Guarino took pride in it. Anything he did had his "stamp" on it. The things he created were an extension of his person, his pledge to his employer and customers that they could trust his work. It wasn't an easy time by our standards. The US had just endured the Great Depression and two World Wars. But as far as Guarino was concerned, he was living the American Dream. "Here in America, you can achieve anything," he'd instruct his grandson, "as long as you work hard and never, never give up!"

Art took this lesson from his grandfather to heart. When he grew up, he embarked on a career in consumer-packaged goods marketing in the food business, determined to work hard and to never, never give up. When Art entered the food and beverage industry, the wine segment of that industry was virtually nonexistent in America. Consumption in countries like Italy and France was about twenty-six gallons per capita, compared to less than one gallon per capita in America.[1] Consumer interest was growing, but the supply of desirable wine was lacking. The only American-made wines on the market were what Art considered non-branded commodity wines.

When Art began his career in the wine industry in the late '60s, table wine was not a common consumer product in the US. "Wine barely existed in the vocabulary of most back then. Although there were a lot of wines available for sale, few sold well because wine was not accepted as an established American drink. As a result, there were only a very few brands that had loyal consumers."

What was then considered the premium wine market segment, which primarily consisted of Almaden and Paul Masson, was very small. Gallo and Italian Swiss Colony were the main players in the popularly priced segment. Dessert wines, like sherry, port, and muscatel, outsold table wines. That was to a large extent because the traditional wine did not appeal to Americans' tastes. Wine is an acquired taste if you did not grow up with it, or rather into it. Table wine was primarily consumed by immigrants and a few high-end consumers.

Art, along with a number of industry leaders in the '70s, felt that wine could become an important element for American family life. Together they saw the tremendous untapped potential for table wine in America and set out to change its standing in the eyes of American consumers. Up until this time, the wine industry in America had been a production-driven industry. This group of industry leaders led the change to become marketing driven. That was the turning point for wine in America. From that time forward, the entire wine industry went on a tear with compounded growth of between 3 and 4 percent per year for the next thirty-plus years.

There were those who would argue that branded wines already existed in the 1970s, but Art disagrees: "Call them what you want, but I don't consider them 'brands.' Real brands are determined by consumers. What makes a real brand is strong consumer recognition and loyalty. In the early years, none of the established wine producers had that!" Art Ciocca wanted to create a brand that offered the best value to consumers. That was the goal, and nothing short of it would do.

Art's experience with his grandfather enabled him to perceive this market need early, and his love for good-tasting table wine cinched it.

In 1969, he seized an opportunity to become a product manager at the E. & J. Gallo winery in Modesto, California, to work for the industry leader. In the '70s, Art was hired to run a subsidiary of Coke New York. And after a few years he led a management buyout in 1981 and created The Wine Group, a company that would have a profound impact on the growth of the industry in the '80s and '90s. Finally, Art was able to bring to life the vision for good wine at a great value. Who could imagine the weekend visits to his grandfather would lead to this?

This kind of vision—to create a new product segment, to develop a table wine that appeals to customers' tastes, to offer it in a larger package, and then create a demand for it—doesn't happen based on an exclusive drive for more profit or product expansion. No, such a vision has much deeper roots in customer satisfaction. Otherwise, it would, pardon the pun, die on the vine.

This customer-centeredness is how Art and his team changed the wine industry. It primarily happened through The Wine Group's flagship wine brand, Franzia. Art focused on making it into a superior table wine product at a competitive price for a specific customer segment. He created enough consumer value to make it the number one brand in American table wine during his tenure as CEO, which ended in 2000.[2]

What's important about Art's story is that he never loses sight of the customer. He maintained a completely other-directed worldview, and he found a profitable solution to satisfy consumers' needs. But he approached it with the customer and his team, not profits, at the center. This is so fundamental to a healthy business. I know that sounds so self-evident that it's hard to imagine a company that wouldn't keep the customer as its focus. But losing sight of the consumer is indeed very common. Such companies or executives don't consciously remove the customer as a core focus, but their or the company's self-absorbed bureaucracy, career mindedness, and short-term-profit or incentive-payout focus creates so much noise and distraction in the system that the customer's voice is no longer heard.

If you want to create value, you need to start with people—with a need, an issue, a demand that customers have. It is in that other-directedness that you find the best ideas for a new business because this perspective ensures from the beginning that what you offer corresponds to a genuine customer need. To put this worldview into action, remember this absolutely necessary first step to creating and growing your business.

The Two Key Components of a Principled Entrepreneur's Company

It Profitably Addresses a Customer Need

The first key aspect of a Principled Entrepreneur's company is that it starts with the customers' needs and provides a profitable solution.[3] This is a focus on the *you* in "How may I help you?" Principled Entrepreneurs like Art think of and know the consumer so well that they can anticipate what they value, create the product they desire, and offer it at just the right price (i.e., profitably).

Companies, and sometimes entire industries, get this customer-centeredness wrong. The German economist Theodore Levitt pointed out such a case when he explained why so many railroads went out of business. "The railroads did not stop growing because the need for passengers and freight transportation declined. That grew. The railroads are in trouble today not because that need was filled by others (cars, trucks, airplanes, and even telephones) but because it was not filled by the railroads themselves. They let others take customers away from them because they assumed themselves to be in the railroad business rather than in the transportation business. The reason they defined their industry incorrectly was that they were railroad oriented instead of transportation oriented; they were product oriented instead of customer oriented."[4]

While customer-centeredness is a pretty easy rule to understand in the abstract, many businesses and entrepreneurs fail because they don't keep it in focus. Because building and running a business involves making many important choices on a daily basis (especially in the beginning stages of a company), this fundamental first step can be overlooked or lost in the shuffle.

Art started with a simple premise: Italians love table wine and so will Americans if it suits their tastes. He tested relentlessly as he executed on this value proposition and adapted as he went along. His value proposition was proven right and The Wine Group became very successful.

This sounds straightforward, but it's easy to put the cart before the horse: getting excited about a new product, service, or process before understanding how that novelty can help a customer. We are tempted to think up a product and only then try to find a market for it. Or we are so focused on profitability that we are guided by it rather than the idea of adding value for the customer. Many successful innovations arise as a response to a problem or desire that a customer already has. And sometimes, it's the market situation itself that forces companies to innovate.

When Art and his management team bought The Wine Group from Coke New York, they did not consider some of the consequences that resulted from not being a Coke company any longer. Probably the biggest such surprise came when Art received a visit from the sales representative of the glass bottle supplier Owens-Illinois (O-I). Art was informed that the company's price to buy glass bottles was about to increase. While owned by Coke, The Wine Group purchased under their volume discount agreement, which was considerable, given that Coke New York purchased Coca-Cola bottles from O-I for several northeastern states. Given the razor-slim margins of the business he was in, this price increase was a potentially devastating blow for Art. Either The Wine Group's profit margin was about to evaporate or the customers were about to get an unpleasant price increase themselves.

The paradigm could be changed—and profitably—by putting the customers' needs first. Art's reaction fully embodies the Principled Entrepreneurship mindset. Instead of fighting with the supplier, instead of retreating and laying off employees to reduce overhead cost, instead of complaining about the situation, The Wine Group team went on to "deal with reality," as they called it. Dealing with their new reality meant finding a way out of a dilemma and going back to their basic conviction: they were there to provide great wine at the best value to consumers. If one part of the product was suddenly more expensive, maybe they could reduce the cost of another?

Efficiency had been a priority since Art had been hired, and there were few improvements left to be made in that respect. The wine they made was also not the issue. By now, that wine was of great quality and produced very efficiently. The focus kept coming back to the fact that The Wine Group was at a competitive disadvantage because of the cost of the glass bottles.

Art's company was not the only one that faced this high cost for their glass bottles. Gallo, their largest competitor, had found a way out using *backward integration*; they had made a major financial investment into their own glass plant in the late 1950s. This was not an option for The Wine Group, who didn't have the scale or resources at their disposal. They were stuck.

The solution developed slowly, piece by tedious piece. A few years earlier, Art's friend Henry Tirone, a large grower of high-priced Sonoma County grapes and the owner of Geyser Peak winery, was stuck with a huge oversupply of expensive grapes he couldn't sell in the grape marketplace. His solution was to make them into wine and sell them in the largest units he could and at a discounted price. The brand name became Summit, and Henry found a way to pour the wine into polyethylene bags that held more volume than glass bottles. The bags were difficult to fill, and inefficient in other ways. The whole operation had to be done manually, but Henry didn't care. His objective was not to make a profit on Summit but to simply liquidate his expensive wine to avoid a write-off. The 3-liter Summit bag was a good vehicle for moving expensive grapes because it moved almost three times more wine than one

Geyser Peak 750ml bottle. At that moment in time, Art had concluded there was no market for this concept as it existed, and even if there were, the manual process would not allow this to be scaled to commercial viability. Nevertheless, he mentally filed away the idea.

Shortly after the fateful visit of the O-I sales rep, Art and his wife, Carlyse, went on a trip to Australia together and, among other activities, went to check out the local wineries, as they always did wherever they traveled. Henry Tirone had told Art that his bag-in-box solution was actually used by several wineries in Australia, and so Art made it a point to look these companies up while he was in the area. Art discovered that these wineries had an automated production line to fill and box the polyethylene bags.

Art and Carlyse, both veterans in the wine industry,[5] were also impressed by the quality of the wine out of that packaging. It was a great solution: the sealed bag ensured that the wine was never exposed to oxygen before being poured. Unlike the glass bottle, this packaging wasn't *uncorked*, and so the seal was never broken. It stayed fresh until you used it up. In Australia they heard a concern from a production manager that bags sometimes leaked. They were intrigued. Could The Wine Group improve on this packaging, and could their customers benefit from it?

On the long plane ride home from Melbourne, Art had begun to think about the applicability of this new concept for The Wine Group. Seeing that automated production was possible had left a deep impression. It opened up the possibility for the high-volume, popularly priced brand The Wine Group wanted to make. If this worked, the cost of packaging would be a fraction of the traditional glass bottle, and it would solve all of Art's problems. But there was a lot to learn about how to truly address the customers' needs and concerns—so the team went to work.

Like most iterative processes, learning came through lots of trial and error. The production department designed a production line and improved packaging integrity—a priority among customers' concerns.

Marketing began designing big, bold graphics that would defeat Gallo's ability to subordinate competitive products. Once this was complete, it was time to test the market reception to the new Franzia 4-liter WineTap. Things didn't go well. Consumers loved the new product, but the retail trade was less than enthusiastic and even turned hostile after leakers turned up in their stores. Cleaning up a few hundred liters of wine off the floor left a few store clerks frustrated with Franzia, and the calls to the sales department were anything but friendly. Every time this happened, the team tried to find out what exactly caused the problem and what could have prevented the leakage. Then they redesigned the packaging with corrective action.

"We must have gone through over twenty iterations," Art recalled. "We'd ship a product and when the team had to take angry calls because it leaked all over the floor of a Safeway store . . . patience wore thin." Art was repeatedly asked to let the team tap out on this experiment. But he stayed the course. "We're making progress; I'm starting to like this! And by the way, we don't have any other options," he'd say.

The Wine Group continued to make incremental improvements to the design of the tap, the production process, the box, and the visuals in response to market reactions. Patience and tenacity were richly rewarded. The new bag-in-a-box packaging reduced the price and increased the quality of the final product significantly.

The Wine Group could now pass on the quality improvements and the savings to the customer and further fulfill its vision of providing good wine at a great price. It was a true win-win situation.

What would the new packaging mean to the industry leader, Gallo? They had invested heavily in the glass bottle backward integration, something companies frequently do to control cost. When faced with the new Wine Group packaging and considering whether or not to follow suit, they must have felt that having some of their product lines in box-packaging would cannibalize their glass bottle investment. A classic "sunk cost" thinking error.[6]

Looking at what happened, it looks to me that Gallo decided not to fight back with product-to-product competition but instead fought The Wine Group's new product on the shelves and used its considerable distribution power to relegate the Franzia 4-liter WineTap to the most disadvantageous space in the stores.

Art reacted fast and within his means. The increased surface area of the new packaging offered much more space for visual product representation than did the label on a wine bottle. So, while they didn't have the clout to muscle their way into good shelf position, they did make the visuals on their box-packaging so attractive and attention grabbing that you couldn't ignore them even if the product was relegated to the farthest corner of the store. They also had those win-win relationships with several distributors that really came into play at this time.

It was beginning to become clear that Franzia's 4-liter WineTap was slowly taking off, and it had a competitive advantage because it cost less to produce. As it rolled out, however, it quickly became evident that selling a Franzia 4-liter WineTap against a comparatively priced competitor was going to be very difficult. Art challenged his team to come up with more ideas and improvements. That's when the breakthrough came. Someone discovered that a 5-liter bag-in-a-box could be made and shipped while it was impossible to even produce a 5-liter glass bottle. This was the game changer the team had been searching for, and it immediately began phasing in the new 5-liter boxes with front panel flags screaming "5 liters for the price of 4." This was the perfect way to shout out the value proposition. It was then that the brand took off and never looked back. The Franzia TV commercial that subsequently ran soon drove additional brand recognition and further legitimized the product.

The next hurdle to overcome was the professional wine reviewers. The wine industry, like many other industries, has a cast of experts that shape customer opinion, and they were uniformly negative about "wine in a box." The leading and most influential expert was Frank Prial of the *New York Times*. Art arranged a meeting and flew to New York with his selling shoes on. Art started the meeting by suggesting a blind tasting of boxed Franzia and Frank's choice of several well-regarded wines in bottles. Frank wisely declined but agreed to taste Franzia alone. Little was said, but Art knew from the expression on Frank's face that he had made progress. That was confirmed a week later when a very positive article appeared above Frank's byline. Prial had a strong following of wine writers around the country. One by one, wine writers everywhere were knocking themselves out to say one good thing after another about the Franzia WineTap.

In hindsight, walking away from conventional large packaging and disrupting the status quo resulted in a huge competitive advantage for The Wine Group and made it the world's top-selling wine brand.

The competition's decision to protect the "sunk cost" of glass production did its part in allowing The Wine Group to break from the pack and took them from a cost disadvantage to a cost advantage, enabling them to become the second-largest wine producer by volume—approximately one in every seven glasses of wine consumed being from The Wine Group.

The introduction of the Franzia WineTap was an enormous success for The Wine Group, but it also resulted in incremental sales for the entire industry. For the first few years, the introduction of Franzia negatively impacted competition, but in the long run it made competition sharper, more focused, and stronger. The wine market as a whole gained an entirely new product category: branded boxed table wine. Customers finally had affordable American table wine they liked.

It all started with the reaction Art had to customer needs. When obstacles appeared—as they always do—he continued to focus on the customer and on his own team. The Franzia WineTap is a perfect example of how to allow the company's team to grow in excellence and find a solution that is both customer centric and profitable. This is what Art did so well: keep the focus on the human person.

But not all customer solutions have to necessarily be novel. Creating a successful solution will not always be a new invention, but sometimes simply a fresh effort—perhaps a market segment expansion or a new segment altogether. The Franzia WineTap story shows how innovation can go hand in hand with the creation of a new market segment. Without the new packaging that The Wine Group perfected, there would not be a 5-liter wine segment today.

Art never changed the winemaking process, but he did "tap" into changes in the wine market. What was crucial was beginning with customer needs and ending with customer satisfaction. If he hadn't paid attention to new and changing customer needs, he could have never ended up creating an entirely new customer segment. The 5-liter wine market cannot be addressed with glass bottles because of stability/breakage issues. It had to be addressed with a new form of packaging. The Wine Group's innovation consisted of finding, creating, and satisfying an entirely new and expanded customer segment! Such innovations start and end entirely with the customer. I cannot tell you how often I meet aspiring entrepreneurs who, in contrast, have a solution long before they understand or define a need.

One of my favorite examples of this happened when I met an enthusiastic young man who came to see me at The Catholic University's Ciocca Center to seek advice about launching a company based on a new product he developed.

We went to the campus Starbucks and exchanged pleasantries before we finally got to the matter at hand.

"So, what's your product?" I inquired.

"Here!"

He handed me an aluminum vial with some powder inside. I opened it, holding the open vial a few inches away from me, not sniffing it directly but sending whiffs of it toward my nose. It had no scent whatsoever.

"Don't worry, this is not toxic; it won't harm you," he assured me. "You could eat it if you want to without any adverse effect."

"What is it?"

"It's an organic powder . . . but that's just the beginning. Watch this!"

As I held the aluminum vial in my hand, he surprised me by pouring water into it. In a nanosecond the thing became so ice cold that I was afraid my fingers were going to freeze to it.

"Whoa! How long does that stay so cold?" I asked with some urgency.

"For a couple of hours. And that's not all. You can dry the powder and reuse it!"

"Wow—that's impressive!" I said while quickly putting the vial down.

"Yes, isn't it?!"

Indeed, I thought to myself.

We looked at each other, smiling in reaction to the unusual qualities of this interesting product. Then I asked him a question that I usually use to begin most of my entrepreneurial ventures and classes: "But what is this product for?"

He paused, as if the question caught him a little off-guard. "I don't know," he said frankly. "Could be used for anything. But it's totally cool, isn't it?!"

Indeed, it was, but I doubted that a customer was going to buy this powder for just "anything"—and certainly not for the price he needed to charge to parlay it into a sustainable business. This product needed a problem that it could perfectly solve. But you can't find that perfect fit if you don't start out with a specific consumer and his or her particular problem or need. That's the difference between having a technology or a product.

Art did the exact opposite: he started with the consumer need, or a consumer potential, and then developed a product to meet that target. Doing it this way ensures that there's someone there to buy your product when you create it.

The Principled Entrepreneur's Products and Services Are Created Through Human Excellence

The second key aspect of a Principled Entrepreneur's company is that its products and services are created by and delivered with human excellence. It is the *I* in "how may I help you?" Principled Entrepreneurs like Art are able to offer just the right product and service because they have put together a strong, market-focused team, which becomes a competitive advantage.

When he first started working in the wine industry, a colleague once joked to Art, "Anyone can make this stuff. The trick is to sell it at a profit!" Back in the '70s, this was an accurate assessment of the industry. Art knew that the only solution was to build strong brands. To do so, the company needed to become closer to the marketplace and much more market focused. In addition, the company had to become more agile, nimble, and responsive to market changes and opportunities. At the time, the company had no real strategic advantages so it succeeded by scrambling through the legs of giants and using superior market intelligence and agility to beat larger competitors to market opportunities. This was an effective tactic, but the company needed much more. This worked out to be an effective means of generating profits and enabling the company to begin to develop the organization. Art knew he needed a strong organization of marketing-oriented people, but more than anything he needed to find the right niche or opportunity to pursue and hopefully dominate. He did just that so when the right opportunity presented itself the organization was ready. After a long, agonizing development period with a lot of fits and starts, the box wine category emerged as the most fertile opportunity and the organization was primed and ready for it.

These are the marks of the Principled Entrepreneur: they don't want to compromise between quality and price; they want both to be good because that's what the customer wants. But good quality and price can be achieved only as a function of consumer value—it has to be priced competitively—in other words, demand drives volume and in turn achieves economies of scale.[7] This is a very difficult problem to solve: the great product that is also a great value. And Principled Entrepreneurs don't solve it by "making cheap stuff," but by creating a quality branded product that can be sold in large quantities. To do this, you require the second key aspect of a person-centered company: a focus on employees.

There's a Great Team Behind Every Great Brand

Art assembled a team and set out on the long, arduous process of creating a national brand. Reflecting the third key aspect of a Principled Entrepreneurship company, The Wine Group team started with the end in mind and thus focused on consumers first, asking derivatives of the fundamental business question: "How may I help you?" The marketing research focused on issues around taste preferences and what the consumer considered higher value as it pertains to wine. It's of course difficult to answer these questions for a market that doesn't really exist yet. It's more of an art than a science. Art's goal was to carve out a market niche for branded Italian-style table wine, where they could distinguish The Wine Group's offering from those of its competitors.

They were masters of branding, knowing that a superior wine wasn't only about great taste but also concerns the visual product appeal and a competitive price. "People taste price, imagery, packaging, and ambiance just as much and maybe even more than the berries and cherries in a product," Art once said. This approach to branding became Art's challenge to his team: deliver superior value to the consumer. Selling and reinforcing this concept was a never-ending job.

"There are two kinds of value," Art once told me. "Demonstrable and perceived. The former one is what you can see, taste, feel, and so on. The latter is a function of the imagery created by advertising, packaging, visuals, and design. Both of them are created by the company's team. Together, they become the holy grail of business: a competitive advantage. Customers want your product because of reasons beyond any specific criteria. They just love it."

Find a Truly Customer-Centered Value Proposition by Asking the Right Question

I learned about this at a surprisingly late stage in my own career. It was 1996 and I was in charge of the international market at Dragon Systems. We had just launched our speech-recognition product and were eager to get it onto shelves. At this early stage, our value proposition was "Superior, highly accurate speech recognition." It was the first such product in the world and we were proud of our innovation.

Wherever I went with the product, people were intrigued. Our product often reminded them of HAL, the wily computer from Stanley Kubrick's classic movie *2001: A Space Odyssey*. I had never before received a negative answer from a retailer until Dixon's (the UK electronic retailer) rejected the request to carry our product Naturally-Speaking in their stores. I couldn't believe it.

I tried to get in touch with the product manager by email, by phone, and by fax but did not succeed in getting a reply from her. But I couldn't let it go. I needed to know why we were rejected. So, I decided to spend a couple of weeks in the UK and introduce myself to the kind folks at the front desk at Dixon's headquarters, a tall building with a lobby where lots of vendors and other visitors like me came and went for their meetings. The only difference was that I did not have a meeting scheduled. I asked them to please let Ms. Stevens (not her real name) know that I was there, who I was, and that I wanted to discuss our product. "She's busy!" they insisted. When I responded that I would return in the afternoon, the response was, "She'll still be busy!"

I went back for a week, twice a day, until one Friday, I was told that Ms. Stevens was going to the cafeteria for a coffee and I had five minutes to talk with her before she had to return to her office. She could tell who I was immediately (probably described as "the tall guy who won't stop bugging us") and perfunctorily offered a chair for me to sit next to her at a lunch table.

"So, you don't like our product?" I went right to the point. "Why did you reject it?"

"I do not revisit my decisions," she declared. "If you came here to convince me otherwise, you're wasting your time."

"Look," I said. "I accept your decision, but please help me learn. I don't claim to be an expert on retail marketing. Just please tell me what I'm doing wrong and I'll leave you alone."

Ms. Stevens proceeded to give me a one-hour marketing class. I learned more in that one hour than I did in business school, and, honestly, during the years of work leading up to that point.

She started off playing what she called the "so what?" game, and taught me that a retail product has to sell itself based on the front of its packaging. Unless the most basic value proposition is answered at first glance, she would reject the product. She did this because Dixon's wanted to minimize the amount of intervention it took from the staff to help a customer figure out which product they wanted to buy. The value proposition we had then, "Superior, highly accurate speech recognition," didn't cut it. Neither did a reference to HAL or *Star Trek*.

What was needed, she suggested, was for us to put the customer in the center. To do this, she told me to figure out exactly who benefits most from being able to dictate text to a personal computer. Only then could our company formulate a value proposition that hit the nail on the head for that specific group. Only that would create what she called "super fans": customers who will love the product and use it well (i.e., to solve a key problem they have) and then tell everyone and their brother about it.

With that extremely useful advice, we came up with a new value proposition: "You talk; it types." For the people who had one of many reasons to want to type without using their hands, our product suddenly solved their problem at a price that seemed far lower than the value they associated with that functionality. It was only once we put the customer in the center of our concern that our products were carried by Dixon's, where they sold extremely well . . . and profitably.

When Your People Are Your Brand

Victorinox,[8] the famous Swiss Army knife producer, is a part of my childhood—the sheer mention of its name brings up wonderful memories. My godmother's husband, Franz, was an executive at the company and the two gifted me some of the most elaborate, innovative pocket knives you can imagine. I loved them, and they made me the envy of my Boy Scout troop.

Franz worked at Victorinox for over fifty years, well beyond his retirement age.

The company was founded as a loose collaboration of local blacksmiths. Carl Elsener, a cutler who, like others in the nonindustrial farmer cantons of central Switzerland, was finding it hard to make a living with this work. When the Swiss military sought a supplier of knives for its soldiers in 1890, Carl designed a simple foldable knife[9] with a few additional functionalities like a can opener, a screwdriver, and an awl. These were all of the essential tools that a soldier would need, he argued. And the soldiers loved it. Thus began the history of the Swiss Army knife and Victorinox.

Carl named his company based on two aspects of its success. One was a tribute to his mother, Victoria, because she provided him with a part of the critical funds he needed to start his factory. The other was the French name for stainless steel—*inox*[10]—which gave his pocket knives one of their key advantages—they don't rust.

Today, it is Carl's great-grandson Carl Elsener IV who leads the company, and the technology and products have vastly expanded from these simple beginnings. Fulfilling the Swiss military order for a year's supply of Swiss Army knives takes the company less than a day. The company produces over 26 million knives per year and has grown into one of the largest employers of central Switzerland with over 950 employees at its headquarters and 2,100 worldwide.[11]

But, according to everyone involved in the company, the most important things stayed the same during all this growth: the company's values and, in particular, the focus on its employees. To the Elseners, their business is not just a family business in terms of ownership. It's a family business in the sense that anyone who works at Victorinox becomes family. The company goes to great lengths to live up to that virtue. The aftermath of the 9/11 terrorist attack had a devastating impact on the pocket knife industry. Not only had airport shops been one of the best sales channels, the fact that passengers were no longer allowed to carry even the smallest of pocket knives on an airplane destroyed demand for them. Sales caved by one-third.

In response, other companies had huge layoffs. Not Victorinox. "Life has ups and downs," Elsener commented on the experience. "We are assured that after seven fat years, there come seven lean years. We made sure to be ready for that." The company asked everyone to stop working overtime, to not cash out unused vacation days, and to reduce shifts selected per employee.

When that was not enough, the company subcontracted its employees out to other local businesses in different industries. All this remained seamless for the employee. They showed up at work as usual, were bussed to the other company, worked there all day, and then were bussed back to Victorinox. There was no change in salary or benefits. Victorinox absorbed all the mediation hassle and payment differential.

This care for and rewarding of its employees is what enables Victorinox to outperform other companies that offer a similar product or service. It's something they have that others can't imitate easily. It took many years, even decades, to develop. The secret to such entrepreneurial success is to develop your people and your team into your competitive advantage, which, ultimately, grows out of your company culture.

Franz, my godmother's husband, passed away some ten years ago. But his widow still receives a Christmas gift from Victorinox every December. "With a personal note from Carl!" She proudly explains, "He wrote to me how much Franz meant to the Victorinox family and that he will never forget him."

Neither will anyone who ever met Franz forget Victorinox. Because, for him, Victorinox was not just work; it was a part of his being. It helped him to become the person he was made to be. And for Victorinox, Franz was a part of its competitive advantage.

The key differentiator for companies of Principled Entrepreneurs is the prioritization of customer-focused, profitable value creation through excellence at work! And that excellence is best achieved through a company culture that is employee-centered.

Principled Entrepreneurs Always Put People First

The economy exists for people. This might be an obvious point, but it often gets lost in the shuffle of doing business. We focus too much on the efficiency of what we do and on the financial results. Our desks were never meant to be our altars.[12] When we start to feel like we are on a "hamster wheel" for short-term financial performance—and I think we've arrived at that point—it's time to rethink and go back to the basics.

I believe the American Dream encapsulates very well what the economy is all about. This is not a concept for "America" only. It bears this name because the US is the birthplace of a well-functioning economy that empowers people to have social mobility, freedom of choice, power of initiative, and the opportunity to flourish.

In other words, the economy is a wonderful network of productivity and exchange. It allows us to bring the value we add through our excellence to solving customers' needs profitably. We must not forget the purpose of the economy. We must not forget that at the core of it all is the human person—all who are involved in this business: the individual customer, worker, and investor. Each is called to be the best they can be. Allowing everyone to be what one does, and to do what one is. The work you do is a part of the excellence you're called to pursue throughout your life, in collaboration with those you work with and for. It is a system that exists not just to allow us to provide for our physical well-being. No, the economy supports us in one of our unique abilities that distinguishes us from all other creatures on Earth: our ability to create. And it does so only as far as it keeps the human person at the center of its concern.

Living Pillar 1: The Economy Exists for People, Not People for the Economy

1. Have there been times when you found work to be a joy or grief? When did you feel that and what specifically caused you to have that feeling? What parts of your work are responsible for each experience? Who taught you to have joy or grief at work? Based on this insight, what three actions can you take during the next thirty days to create more occasions of joy at work?

2. How does your life story lead to your work interest? What experiences (like Art having served in the military and worked at Gallo, General Foods, and Coke New York) do you still need to "collect/accumulate" to get ready for your great fulfillment in what you do for work?

3. Who are your customers? Define your market niche and find indicators that validate its existence. Who are these customers and what do they value?

4. How do you profitably address a legitimate customer need? What is the "WineTap" opportunity in your industry or

market? What does your brand represent to your market niche and how does it answer the "so what?" question?

5. How are the goods you produce truly good? How do the services you provide truly serve? Be specific.

6. How is your team your competitive advantage? What can you do to make it (more) so? How can you put people first? What repeatable two actions can you take and practice during the next two months to put your people first?

4

Pillar 2: To Work Is to Create; To Create Is to Be Human

Work gives you meaning and purpose and life is empty without it.
–Stephen Hawking

When we work, we do not only *make* more, but we *become* more. The Principled Entrepreneur is primarily a creator—someone who pursues their excellence by creating value for others profitably. That value entails supporting others on the team in their pursuit of excellence and appropriately rewarding all stakeholders physically, mentally, and spiritually.

How does Pillar 1—that the economy and businesses should exist for people, instead of the other way around—work in practice? The answer is Pillar 2: to work is to create, to create is to be human. This chapter explores how a Principled Entrepreneur *creates* goods that are truly good for their customers, and services that truly serve them.

They *support* the excellence of their employees so they can become the company's competitive advantage[1] in creating value for their customers. The returns generated are appropriately used to *reward* and encourage everyone involved in creating them. These are the three key objectives of business, entrepreneurship, and work in general: CSR. In that order and priority.

Milton Friedman's famous statement[2] that the only social responsibility of a business is the creation of shareholder value is held up as "proof" that business is only about money and that the pursuit of business is an inherently selfish undertaking. This is a characterization that I cannot agree with, but still many within and beyond the business world hold that misconstrued perception.[3] Some act on that impoverished, purely materialistic view of business and the economy. The results of such narrow-minded efforts end more often than not in the news headlines and reinforce the belief that business is inherently materialistic and selfish.

As a reaction to some of this faulty "money only" approach to business, critics came up with CSR—which usually stands for Corporate Social Responsibility—the idea that a successful company ought to "give back" to the community or society by measuring what it does for its various stakeholders. Principled Entrepreneurship proposes an alternative or answer to conventional CSR: Create, Support, Reward. It stands as an alternative, or an answer, to the Corporate Social Responsibility thinking that's so prevalent today.

I find that current approach wrongheaded, because it only reinforces the idea that business itself is all and only about the outcome: money. The effort doesn't "fix" the false view and exercise of business but tries to balance the "evil" of business with the "good" of CSR, almost as if business should "atone" for itself with donations after the fact.

Moreover, CSR doesn't solve the problem. The "added aspects"[4] that CSR obligations ask for are extrinsic to the actual "doing" of business. These newly introduced aspects compete for the money that the business[5] generates. There's still a hyper-focus on money and profit.

A great paradox is created if we do not understand that business exists to serve people, if we don't grasp the deeper meaning of what it means to work. It turns everything I do into a materialistic scheme. It ultimately makes money the only measure that I share in common with those around me. The value of excellence, teamwork, the creative process, innovation, and products are ignored.

This paradox could be called "financialization." It is the exclusive obsession with the monetary aspects of business, the economy, and life. We abhor another person's focus on "only" money, and in response do exactly the same. This is a foundational mistake—and not only of some in the Corporate Social Responsibility movement but also of many other proposals and attempts to improve the current free market system. Solutions that promise to rectify what ails our economy often work within the same myopic paradigm and sometimes make it worse. I would suggest that what is needed is a change in focus—a return to the basic idea and purpose of business: the human person, our (creative) work, and the value created for customers.

In my view, what makes the free market system better than other economic systems is not primarily money, but the creative freedom and excellence of each individual that it enables. Money or profit is a part of that—a vital, even nonnegotiable part—but it's not what animates our pursuit of excellence. We pursue excellence for the sake of excellence. And there are many examples of this at work.

The Creation of a Breakthrough Tire

François Michelin, a great industrial leader, was the grandson of Édouard Michelin, who cofounded the now-famous tire company Michelin et Cie with his brother André in 1889.

François told my friend Alexandre Havard the story of how he felt his grandfather gave Michelin its unique corporate culture. It is a prime example of applying the CSR of Principled Entrepreneurship: to create innovation through human excellence, to support human flourishing, and to reward everyone involved in the endeavor.

Many years before François was an adult and worked at his family's company, a man appeared at the factory's doors and asked for a job. The HR manager wanted to know about his professional qualifications to which the young man, Marius Mignol, responded, "None." Marius had no formal education. The only experience he had so far was helping out at the local printing press. The HR manager felt bad for Marius and hired him to work in the printing department of Michelin. Once Francois's grandfather Édouard heard about the new employee, he scolded the hiring manager for his decision—not for hiring Marius, but for sending him to the print shop. "Don't you realize that we won't get to know this man by having him do what he already knows? And not only that—he will not learn anything new about himself either, about his potential, by simply doing what he already knows. Remember, you have to break the stone to discover the gem inside! Send him to work in the international department!"

A few months later, Édouard went to check up on Marius to see how he was doing, dealing with all the international transactions in foreign currencies. He was astonished to discover that Marius Mignol devised for himself a slide rule to more quickly and accurately do the currency conversions. "This man must be a genius," Michelin thought to himself, and assigned him at once to the engineering department.

At that time, the tire manufacturers could not keep up with the rapid advances in new and faster engines. The most modern tires could not withstand speeds of over 80 kilometers per hour, and the new cars could already reach 100 kilometers easily. The tires were the weak point of the car industry. Mignol was put on the team that tried to solve that problem. This ended up being a very consequential decision. "You know," Michelin wrote in his book *And Why Not*, "sometimes it is the ignorant person who has the advantage over someone who has learned, in that he does not live in the graveyard of ideas." It did not take Mignol long to find a solution. Fueled by his passion, observation, and hard work, he invented a basic radial tire design that placed the metal cords directly from bead to bead and aligned them in parallel. The strength of the structure came from steel wires running with the cords. Problem solved! A lad without any formal education solved an engineering conundrum that vexed the PhDs.

This is the essence of the Michelin corporation to this day: Allow employees to develop in real time. Do not hire primarily based on schooling or degrees but put people to work and allow them to discover their strengths on the job. Don't create predetermined job tracks that create rigid silos in the company but allow employees to unleash their passion at work, to grow into the job and overcome the challenges they encounter along the way, and to fully become the best version of themselves. There are no predetermined career paths at Michelin, only paths of greatness, risk, and passion. "It is only free thinking that is entirely worthy of a free man," Michelin would later write. His grandfather's story gave young François the vision for his own career and taught him the essence of the company culture at Michelin Tires.

Young François studied mathematics before joining the family business in 1951 as an engineer, and after working in various roles he eventually became the CEO in 1959. Marius Mignol was still with the company when François started working there. He recalls that, one day, when he was uncertain about his future there, Marius told him, "If you don't like tires, get out of here!" Well, François did not just like tires; he loved them. "What a fascinating object [they are]! The car is a marvelous symbol that epitomizes the whole history of humanity all on its own: the marathon, Roman roads, the horse."

François Michelin strongly believed that the men and women of Michelin are the company's competitive advantage. He went out of his way to get to know his employees. He engaged them in conversations about themselves, and encouraged them to go deeper. "What is really important is to be found deep within oneself," he would advise his coworkers. Throughout his tenure, he supported the flourishing of his workforce in their jobs and ensured they received superior training. Because of that, he fully trusted them to carry out their missions and was comfortable to give them decision power and responsibility. He loved to tour the shop floors and visit the sales force, to talk with the people who design and manufacture the products or those who are in direct contact with customers. During his fifty years at the helm, everyone who met or worked with François Michelin remembers a man who listened to others carefully, had exceptional analytical skills, and would encourage them to "become who you are." François Michelin inspired dedication by sharing both successes and challenges and by giving people the opportunity to experiment: "If you can learn from a mistake, it is an opportunity to grow and make progress."

To him, his position as CEO was simple: keep the vessel on course, protect and support passengers and cargo, anticipate events in the world and the conflicting currents of the market but always taking care to satisfy the three groups of people who are entitled to hold him accountable: the customers, the employees, and the shareholders.

Michelin and his company thrived and he had much to say about the system of the market economy. "Human beings are the only self-teachable beings on the planet. In their hands they have all the means to better themselves or destroy themselves. To grow, they have to constantly weigh the consequences of their actions. Capitalism gives them this opportunity to be responsible."

For Michelin, the matter of the economic system had no ambiguity about it at all: The system is made for man, and not the opposite. Capitalism, he maintained, is a system that educates man and allows him to flourish as a human person. Not that there are no laws or sanctions, but people are allowed a wide scope of activity. A good system has a minimally necessary framework.

It was not only upturns he experienced during his tenure at the company. Like everyone else, Michelin experienced difficulties due to the oil crises at the end of the 1970s. The company had to restructure and reorganize. At times, he even had to reduce the workforce, but he did so very reluctantly and only as a last resort. "Employers who think only of laying off people are not employers. Dismissing someone is a terrible human drama." He felt that when someone leaves the company, it is a part of the company's very substance that is going away. "Every time we had to do it," he recalled, "was a real ordeal for the company."

Even in these circumstances, François Michelin remained confident in the company's strategy based on innovation and a focus on individual persons and their development.

Principled Entrepreneurs foster an environment in which each person can flourish and excel—individually and as a group—through creation, lending support, and offering fair and lasting rewards.

This logically flows from the first principle: if work can help each of us to personally reach our full human potential, then it would only follow that I would like others to have the same opportunity. Your own excellence is always connected to that of others. Mignol's excellence benefited the HR manager who hired him. It was good for François Michelin who had not even begun working at the company. And Mignol's excellence has benefited you, who are reading this right now, many times in your life. Without a Principled Entrepreneur like Édouard Michelin, who actively supported and promoted excellence in others, that exponential process would not have occurred.

At the core of our work with others is our intent for them, what we wish for, or from, them. As Pope John Paul II liked to point out to those of us who worked for him, it's all about love. In English there's only one word for love, so it sounds odd to "love" your customers, coworkers, and investors. The expression in Italian is more nuanced. You would not say *"Ti amo"* ("I love you") to an acquaintance or an employee; that phrase is reserved for familial and romantic love. You'd say *"Ti voglio bene,"* meaning "I want your good!" The late pope often said he loved that expression because it points to the root of love:

wanting the good of the other.[6] When we love someone, we want their good, especially their ultimate good. If I love you, why would I make you do something, give you something, or do something to you that would hinder your fulfillment?

I know it sounds unconventional to bring *love* into the conversation when talking about building a company, but it's well worth it.[7] It's important that not just your customers feel loved; it's a game changer for employees as well. Édouard Michelin treated Marius Mignol with love. Giving others the chance to be creative—to actualize their potential—is to truly want their good. To do outstanding work, you first need love. You cannot do good work in a hostile environment. And this is not an outdated sentiment. Whole Foods used to have a set of management principles that begin with love.[8] We're talking about the compassionate kind of love, like empathy. What matters are the small things, because they add up. Think of random acts of kindness supported by a company structure.[9]

Creation is a team sport. No individual can sustainably invent, produce, market, and sell its products alone. It is not just physically impossible, but also impossible in terms of expertise. Marius Mignol learned from and was supported by others on his team. They trained him, explained to him how tires worked, what their shortcomings were, and what the materials were. Each one of us has a certain natural talent reinforced by training that makes us more excellent at a certain job than many others. What is required of us is a *contribution mentality* so that we seek the common good of our team, our customer, and society in all we do. It's not about getting something *out* of the work or not. Mignol probably made a good living at Michelin, but I am sure that in his mind, his most treasured reward was the contribution he made to the safety of drivers around the world. We ought to be rewarded for our excellent work and profit from our business—that's what distinguishes it from a hobby—but the intrinsic focus is not on getting the largest reward; rather, it's on adding value and contributing to the greater good.

The First Objective of a Company Is to Create

Have you ever considered that work is creative? The act of creating is what work is all about: seeing a need for a new (or better) product or service, and innovating to meet that need. We usually call that "entrepreneurship," but turning an idea into reality should be a part of any work.

Work Makes Us More Fully Human

Have you ever been unintentionally unemployed for any length of time? The suffering you experience goes beyond a lack of income, which would be already bad enough. What you feel most profoundly is a loss of dignity, a kind of meaninglessness. You feel like a piece of your humanity is missing. This happens even when you receive unemployment benefits. Having a job or career that you enjoy is one of your most fundamental desires. According to recent Pew research, it is more important to teens than helping others or getting married. That feeling varies over a lifetime, but what this indicates is the innate desire you have for meaningful work of some kind. We are not meant *not* to work. If you don't work (whatever form that takes), you suppress an aspect of your humanity.[10]

There is a danger in looking at work only as a way to make money. Ignoring the deeper meaning and purpose of work has negative consequences. As Tomas Chamorro-Premuzic wrote in the *Harvard Business Review*, "Quite simply, you're more likely to like your job if you focus on the work itself, and less likely to enjoy it if you're focused [only] on the money."[11] When we do not work, and do not work joyfully, we lose a key aspect of our humanity.

I've seen the same thing happen to people who stopped working because they had made a financial fortune. We wither away without work because, in working, the path is the goal, and the goal is the path. Work is a transcendent aspect of our humanity. When we work, we don't just make more, we become more. Think of the famous NASA custodian: "I'm not mopping the floors, I'm putting a man on the moon."[12]

When our work satisfies an important customer need, we benefit not only the consumer, but ourselves as well. We get great satisfaction from the work, from the "other-directed process" of helping our customers. We also enjoy the collaboration within our company, our team. It makes us grow as a person. Through work, I live up to my potential and become the person God created me to be. That is the ultimate reward and reason for our work.

There Are No Shortcuts to the True Benefits of Work

A disturbing trend is that some of us no longer want to "work" in the creative sense. An increasing number of people I meet no longer want to create income or wealth by their own physical or mental work, through innovation, building, service, or creation. Instead, they pursue the dream of making it big in the stock market or a windfall from some financial scheme. I believe this unfortunately represents a growing trend in a growing sector of society. A deep-seated change in attitude: we seek to harvest but we refuse to do the work of sowing and creating. This is a very dangerous trend because taking work out of the center of generating our income, as tempting as it is, leads to the same disastrous results as taking the human person out of the center of the economy.[13] It is to miss the entire point. The economy and work are not a means to an end. The prosperity that ensues from work is only half the part (if that) that will give us satisfaction and happiness. The very activity of work itself is an integral part of human flourishing. Without it, we languish.[14] Yet I see more and more people around me who dream of a life of little work and lots of money.

The vision of less and less work is not new. John Maynard Keynes predicted fifty years ago that by now—the early twenty-first century—we would all have a fifteen-hour workweek.[15] (And the idea is still popular, judging by the success of Tim Ferriss's book *The 4-Hour Workweek*.) But this vision will never be a reality in a prosperous economy. Keynes's grandnephew is working fifteen hours a day as a professor. And Tim

Ferriss works sixty hours a week.[16] Work is about creating value and, as I've written many times already in this book, we measure value with money.

We may dream of super efficiency and automation,[17] but the truth is that the more money people earn, the more hours they work. The poor are the ones who face chronic underemployment. They're the ones who face involuntary "fifteen-hour work weeks" and five-day weekends. And as a result, they suffer mentally, socially, and financially.[18] Working so little is not something people choose to do. It's often a situation they're trying to escape.[19]

There is no substitute for work because it is an essential part of who we are. Everyone deserves to work and ought to have the opportunity to work. Principled Entrepreneurs recognize that this is essential for a free and prosperous economy.

Human Creativity Fuels the American Dream

One of the key results of avoiding work is that we no longer create new value. When that happens, we compromise our own freedom and social mobility. Creating value is akin to creating new money. When we no longer create wealth, the economy becomes a zero-sum proposition and we have to resort to redistributing the wealth that already exists. Unfortunately, this is becoming an attractive solution to many.

Could anyone have imagined that thirty years after the collapse of the USSR, people in the United States would be seriously considering socialism?[20] This change is not only due to the lack of creative work. It is also a result of the widespread abuse of the market economy. In fact, many of our contemporaries, especially young people, don't see a free market economy when they look at our current system.[21] In a 2020 college student survey, 45 percent of respondents defined capitalism as "an economic system in which corporations utilize grants, special tax breaks, political connections, and special rules that favor them over competitors to earn profits"—a definition of crony capitalism.[22]

I came to America thirty years ago for many reasons, but certainly a key one was the economic opportunity. And so many others do the same. The American Dream! Social mobility, "making it"—it's the quintessential American promise. A society that is not afraid of competition, that roots for the underdog, a system that gives everyone a chance and celebrates their success.

This dream is very much alive today,[23] but the illusion of wealth-without-value-creation,[24] or "financialization" as I would call it, risks turning a nation of hard workers and creators into a nation of opportunistic gamblers in a zero-sum game.

Principled Entrepreneurship is about ensuring that doesn't happen. We are mindful that the first objective of work and of a business is to create, because creativity is the path to excellence. In a more global sense, entrepreneurship is not simply about creating a product or a service but, more importantly, about cultivating an environment for human creativity.

I love Peter Drucker's description: "… by applying management concepts and management techniques (asking, What is 'value' to the customer?), standardizing the 'product,' designing [creation] process and tools, and by basing training on the analysis of the work to be done and then setting the standards it required, McDonald's both drastically upgraded the yield from resources, and created a new market and a new customer. This is entrepreneurship."

I would propose something even simpler. *Everyone* can have a mindset like the one Drucker describes. Indeed, we'd be greatly blessed if we had such entrepreneurs working at all levels in our businesses.

Friedman's declaration of "the business of business is business" is a gross oversimplification. I prefer instead the observation of my colleague John McNerney:

The business of business properly understood is necessarily personalistic.
The human person acting as an entrepreneur or working in business is

not merely a froth and bubble in the stream of history but is a freely act-
ing (creating) person motivated toward specific ends. The business per-
son can be seen as an exemplar of what it means to be a human being.
Commerce is not necessarily, as W.B. Yeats suggested, just about fum-
bling in the greasy till and adding the halfpence to the pence. Business
is not an end in itself, rather it creates space in which the human person
can realize their personal dignity and excellence in creative action. As
human people we live in an existential tension searching to become who
we are. It is a part of a whole; of who we all are as persons.[25]

When we are creative, we don't simply make more; we also grow
ourselves, both as individuals and as teams. The value we generate
is both *within others*—in the products, services, and relationships we
create—and *within ourselves*. Only humans have that creative potential,
and that's the reason why an investment in the human person is an
investment with infinite returns. This is the marvel of human work—like
the miracle of the loaves and the fishes—and, by extension, why business
is an inherently moral undertaking.

The Second Objective of a Business Is to Support

Principled Entrepreneurs create companies whose competitive advantage is human work and ingenuity. This is achieved best by ensuring that
everyone on the team has complementary strengths, and that everyone
on the team is supported to pursue their unique excellence. If creating
is so good for me, I ought to want others to have the same opportunity
to realize it for themselves. By building a company that grows through
the flourishing of each employee, we create a company that is sustained
by human excellence. Putting the person in the center of concern of the
business is a very successful strategy.

Support the Teams to Pursue Complementary Excellence

There is personal and team excellence; the latter puts the former to shame. No one in business is successful alone. Entrepreneurship is by definition a team sport. The pursuit of group excellence is maybe the entrepreneur's most challenging and most rewarding task. Making one team out of many persons, matching their talents and gifts to compensate for one another's blind spots, only makes the result more excellent and productive than if each was alone. Unity from plurality is divine!

The effective business leader is not a soloist but more like an impresario. They let the product and the team shine through the common excellence achieved in pleasing the audience. If this is done well, it actually becomes the team's or the company's competitive advantage. The trick is to nurture and empower others to grow in their excellence. If the team is created well, then everyone's excellence combines into that perfect orchestra that creates amazing music together, and enjoys doing it.

François Michelin had a veritable curiosity to find out what someone's excellence was. He never doubted that absolutely everyone had one. Can you imagine working with someone like that? Someone who is convinced with every fiber in his body that you are best at something, and is proactively supporting your quest to find it? Michelin's faith in humanity, his trust in the potential of each person, is exemplary and makes him one of the great role models of Principled Entrepreneurship.

Art Ciocca similarly led by example in the pursuit of excellence. He had experienced a lot of politics and bureaucracy and was fed up with double standards at work. He wanted to have a transparent company, a place where everyone was open to learning and changing in pursuit of both personal and group excellence. I believe that one of Art's great achievements is that he made others better through his leadership, how he developed and enabled them. The excellence he inspired was pursued even when he wasn't physically there.

All of us are always on a path toward excellence, but we are also never quite there. That's because self-actualization is not a goal but a path.

Excellence is something that never is but is always just becoming. It is a process that relies heavily on feedback and correction. It is not a comfortable process. Receiving honest feedback about one's work and how to become better at it is tough medicine, but the only one that works.

One of Art's great frustrations with politics in the workplace is that it smothers excellence. So, when he became the CEO, he put excellence at the center and expelled politics. He promoted some of the people who had brought him the best solutions earlier, the employees who had a can-do attitude and fixed things. Being a member of such a team—one that learns and grows together, that offers support for everyone in the group—provides tremendous meaning and a sense of purpose to everyone's life.

Teamwork Creates Spontaneous Order

If an entrepreneur creates a company where there are no "employees" but only team members—where everyone is there to become a better version of themselves, to pursue personal and team excellence—good things will happen.

Art assembled a team out of his "inherited" staff at The Wine Group. Everyone on that team wanted to become better at what they did. In self-interest, they wanted to make better wine and create a great company that would support their own career and excellence. That team at The Wine Group created unforeseen advances and growth in the wine industry. Not because of a specific plan, but because each of them added up into a group that was mutually complementary. A group that was far more than the sum of its parts. Art often told me that he's amazed at what happened at The Wine Group. He did not plan it. "Our company's success just kind of happened, like a miracle," he'd tell me.

We have to have faith and self-control to let this "overnight success" happen, because it's not the result of top-down planning and micromanagement. But when it does happen, it sure looks like a miracle: suddenly a group functions perfectly, cacophony turns into the most beautiful symphony, obstacles turn into opportunities—all because each member of the group is allowed to use their free will to contribute, to enter into the give-and-take of human excellence. This is spontaneous order.

There's spontaneous order in nature—flocks of birds flying amazing patterns in the sky, a pack of wolves creating its hierarchy, a tree developing a pattern of branches and leaves. This seemingly spontaneous order is actually programmed by the laws of nature.

Society is like that, except that humans are more than animals. Our free will enables us to rise above our instincts and ingrained tendencies to a certain extent. We can make decisions that go against our natural inclinations and aim at our transcendent aspirations. Each individual has that ability, whether we always use it or not. Human dignity is defined as the innate value we have simply for being a person. We have a kind of spark in us that is very different from any other creature. If we are allowed to, each one of us learns from past decisions and mistakes and grows, makes better choices next time, and learns to pursue personal excellence. This pursuit of excellence is part of our human nature, and society does well to allow everyone to pursue their excellence. As a matter of fact, the offering of that ability to everyone is called the common good because it benefits everyone when we all flourish. There are some very interesting studies that talk about "network effects" in society that remind me of the "flock of birds in the sky" phenomenon.[26]

Companies are by definition not caused by spontaneous order. They're always planned. But you could argue that cooperation and competition between them can be spontaneous order—things like industry clusters and expertise areas. Or efforts like *open source software* and *wiki pages*.

Some companies try to use something approaching spontaneous order happening at various levels. Gore-Tex is famous for having a very *flat* organization; the CEO even calls herself the non-CEO. She presumably does that because she is trying to encourage human ingenuity in an environment of freedom and spontaneity. Not *pure* spontaneous order, but as close as it gets in a business. A business is kind of a small society. Similarly, to encourage spontaneous order to occur, and to provide an environment of freedom of action, the leadership of the company first of all has to believe in the fundamental goodness of humanity—not just in general, but the goodness of the very people working in that company. It is forever our temptation to interfere with people, to distrust them, to micromanage and control them. This is so both in society and in business. But the greatest achievements and advancements happen through spontaneous order—when we are allowed to do what we want to do, what we perceive as good, when we're supported to pursue our individual excellence in concert with those around us doing the same.[27] That is when our work transcends: when we work in harmony, each pursuing our excellence in an environment that fully supports and integrates our effort into the overall team, all without being forced to do another person's will.

Your Ergon: Being the Best Version of Yourself

Great teams add up to more than the sum of their parts. Have you ever thought about how that's possible? It doesn't simply happen when everyone gives their best. It also requires you to give your best *at what you are best at*. And it requires everyone on the team not to be the best at the same thing. Creating strong, supportive teams is one of the cornerstones of Principled Entrepreneurship and it starts by understanding what personal talent, potential, and excellence is. Let me explain.

In Greek philosophy, there's a concept called *ergon*—it's where "ergonomics" comes from. As defined in Aristotle's Ethics, it's the distinctive work of an actor, the thing that is proper to its nature. For example, a hammer could be used as a door stopper and a door stopper as a hammer—but each is the best fit for the job it was designed for in the first place. A hammer's ergon is to drive nails into wood and a door stop's ergon is to stop doors from swinging back and forth.

But you are not just a generic hammer or door stop. You're especially not a generic human being. You are a unique, *unrepeatable* creature made in the image of God. There is no one else just like you. That means you don't just have a generic human ergon. There is an *ergon*, a distinctive work, a "good that only you can achieve." This notion that I could do something better than anyone else was hard for me to get used to at first.

My ergon is to communicate and make ideas understandable to others. I have a strong sense of empathy that enables me to see things from someone else's perspective—like a customer, a partner, or an employee.[28] I have used this for many years to lead and build companies, to rally employees, to create products, and to sell and market to consumers.

Now I use it to convey ideas in the classroom. I use my specific gifts for it. And I try to minimize, or avoid, some of my weaknesses. I am a big ideas guy—I don't do well with small details. I struggle with accounting and other minutiae.

I feel that God gave me very specific, unique opportunities and experiences that helped form me this way. Good ones and bad ones—but they made me unique. I'm "unrepeatable," as my friend Luke Burgis would say.

So, what is your unique ergon?

Think about what it takes for you to find and pursue your uniqueness. Find out what you—only you—can offer the world. And once you know it, pursue it to deliver at your peak excellence, and enable everyone around you to do the same. That's the way of the Principled Entrepreneur.

Hiring for Ergon

A key role of management is to align and nurture the ergons of the various employees, groups, and departments to ensure that they all add up to the overall culture for the company. It's like balancing an equation. The contribution of each part is unique and predictable, so that in concert with the other parts, the equation is in balance.

What makes the difference is people's personalities—something each and every one of us brings to a job. No matter the demands or the training, certain behaviors and attitudes cannot fully be learned. Some people have a knack for numbers and some don't. Some are brilliant at language, some always see the glass as half full, others excel in feeling empathy and turning that into product feedback. Still others are so convincing that they could sell sand in the desert. These are not skills that can be learned—they're natural talents.

So, when you are creating culture and need to fill a job, it pays to start off with the following questions: What talents should the person doing this job have? What natural traits do we need from the best person for this job? What attitude is critical for this position? What character do we want this person to have? Skills and knowledge are secondary—you can easily teach skills. It's the natural talent question that will make or break this job.

The reason why this approach is more effective is that it does not lump skill, knowledge, and talent together. Talents such as "handles change well," "is a self-starter," or "is good at customer service" undoubtedly require skills and knowledge, but without natural talent, no amount of training will help. Training those who have talent, on the other hand, will provide significant improvements easily.

What does this mean for creating a culture? It means that you should select your employees not primarily based on skill and knowledge but rather on talent and character. How? Start by describing the ideal. Create a job description based on a person's talent and character. Maybe look at your top performers and analyze what they have that others don't. Discovering what sets them apart is usually an intuitive process—gauging the "feelable" stuff we immediately notice when we talk with someone. Then, complement the job description with the required outcomes. What does this person need to achieve? What is the final result you would consider a success? This together makes up a great job description. Here's an example:

> Job: Helpdesk Technician
>
> Talents needed: Inquisitive person who loves to solve problems even if data is scarce. Conceptual thinker with a love for detail. Good at verbal expression.
>
> Attitudes and culture needed: Only happy when (s)he can help people. Empathy. Loves people (extrovert).

It's important to understand that this approach is not trying to judge "the person" but rather pinpoint their talent and type—like the Myers–Briggs test. It's not a value statement about the person but rather a tool that allows both the person and the company to win. The person is in a job at which they are more likely to succeed, and the company has a culture with more successful employees.

What if you have an existing team and try to apply this approach? Instead of evaluating your employees' competencies in the next evaluation cycle, try to talk about talents and non-talents. This initially can be tricky, so it might be a good idea to start first with the management team—maybe the CEO—to break the ice and create a culture of trust.

My talent is verbal and conceptual. I relate well to people. I can talk up a storm. I see overall patterns and am good at integrating them. I am a generalist. My non-talent areas are in details, numbers, and minutiae.

The idea for me is to have a job where I can develop my talents and my non-talents are the strength of my teammates. Whenever I lead a company, for example, I immediately get two key positions filled around me: a CFO and a special projects person. The CFO compensates for my lack of accounting and finance talent. I usually try to hire a person with a strong sense of what is right, someone who is not afraid to speak up when they see an issue, even if it's uncomfortable.[29] I look for a real numbers person who cannot stand it when there's even the smallest discrepancy, a perfectionist. The special projects person follows up on things I do to make sure the details are covered. This person needs to like to finish things and have patience. A good sense of humor and perspective on life helps as these are often stressful and difficult projects and I do not always have realistic expectations. This person has to be comfortable to manage up and deal with someone who can be intimidating in both size and amount of enthusiasm (that would be me).

Andreas Widmer
Talent Areas: Language and verbal agility; Contagious enthusiasm; Presence; Pattern recognition; Integrating concepts and ideas; Empathy
Character: Jovial; Positive; Conflict-averse
Non-Talent Areas: Attention to detail; Dealing with numbers; Exact processes; Engineering and technology

You see how this works? Creating a culture of sustainable performance does not come from mimicry or tasks; it comes from our pursuit of excellence, each in our own way, with our own talents and strengths adding up to pursue a common goal.

The difficult task of the Principled Entrepreneur is to gain an understanding of everyone's ergon, define the team's needs in terms of different ergons, and then put that team together with persons having complementary ergons. This is one of the "art" aspects of Principled Entrepreneurship in that it's certainly not a science, and is somewhat objective. Nonetheless, following a clear process, putting the thinking in writing, sharing it with others, and receiving constructive feedback and introducing this as a concept and vocabulary when discussing the team brings one well on the way to creating great teams.

The Third Objective of a Business Is to Reward

A reward is something we receive for something well done. At work we are expected to do a good job and to add value through our work, and that is rightfully rewarded. Usually, the pay for our work is in direct proportion to the value we add—value in the sense of "value add" for the customer, which is made explicit through higher profits. The more we contribute to the company's profit, the more the company pays us.

While that sounds very straightforward, it has not always been this way, nor should it always be this way. Let me explain.

1. We don't all have access to the same part of the value chain that adds the most critical components to it, for which the customer is willing to pay a high price. Some of us work in very basic manual labor or service provision that is necessary for the overall delivery of the value-adding product or service, but it's not the *singular* aspect that finally makes it of such great value. Think of mining for cobalt, or cleaning the office or the streets, the maintenance of our infrastructure, and so on. These jobs are not measured with the "high profitability" product delivery, but without their constantly being provided for, the final product or service could not be delivered. The contribution of such work might be aggregate, or foundational, but that needs to be rewarded in terms of what it means to us more than just its particular contribution to the last mile of value add of a product. That means that there has to be equity in how much each person gets paid along the process of creating a product or delivering a service that acknowledges the ultimate value of the product to the end user.

2. Reward ought not to be exclusively measured by productivity or contribution to the value added. A donkey can pull far greater weight than I can, but you don't reward a donkey more

than me if you ask me to pull a cart. A computer can do a faster job at a checkout than a human, but it is (I hope) obvious that we would not pay a computer more than a human being for doing the same job. This has to do with human dignity. Humans are on a different pay scale. We pay a person a reward adequate for a human being, not comparable to an animal or an inanimate object. That means that we pay them first based on the fact that they're human, and second based on how productive they are or how much value they add.

All this is to say that reward is as human a category as the creating and supporting objectives of work. It must be as person-centered as the rest of the company. If we only measure profit and exclusively pay on access, productivity, or financial aspects, we won't develop people and we don't further human excellence, which is the core objective of work. This also means that money is not the only reward by which employees are motivated. Since currency is our universal measure of trade, we like to be rewarded with money for our work because it easily translates into other, tangible things we need or desire.

"So, what motivates you?" I asked Art during one of our conversations. "Most people looking in from the outside would think you did this for the money, right?" He did not hesitate in his answer.

"Years ago, the easy course would have been to sell the company," he explains. "We even received several unsolicited offers. It would have been equally easy to take the company public, with extraordinary payouts to the current owners. But we never once seriously considered either of the options. Selling out to a competitor would probably have achieved the highest economic return but it would have resulted in the loss of jobs for a lot of valuable employees who were instrumental to our success. Going public would have been totally unprincipled, given our previously stated positions that cyclical agricultural companies don't belong in the public arena. Instead, we chose to be dedicated to investing in the growth of brands, facilities, distribution networks, and an organization with enduring values." I actually think that Art represents the majority of entrepreneurs with this statement. The true reward they're after is not financial; it's excellence and creating value.

Good Stewardship as an Integral Corporate Value

Art has always believed "to whom much is given, much is expected." He put this belief into practice by making it a key cultural value and aggressively promoting it to his organization. The shared value within the company is to pass along values that will enable the company to last for generations to come. The Wine Group management wanted to make sure that future management and team members of The Wine Group would also keep the course they chose. They wanted to codify that excellence, and long-term success of the company was a greater reward than short-term bonuses and fast cash-outs. They wanted stewards to manage the company, not traders.

They also decided not to create financial incentive plans for their employees. In a business that deals with an agricultural product, the key influencers over major profitability issues of the company are Mother Nature and the management. Art believed that smart decisions are made with the long term in mind and that it would be counterproductive to establish objects for employees in such a rapidly changing cyclical agricultural environment. If the company was well managed, employees should receive high and rising wages. If this would be the case, Art knew from experience that they would take pride in delivering superior performance.

The focus therefore was on management. Instead of annual incentives based on individual employee performance in a rapidly changing environment, Bill Jesse, who ran another subsidiary at Coke New York and eventually joined The Wine Group board of directors and became one of Art's closest advisors, developed a totally unique incentive program designed to reward team performance of the top management group. The fact that they were a private, management-owned company and that they wanted to make sure it remained that way made the task a bit more straightforward.

Art did not want to start off the performance plan with a calculation or numbers. The plan should first and foremost promote long-term value creation rather than short-term individual bonus optimization. Therefore, he started off by memorializing the following stewardship goals in a set of binding recitals for the company and its owner-managers. Current and future owners of The Wine Group would agree that their tasks and objectives were:

1. To maintain an independent, management-owned private company that will prosper and remain competitively vibrant in the wine business;
2. To ensure that the Company remains in a healthy financial condition with a view to continued enhancement of the long-term value of the Company;
3. To motivate the owners to manage the business as stewards of the assets of the Company, not only on behalf of current owners, but also on behalf of future owners and other stakeholders in the enterprise;
4. To ensure that current management aggressively develops successor management that is both skilled and committed to the objectives and principles embodied in these Recitals;
5. To provide appropriate mechanisms that will enable successor generations of management to become owners of the Company; and
6. Consistent with and promoting the objectives and principles stated above, to provide appropriate mechanisms for owners of long-standing to be appropriately rewarded for their contribution.

Ever since their establishment, every Wine Group shareholder has enthusiastically agreed to these recitals, which gave them further incentives to act like owners rather than hired guns.

In many other companies, the two roles of owning and controlling the company have been divorced for various reasons. This can result in the cliché of the company management making all decisions exclusively to please shareholders. I believe this can represent a big problem because a shareholder is not the same as an owner, at least not in most cases. A shareholder, or the subset I would call "share-trader," is trying to maximize their money, now. An owner is trying to create long-term value. These objectives might at times overlap, but they certainly diverge over the long run. Owners worry about company morale, culture, reputation, the work environment, investment in long-term R&D—things that the transient shareholder would happily forego if they were to score a great gain in value over a month instead.

The management either works for the long-term-oriented owner or the short-term-oriented trader. If it's the latter, managers end up working more for Wall Street than Main Street, getting paid by the stock market rather than their own company. The lion's share of such an executive's payday derives from the quarterly stock market price fluctuation of her company over a period of one to five years rather than the actual performance of that company's business.

Art's recitals made sure that this never happens at The Wine Group.

The six recitals don't follow the same outline as the five pillars of Principled Entrepreneurship, but they fully incorporate what I would call the "Principled Entrepreneurship mindset" and reflect both the team's personal values and the particular needs of the company and wine industry. In other words, they reflect the application of Principled Entrepreneurship in a particular company in a specific industry—just as it's meant to be done.

This is what the title of this book insinuates about Principled Entrepreneurship. Using the analogy of painting—this is not "paint by

numbers" but it is actual "fine art." Each one of The Wine Group recitals reflects several of the Principled Entrepreneurship pillars. For example, their focus on remaining a private company that will "prosper and
remain competitively vibrant" draws from the fact that the economy
exists for people. But that principle doesn't necessitate that all companies should remain private. But looking at their particular situation, The
Wine Group team determined that to bring the best product at the greatest value to their customers, as well as allowing their team to focus on
the cycles of agriculture rather than the writhing of Wall Street and the
financial market, it is best to be independent and management-owned.
It also draws on the culture principle in that Art wanted to create a
culture free from company politics and outside interests that would, in
a sense, distract the company from focusing on its core concern: producing quality wine at a great price that creates a substantial consumer
value. As an independent company, the internal culture of the company
could keep its focus on what mattered most.

And so it is with every one of their "recitals." Each reflects various
aspects of the five pillars of Principled Entrepreneurship. It is important
to first address the "mindset" in a company before defining the rewards,
because the mindset guides the desire for reward.

You might think that Art could do this only because The Wine
Group was a private, management-owned company, and that this could
not be done in a publicly traded, or Venture Capital funded, or any
other company. And that is true. But this is not really the point. The
point is that Art and his team found a perfectly personalized way to follow and implement each of the pillars of Principled Entrepreneurship
in their company. Principled Entrepreneurship is a mental model that
doesn't give ready-made action points but, rather, a common way of
thinking about and approaching opportunities and challenges.

How The Wine Group Structured a Long-Term Reward System

The Wine Group's reward system is designed to provide significant financial rewards to owners and managers who support the company's recitals and make a significant contribution to creating incremental value. There are no cash bonuses or other incentives. The only goal is long-term value creation.

The management team continually identifies and offers new employees that distinguish themselves by contributing to long-term value creation and living out the culture of the company the chance to join the management-ownership of The Wine Group. The path to a cash-return on ownership of a high-level executive is nineteen years. The value of the company is determined annually after completion of an external audit using a conservative multiple of their revenues minus expenses excluding tax and interest, and deducting funded debt and the value of scheduled but unredeemed equity plus cash. This value is then averaged with seven prior years to determine the current value of the company. This approach has a plethora of positive effects. For one, managers are not rewarded for volatility, and only people who positively contribute to the long-term health of the company can benefit from the created equity. "Managers that depend on this kind of multi-year rolling average valuation that we use are motivated to focus on long-term decision making instead of short-term earnings manipulation or financial engineering," Art explains. There is no quick payday for executives at The Wine Group.[30]

Incentive structures and their unintended consequences are one of the great dangers in business. Art was well aware of that. Ultimately, there will be managers with a harvester mindset, no matter how well you screen for creators. That's when carelessly designed incentive and stock option plans can wreak havoc. Too often, such incentives represent only upside and no downside, meaning that the manager wins if the company does really well, and stands to lose nothing if the company does really badly. The manager would lose potential gains if the company does not perform well, but there's no material downside for an overly risky or reckless plan. That incentivizes management to take foolish chances.

"My team and I have done our best to construct a sound foundation, efficient facilities, enduring brands, and a set of lasting values, but in the end, it all comes down to people. We are willing to stake the important judgment we made about the long-term direction of the company on our faith that noble values will rise to the forefront when choices may have to be made between self-interest and stewardship responsibilities," Art told me during one of our calls. "We have built a business by betting on great people with a specific set of values. Because when the business gets tough, good people and noble values prevail."

The customer, and the team that creates the product, represent the key focus and purpose of the company. Everything else flows from that.

It is a unique but brilliant way to ensure everyone has both the motivation and incentive to focus on the long-term health of the company. While this kind of plan is more easily implemented in a privately held company, it certainly also works and applies to public firms. The best approach is to start this kind of program when you start the company. It is more challenging to bring this to a large, existing organization, but the upside and benefits of a large company are also that much greater.

The beauty of Art's model is that, once it's implemented, it attracts managers who are motivated to be part of an ownership team that concentrates on sustainable value creation by rewarding long-term decision making. It becomes a self-selective mechanism that increases the quality of your team.

What Art was able to do in his company is turn the proper understanding of human work as creativity into a cultural value and therefore ensure the continuous re-invention and revitalization of the company and everyone involved in it.

Financial Reward in Context

The difference between a hobby and a business is that the business activity creates sustainable financial return, or surplus. The difference between a charity and a business is that the business creates a surplus financial value, while a charity creates value that needs financial capital to be realized. A business creates the money through profits;[31] the hobby and the charity spend it. There is a need for all three—and more—but it is important to know the difference and run each activity accordingly.

But profit has received a bad name lately. Many point out rightly that excessive profit seeking—profiteering, they call it—results in some of the behavior we try to avoid in a free market. I would argue that we have and should use laws to fight misbehavior. Only a very small percentage of people are criminals. Should we abolish profit because of that? Of course not. Let's not create the whole system around their behavior. Businesses all over the world pursue profit perfectly legitimately and by offering excellent products and services.

How much profit to make, or what to do with the profits your business generates, is a different question. The core issue at first is whether your business is making a profit or not. If it is not, and if it doesn't look like the business is realistically moving toward profitability in a reasonable time frame, then the business is not sustainable and the resources should be allocated somewhere else. Not every business is a good idea, and sometimes what used to be a good, profitable idea is no longer so. It is okay to shut down a business when it no longer provides a sustainable financial return, or when there is no reasonable path for it to do so. But the success of a business does not result from an obsession over profit.

Think of it this way: profit is to business what white blood cells are to the human body. I don't run around counting my white blood cells all day long, nor do I obsess about producing them. But if I end up in a situation where I don't have them, I'd die in short order. They are a vital by-product of a healthy life, not something I should myopically focus on. That doesn't make profits bad. It makes them vitally necessary, but not an overarching concern on a daily basis. In my thirty years of working with entrepreneurs, I can count the ones who hyper-focus on financial profit over the actual business on one hand. And even fewer made an outrageous amount of profit with their business.

But public opinion seems to differ. When a random sample of American adults were asked the question "Just a rough guess, what percent profit on each dollar of sales do you think the average company makes?" the average response was 36 percent. [32]

No wonder there's a call for a more equitable system. Right? If there's so much profit at corporations, then let's share in this bounty more equitably. The truth is, however, that the median US company makes about a 6.5 percent profit. An increase of any financial burden could mean certain bankruptcy for many small and growing companies.

When a business does create a financial return, everyone involved in it has a right to be rewarded financially for their work and involvement. That is one of the reasons why the third objective of work is to reward the participants in your business. However, it would be a mistake—and a violation of Principled Entrepreneurship—if the "reward" of our work would be exclusively financial. In fact, there are various kinds of extra-monetary rewards that may result from good work: emotional, intellectual, social, spiritual, and physical. All of these are pursued by Principled Entrepreneurs, but one common denominator we all have is that while we measure our emotional, intellectual, social, and other "good" in varied ways, we can all use money to, in a sense, "buy" the kind of "good" that we're lacking.

In other words, it is completely appropriate for Principled Entrepreneurs to be focused on profitability and financial reward; it is actually required for success. But making a profit or receiving a financial reward is not the end in itself. Money once generated by a company—the value we have created and then "garnered" as a team—exists to be distributed and used, but it is by far not the only or most important result of what a company does or how it fulfills and rewards its stakeholders. [33]

When asked what surprised him about humanity the most, the Dalai Lama once observed: "Man. Because he sacrifices his health in order to make money. Then he sacrifices money to recuperate his health. And then he is so anxious about the future that he does not enjoy the present; the result being that he does not live in the present or the future; he lives as if he is never going to die, and then dies having never really lived."[34] What he describes is that the pursuit of profit for the sole purpose of profit is a fool's errand.

The appropriate approach to financial profit is the right understanding and balance. Money is the objective transfer-value of humanity. It allows us to transfer value from our intellectual activities (someone giving an academic dissertation and getting paid for it, for example) to our emotional needs (that same person using the money earned to throw a party for five friends). As such, the fact that business is the only human activity that actually creates money makes it a central concern for the well-being of us all. Business creates prosperity when it is profitable. Not the government, not universities, not churches, not social clubs. *Business* creates prosperity. Every other institution can only redistribute or consume it.

Satisfied customers create more sales, and more revenues provide the company with profit margins that gives it the freedom to continuously improve the work and company environment, pay high and rising wages, and generate above average return on investment for the owners. These things matter. But to Principled Entrepreneurs, they're the third, not the first, objective of a business. Good profits are the result of creativity and human excellence. Good profit results from new value created for members of society through a voluntary exchange. In contrast, what I call bad profit would be financial benefit from transactions that are forced on one or both parties, realized through fraud or by restricted competition and straight out transfer or confiscation of wealth.

Principled Entrepreneurs reward financially and they pay specific attention to rewarding their team members based on their human dignity, their contribution to the culture and productivity of the company, and, last but not least, for the pursuit of their personal excellence.[35]

What is needed is a realignment of incentives along the way that The Wine Group did it. It works for both private and public companies, and always includes a reward system that focuses on the long-term value creation of the company.

The financial part of the reward is usually given in cash or some form of equity. There is no "one" formula to figure out this split. The key is to find the best balance for your company by creating reward and incentive plans based on long-term value creation and a recognition that we pay for more than productivity. There are contributions that are not productivity oriented, but are just as valuable and important, such as contributions to the company culture, inspiration, quality awareness, cohesion, and so on. We do well to be aware that we're rewarding human beings, not machines. And money is not the only factor in human motivation.

Unprincipled businesspeople evaluate success simply by one reward alone: exit value. That pretty much boils down to an IPO or a sale. There's nothing wrong with a sale of the company; "exit value is legit for some companies, but shameful for others," as Art likes to point out. The key is to not hasten an "exit" because of a desire for short-term financial gain. That was not the aim of The Wine Group, nor is it the goal for most Principled Entrepreneurs. There are many more options available than seeking an exit, and some of the most successful entrepreneurs, like Art and his team, took different routes—it's just not talked about or written about as much in the press and entrepreneurship literature.

9 Steps to Create, Support, and Reward

So, how can we implement Pillar 2 in our companies and teams? There are a few fundamentals to keep in mind as you apply this approach.

1. **Define the company's objectives.** A good way to start or "restart" a company, depending on the situation you're in, is to formulate your own company recitals. These should be unambiguous and actionable.

2. **Reset the performance measurement clock.** This approach does not work alongside a run-of-the-mill quarterly or even yearly management incentive program. Implementing a rolling, multi-year valuation model is critical to promoting long-term decision making. Public companies may continue to conform to the quarterly and annual reporting cycle, but change their equity-based compensation programs to a rolling, multi-year average valuation model. The length of the rolling average model will depend on the cycles and nature of the company.

3. **Ditch the job descriptions and replace them with outcome objectives.** Allow teams to self-organize and redistribute authority and responsibility among members every time there's a new person joining. Make ergon a "thing" by using it in the annual review process and develop plans to further each team member's ergon.

4. **Reward and connect long-term decision making and succession planning.** Instead of allowing owners and managers to cherry-pick timing and/or quickly monetize equity interests upon retirement or leaving the business, establish the value of the equity on smoothed long-term results and provide for a value-at-risk multi-year payout. This ensures current owners and managers recruit and train the best possible subsequent generations of managers to deliver future value creation and liquidity enabling the business to redeem equity interests over multiple years.

5. **Incentivize sustainable value creation, not value redistribution.** The incentive plans and ownership structure

must reward expanding the pie, not quickly grabbing for the largest piece of the pie and/or creating unsustainable short-term events that yield short-term rewards. Buying short-term performance at the expense of future periods is nothing more than wealth redistribution from continuing owners and managers to those managers or investors exiting the firm.

6. **Turn managers into owners, not traders.** Eliminate transitory company valuation and instead implement a sustainable valuation method. Make sure that incentives don't encourage your management to pursue needless acquisitions or take other financial measures that make only short-term sense. Some management-led acquisitions look good only at the moment of execution and become a drag on the company after the deal goes through. Capital deployment without quality returns results in a downward pressure on valuation, whether debt or equity financed. Projects must make economic sense. To ensure that, include a cash addition/debt deduction feature in the determination of company value. This makes sure that frivolous and pet projects receive no consideration. Using an appropriate valuation horizon and methodology ensures acquisitions must be at reasonable multiples and integrated quickly to prevent a decrease in the company valuation.

7. **Unleash entrepreneurial behavior.** Principled Entrepreneurs try to reward value creation rather than value redistribution whenever possible. Place no constraints on the creativity of the owner and managers. Think of ways to create incentives that foster product and service innovations. There is a time for organic growth and a time for growth through acquisition. The timing is a function of the marketplace and numerous other factors. It's impossible to make a general call on this with the minute details. But one thing is sure:

maintaining a Principled Entrepreneurship mindset in making the decision is critical.

8. **Recruit, train, and promote like-minded owners and managers.** Make sure your plan is so strong that it turns off people who you're not interested in. Mention those aspects of your vision that maybe not everyone wants, such as having a long-term career with a single company or possessing an owner—rather than a harvester mindset. The Principled Entrepreneurship model is not for people who are interested only in swinging for the fences or for harvesters who want to close out their position at the closing bell every day. The specific rules you create need to be suited to your company's situation. Public companies and startup situations would certainly have different reward rules and plans. But in both cases, and all of them in between, you will want to attract owners and managers who are inspired with a long-term, sustainable, and value-creating business model.

9. **Time is of the essence.** Often, there is a misplaced belief that long-term means slow. Nothing could be further from the truth. Principled Entrepreneurship requires crisp execution and clear, measurable progress. What ultimately produces long-term sustainable value is repetitively consistent, excellent short-term performance along a long-term path. Long-term focus is not an alibi for poor or inconsistent short-term performance, nor is it a "hall pass" on accountability. However, a clear articulation of the short-term metrics that measure progress toward long-term goals is critical.

Principled Entrepreneurs take these traits to the next level: they take personal responsibility to promote creative excellence, not only for themselves but for everyone the business touches, including employees, vendors, investors, and customers alike.

Living Pillar 2: To Work Is to Create; To Create Is to Be Human

1. Are the goods your company produces truly good? Do the services your company provides truly serve? How can you make it (more) so? How is what your company/work does good in and of itself?
2. What is "something you don't already know," as Michelin called it with regard to Marius Mignol, that you should start doing? What can you do to discover strengths you didn't know you had? Make a plan to start building on your strengths within the next six months.
3. What is your ergon? What virtues do you need to train to reach it better? What vices do you need to avoid? Find small things to do or not do to achieve these virtues or train in strength to avoid those vices.
4. Go through all the jobs on your team (and all new jobs you list) and find words to describe what ergon is needed for that job. Use that language in your performance review process and in your job postings.
5. What is the genius of the person who works next to/with you? How can you help them pursue their individual excellence? Think in terms of things you can do—or stop doing—to help the person(s) who works with you to flourish. Specifically ask them: "How do I make it easy for you to do great work?"
6. Do a strengths/non-strengths inventory for yourself and then discuss it with your colleagues before you introduce the same language/exercise with the whole team. Discuss how you can/ do create teams that put people with complementary talents/ gifts together to help them create super-effective teams.

7. How do you love (*Ti voglio bene*) your customers, colleagues, suppliers, and investors? What are five specific ways you can show that you want their good?

8. How much is enough? List the key rewards you want to get out of your work. Think of the perspective of your entire lifetime, not just this month or year, and don't list only physical rewards. Rank these rewards and match them to your current work. What areas of your desired rewards are you scoring high in? Where low? What action can you take in the next twelve months to create a work situation that reflects your priorities? Discuss this with your team and see what you can do as a group to help each other gain your rewards.

9. How and when have you experienced "spontaneous order" at work? Analyze the situation and make a plan to re-create that situation.[36]

10. Describe your American Dream in detail. Your description of it has one limitation: achieving it must include your work. Where are you on that path? Make a list of action items to reach the next step on that journey—actions that you can take within the next month or quarter.

11. Are the values and objectives of your investors in sync with your company's management? What are those values and objectives? Can/does your team create a written and agreed-upon list?

12. Take, and have your team take, the MCORE test and use it as a topic in your work division, job planning, and performance review meetings. Discuss ways to include the findings in the incentive plan of the company.

5

Pillar 3: Culture Eats Strategy for Breakfast

You don't build a business–you build people–
and then people build the business.
–Zig Ziglar

The most consequential endeavor a Principled Entrepreneur undertakes is not building a product, but creating a wholesome company culture.[1] Culture is the DNA of the organization that goes on to create many more products and services. It is created not with slogans and HR manuals, but through your actions and deeds.[2]

How does Pillar 3—the idea that corporate culture is paramount—get implemented in a company or a team? The founder or leader of the organization has to consciously focus on modeling the values and virtues she believes are essential to the task of creating the best product and experience for the customer, employee, investor, industry, and community. Once Principled Entrepreneurs create such a culture,[3] that culture becomes the company's competitive advantage.

The distress call from Lou came at 2 PM. For the next hour, Art, Lou, and the winemaker met to examine and evaluate bottles of vermouth pulled at random from the warehouse. They opened dozens of bottles, tasted samples, and carefully examined the appearance of the product. The taste was fine, but the appearance was not consistent with their company's standards. (Though Art was sure the product was perfectly safe to consume.)

What happened? Making vermouth is a complicated process—really an art form. It requires carefully mixing several herbs and spices together and stabilizing them before blending them into a fortified wine base. A winemaking error had caused a precipitate to deposit a light, hardly noticeable sediment at the bottom of each bottle in 25,000 cases of Vermouth marketed under the Tribuno brand. It couldn't have happened at a worse time. The company was highly leveraged and the huge cost to dispose of the questionable batch was a potentially crippling blow for this fledgling enterprise.

Based on input he received, Art concluded that they could most likely "get away" with shipping the mildly off-condition product to consumers. Just three months after leading a successful management buyout, Art was newly in his role as CEO of The Wine Group and already facing a challenging decision. The biggest problem was that shipping inferior vermouth would be totally inconsistent with the cultural values Art was trying to instill in the organization of which he and his team had just become owners. Shipping the product would solve a short-term problem but he was afraid it would create a bigger long-term issue with credibility.

After a pregnant pause, Lou hesitatingly asked, "So what do you want me to do, Art?" Art answered, "I'll get back to you before the close of business today." In the meantime, he had a very difficult decision to think through. He needed to decide what to do with the 25,000 cases of compromised vermouth, and he needed to do so quickly. On the one hand, he felt in his gut that the right thing to do was to destroy the questionable product, thereby sending the right signal to the organization relative to "walking the walk" with regard to their newly developing cultural values. This was clearly best for the long term. But The Wine Group had to survive in the short term and destroying the product threatened that.

Art's conviction never to go public with his company cemented at that time. "That's when it dawned on me," he says, "that many of the company values we believed in were very difficult to fully sell to the organization in a public company environment where short-term earnings were the driving force. Sure, we would buffer our people from some of that, but on balance, employees at all levels are smart and perceptive, and unless we walked the talk, the rank and file would see right through us. Becoming private gave us a chance to start with a clean slate. It put us in the spot to be unequivocal about our values and to set a good example as owners. Becoming owners transformed my partners and me; becoming private transformed the entire organization."

Tribuno Vermouth was viewed by management as a "cash cow," which meant the company would defend it, but not invest heavily in its growth. This strategy did not change with the management buyout. This was not the first time The Wine Group had faced the problem of something going wrong during the vermouth-making process—though it was a first as a freestanding private company under Art's leadership. Twice before something similar happened under the ownership of Coke New York (KNY), and both times KNY management directed Art to sell the compromised vermouth to avoid the hit to short-term quarterly earnings. Those occasions, when Art advised his boss, the executive vice president at KNY, he was asked only two questions:

Was there a health risk?

What would destruction cost?

When Art advised that there would be no health risk and destruction brought a net cost of $250,000, he received a two-word directive: "Ship it!" Understandable business decisions. But in direct contradiction to The Wine Group's first core value—"offering the best consumer value."

What irked Art most about the action he was ordered to take in those previous instances was that it made him look like he was talking out of both sides of his mouth: preaching a cultural value on the one hand and flagrantly violating it on the other. This troubled Art to no end, but he followed orders and accepted full responsibility for the decision. Now, however, as an owner of the company, Art wanted to make a better decision.

At 4:45 PM that day, Art called Lou back with a two-word answer: "Destroy it!" Early the next day, he pulled together his top management, several of whom disagreed with his decision, to explain his position and develop a plan for communicating this to the organization. By the end of the meeting, everyone agreed they hadn't bought the company to sell marginal products or take short-term profits at the expense of the long-term future of the company. Art was pleased that his team ended up on the same page and, more importantly, as new owners of the company, they knew this would send a clear signal. This was no longer KNY and they were in it for the long term. There would be no shortcuts. Art was content with what they had accomplished, but there was much more to come.

Doing the right thing pays off, especially in the long term. Twenty-five thousand cases of vermouth is the equivalent of thirteen fully loaded railroad freight cars. That amount was impossible to destroy inconspicuously. Art understood this but had not at first considered what profound repercussions this action would have on the entire organization. As the vermouth destruction began, the informal underground communication network began to beat out a message that in effect said, "These new owners are serious about the culture they profess—we better get serious too." The message hit home and within days a new spirit of teamwork and excitement infused the organization. The change was palpable. This new energy was a totally unexpected bonus for Art's team. All Art had wanted to do was set a new tone. No one in their wildest imagination dreamed this would dramatically improve overall company performance. This spirit was best described by a company welder who said, "It makes us feel like we're all in this together. We're going to sink or swim together."

People throughout the company, at all levels, now began to take real ownership of their work. Overall performance, which was already improving, took a significant turn for the better. This was the dawn of an incredible transformation.

Transformation was also joined by innovation. Unbeknownst to anyone, the head winemaker, Jim Walls, began working quietly on a creative idea to ensure this problem would never happen again. He completely took ownership of the situation and went to work with an outside flavor company to develop a concentrate of the exact herbs and spices needed for Tribuno. And it worked! This meant that The Wine Group could purchase a ready-made concentrate and simply blend it with fortified wine without risk of another precipitate depositing a sediment in the bottles. This not only eliminated the big risk of another blending issue, but Jim's initiative set a good example for others about the value of what I have called an ownership mentality. He humbly and quietly made it known that the Tribuno blending problem was solved. This success was celebrated. Principled Entrepreneurial behavior paid off. Art and his team finally owned The Wine Group and could now make decisions that supported their vision. It was a happy day for all.

Establishing The Wine Group's 10 Cultural Values

Management theory has developed and focused ever more closely on the human person during the past fifty years or so. Initially, management was focused on the process inside a factory and thus paid more attention to the machinery than the people who operated it. This has slowly inverted over time so that, today, the key concern of management theory is how to motivate and inspire team members to become more innovative, collaborative, and effective.

This development roughly follows the increased recognition of the human person as the key asset—the competitive advantage—of a business. When companies competed during the Industrial Revolution, the focus was on manufacturing process and efficiency. Then came the focus on the product itself, and so marketing became the leading interest. Ries and Trout are probably the best examples of masters of marketing. Their book *Positioning* remains as relevant today as it was when it was written in 1981. Then the focus became strategy, led by great thinkers like Michael Porter, who defined competitive advantage and other invaluable insights. None of these theories are wrong, nor have they become obsolete. But they don't focus on the core of the company: the human person, especially those working within the company. The movement of corporate culture management[4]—if we can call it that—is finally focusing on what was the most important part of any company all along: the team, and its excellence.

"Our team never set out to develop a style of working together," recalled Art. "It evolved as we wrestled with difficult issues and learned to work together to achieve optimum results. We found that having a small, close-knit team of top managers with deep expertise in their field and a broad perspective on the overall business gave us a big competitive advantage."

In addition to keeping expenses low, The Wine Group was much more responsive to rapidly changing market conditions than its bureaucratic competition. "This was particularly important in the earlier years, when we were more commodity- than brand-driven," Art continued, "because it enabled us to quickly match up market opportunities with grape and wine purchases and beat our competition to the market time after time."

At one point, less than three months after the management buy-out, The Wine Group's new White Zinfandel wine cooler was growing smartly as was the entire Zinfandel category. At the same time, the grower relationship team reported that the entire Zinfandel crop was coming up short. Convinced they had discovered this vital piece of information ahead of their competition, Art took a chance and directed grower relations to "lock up" every uncommitted ton of Zinfandel available on the market and thereby deprive the competition of the opportunity to deliver a competitive cooler for a year. "This kind of market responsiveness is just one example of a core cultural value we had at The Wine Group," he explained. "In the course of doing business, we tried to learn our strategic advantages, built values around them, and organized ourselves for the mission at hand."

Art's approach to Principled Entrepreneurship is not an exclusive focus on culture, but company culture plays the central role. It has several elements, most of which are more of an art than a science—that is to say, they are judgement calls that depend on the specifics of the entrepreneur and the company. There is a rough process to follow and a mental model[5] to use for guidance, but in Principled Entrepreneurship, solutions are as individual as the customers and employees we do business with.

The price one pays when you put the human person at the center of business is that there are no one-size-fits-all solutions.

Here is the process Art Ciocca recommends to start or manage a company as a Principled Entrepreneur:

1. Create a set of cultural values for the organization. Values should be logical, supportable, easy to explain and understand. One of a leader's most important jobs is communicating

values, practicing them, and recognizing and rewarding them in others. These values come from:

   a. personal values of the leader/team

   b. general business/career experience of the leader/team

   c. the specific needs of the industry

2. Create a vision for the organization that fits the market and company.

3. Create a strategy that delivers on the vision.

4. Create a hiring method that finds employees with the right character and talent.

5. Create a culture of excellence.

Art has a slogan: "Either create a strong culture or you'll have to manage tough." A strong culture empowers people and unlocks their God-given talent and empowers them to rise to the occasion to make good decisions. The price of a weak or toxic corporate culture is constantly having to monitor and discipline people who, in a healthier environment, would show a lot of initiative and teamwork. Either measure, evaluate, watch, and enforce constantly or empower people to be who they are and become good at it.

You can see why, as the title of this book suggests, the Principled Entrepreneurship approach is much more of an art than a science because there can be no pat formulas. It requires a human mind and heart, critical thinking, and problem-solving ability. In the short term, this is more arduous. But long term, this process allows all team members to develop on the job and contribute toward the excellence of the joint undertaking. No one in such a system feels like they work *for* anyone, but rather that they work *with* everyone. When this process is done well, each of the steps reinforces, complements, and relates to the other steps.

In time, The Wine Group articulated the following core cultural values that drive its business and that are a road map of sorts for all its employees. These company values are a mix between Art's personal values and the values needed for the company to do what it does with excellence. They're offered here as an example:

1. Offering the best consumer value
2. Putting performance first and eliminating politics
3. Encouraging everyone to take a proprietary interest in their work
4. Keeping it simple—reducing complex problems to simple solutions
5. Being responsive to the market (both the market for purchasing grapes and the market for selling brands)
6. Exercising entrepreneurial risk taking
7. Thinking outside the box to imagine new ways and to innovate solve problems
8. Operating with the highest integrity because good ethics are good business
9. Being proud but never arrogant
10. Being good stewards of gifts received

When a company stays focused and committed to its values, the behavior in line with these values gradually becomes second nature. Team members don't even have to think about them anymore—they act that way automatically. In philosophy, a well-trained, good action is called a virtue. That process of repeated action is how values turn into virtues. And when the company has a whole set of values that complement each other, add value to each other, and become virtues, the result is character. In a person, character expresses individuality—your beliefs, goals, inner strength, and attitude. A person's character is perhaps the most important aspect of self-determination. For companies, character becomes their brand. And brand is the holy grail of business.

The values that developed under Art's watch were 100 percent focused on building the business for the long term.[6] He told me on many occasions that he believed that by thinking long term, the company could improve the lives of all its constituencies better. By constituencies, he meant consumers, employees, middlemen, the supply-chain people, and, lastly, owners, including all of these people's families. That's a lot of people! I think Art did this masterfully and the beauty of this is that, in the process, he and his team contributed a lot to society not only through their products and the multiplier effect this has in society, but also through their volunteer work and charity in the local community—something they could only do because of their economic success. That is why it's called *the American Dream*. It benefits everyone.

What Makes for a Positive Corporate Culture?

It is difficult to define a good corporate culture, yet it's very easy to recognize it when you experience it. Culture is the stuff we do beyond the basic rules, beyond what's legally required. It's what reveals our business character. It's how we answer questions such as:

- What do we celebrate as success?
- Who do we try to emulate?
- Who do we esteem?
- How do we speak?
- What do we measure?
- What do we reward?
- What do we use our money for?
- How do we compete?
- What is our ultimate goal?
- And what do we do when no one's looking?

Great corporate cultures may look quite different from one another because they have situation-specific values and emphases. There is no cookie cutter for building a great corporate culture, as we've said. But what great company cultures have in common is that they all promote creativity, trust, cooperation, excellence, and joy.

I'm convinced that what ails many failing companies is the absence of a positive corporate culture. As we saw earlier, recent Gallup research shows that 51 percent of US employees don't care about the success of their company. Another 16 percent are actively disengaged and trying to hurt their employers. They hate their jobs and their bosses! That's usually not the fault of the employees; the blame rests with the leaders, because what the leader says, and especially what the leader does, sets the example and pattern for the rest of the company.

Art chose product quality over profits, which is better for the company's reputation and revenues in the long run. The employees were shocked—and impressed—and this decision set the tone for the company's values moving forward. The initial hit to earnings was repaid many times over by improved employee morale and productivity: The employees embraced the pursuit of excellence and started working with an ownership mentality because they identified with the most essential corporate virtues Art modeled if for them. The lesson from this is that managing a business is not just a material exercise, but an immaterial one as well: you want to unleash the human spirit in your company to achieve incredible results.

Do you have a negative, or even toxic, corporate culture in the company or team you lead? If you want to change the culture, you have to change yourself first. The company is, in a sense, an extension of yourself. We can't change others if we are not aware enough to change ourselves. That is why it is always a good idea to look at our own values and how we live them out, or not. People want to find meaning at work, in corporate values and virtues, and they are highly allergic to hypocrisy. Giving lip service to some foundational values and then not living them out is the kind of thing that makes employees disengage . . . and it's poison for good brands. Here are several key ways to build a positive corporate culture.

What Are Your Personal Values?

Psychologists believe that having purpose—a *Why*—is one of the most critical ingredients of resilience and, ultimately, success. Psychologist and Holocaust survivor Viktor Frankl credits his sense of purpose in life—his values, his *Why*—as the key factor that allowed him to survive his awful experience in a Nazi concentration camp. What is true for this most extreme of environments is also true for any other. But this is not easy. It's difficult work, because as Socrates observed, the real battles in our life are fought in our interior. Based on these insights, there is general agreement that "to be authentic leaders, managers must be able, first and foremost, to identify their own purpose."[7]

Our personal values have a lot to do with the employees we have and attract. One-third of US workers have changed jobs in the past three years.[8] There are many reasons that can contribute to job change, but given the data from the same study that only 27 percent of workers strongly agree that they believe in their organization's values, I think it suggests that the values and culture of the workplace affect this kind of churn. The trend toward shorter employee tenure has been going on for decades, but I think the feeling of disconnection is one of the overlooked reasons.

As a leader who is a Principled Entrepreneur, it is you who provides the spark for the company's purpose. And you can't fake it. You can't give what you don't have. If you don't make your sincere values the foundation of your company, you will inevitably declare one message with what you say but act out a contradictory one. It comes down to you examining your own personal behavior. Is it in accord with the values you profess? Personal, core values are your deeply held beliefs that manifest themselves as attitudes or automatic reactions to what's happening around you. This goes beyond the corporate social responsibility platitudes that too many executives use to generate huge financial windfalls. Before you start to lead a group of people, you need to critically examine the core values that actually reflect how you see the world, what you believe, and how that affects the groups of which you are a member.[9]

The first two pillars of Principled Entrepreneurs are examples of such a worldview. The conviction that the economy exists to serve people rather than the other way around is foundational in how we go about our work. If a business puts the customer and employees at the center of its concern, we have a very different kind of company and work environment than if it puts short-term share prices or profits at the center. The three objectives of Pillar 2—create, support, and reward—show that companies are indeed supposed to generate a profit, but not at any cost or exclusively, and that the primary focus is to be on the human person. Profits are legitimate if they're the result of creating value for customers, especially if that value add is created through the excellence of the company's employees.

Recognizing what work is all about is another core value: understanding that what we do at work is a uniquely human privilege, that we are made in the image and likeness of the Creator and that we have the awesome opportunity and responsibility to participate in the continuation and guidance of our world. We human beings have the unique ability in work to transform matter into resources and thereby create value, beauty, and wealth. As we have seen, because of this *creativity*, work can make us more fully human by actualizing our potential and allowing us to flourish into the best possible person we can be.

But of course it is not work alone that makes us more human. Work is a good value in the right measure. Workaholism by contrast is an anti-value; it destroys our humanity. Some think our culture has already gone too far in this direction: "A culture that worships work is setting itself up for collective anxiety, mass disappointment and inevitable burnout."[10] The data on employee disengagement and burnout seems to bear this out.

Entrepreneurs and business leaders who understand and live out the full potential of human work will create opportunities for their employees to flourish through their work. This vision will translate into a culture that pursues and celebrates human excellence and creates a learning environment where each individual is encouraged and helped to find and hone their personal talent and balance.

Core values in Principled Entrepreneurs' companies often reflect themes along these five pillars that we're exploring in this book:

1. The economy exists for people: person-centeredness, customer focus, and employees as a competitive advantage
2. To Work Is to Create; To Create Is to Be Human: the objectives of a business are to create, support, and reward the pursuit of personal and team excellence
3. Corporate culture: authenticity, servant leadership, walking the talk, and transparency
4. Win-win solutions: subsidiarity, efficiency, empathy, and meritocracy
5. Always think like an entrepreneur: deferred gratification, solidarity, sustainability, and a focus on constant creativity

The five pillars provide a basic set of corporate values, but there is also a need to have more specific values that pertain precisely to your company or team. The way to discern those specific personal values to focus on, or to transfer them to your company, is to ask yourself a very specific question: What is the ultimate aim I want this company to have?

Model Your Own Core Virtues

Remember, culture is what you do when no one's looking. Our personal core values are most apparent in high-stress situations when we don't have time to think about appearances. These values always become apparent, especially when they don't align with what you declare the company values to be. In his *Harvard Business Review* article "How Corporate Values Get Hijacked and Misused," Ron Carucci writes that employees want the declared values of a company to be sacrosanct. If leadership violates them with its behavior, it leads to widespread misuse or abandonment of these values, with the result that only "23% of US employees strongly agree that they can apply their values to their work every day, and only 27% [actually] 'believe in' their organization's values."[11] In short, corporate values in the US are declared but largely not lived.

That's why you need to explicitly identify and live out your core values now. Create a way to practice them every day in the smallest of your actions until they become a part of you. When that happens, they will become virtues that will in turn inspire and "infect" your entire team with them. Values that turn into virtues—actions that we do automatically—are what add up to character. You can always count on people with well-formed character to do the right thing, whether or not anyone is watching. That's really the description of the perfect employee, but they're hard to come by, and even harder to create. Character is much more difficult to form than something like skill. That's why Principled Entrepreneurs try to hire for character rather than just skill.

The reason why I make students go through the exercise of finding and defining their personal values is because virtue and character start with us, not with others. We cannot give what we don't have, nor demand what we don't do ourselves. The values of your company are not created democratically. The startup entrepreneur brings not just the business idea to the company but also their own values, which they purposely or unconsciously infuse into the company culture. In fact, the building of the specific company culture has a far greater impact on the future of the company than does the original business idea. It falls to the founder or leader to set the tone and expectations for behavior. Most do so without even thinking about it—for better or for worse.[12] People just naturally act out their beliefs and that pretty much establishes the corporate values. But that can be a gamble. I've seen many entrepreneurs who are shocked when they see the culture that the company reflects back at them, having never before been conscious of their own deeply held beliefs and values.

Others, like Art Ciocca, take some care to determine these values first personally, then take great care to verbalize and embody them in their company. These values had a profound effect on the actions Art took at The Wine Group, as in the case of destroying the faulty ver-mouth. Putting people and excellence above making a quick buck is easily said, but it takes great character to actually do it.

The Wine Group management, who were the only owners of the company, decided that they wanted to put in writing their common val-ues and objectives with regard to what kinds of priorities "the owners" would give to the executives and employees. The intention was for the team to codify a unique culture for The Wine Group that focused on a stewardship mentality—rather than one of ownership—that could sur-vive many generations of owners and managers. These recitals would in a sense precede, or set the stage for, the financial incentive plan for them. They wanted to make sure to put their money where their mouth is.

While discussing it, they agreed the first and most important group that needed to agree on a code of behavior—on a culture, if you will—were the owners: themselves. They then created a membership agreement that each shareholder has to sign that attempted to memorialize their stewardship goal. They called it The Wine Group "recitals," for current and future owners as listed on page 81 in the previous chapter.

How many companies have such "mental model" guidelines for their owners? As I already said, it is Art's attempt to instill culture not just in the overall team, but to ensure a specific kind of behavior for the owners who ultimately make the more critical or far-reaching decisions in the company.

This list of six clearly defined recitals makes the culture definition very specific for management. The logical next step would have been to create a similar document for the employees. But The Wine Group never had a document like that for the employees. Art told me that in the beginning he spent a lot of time developing procedures manuals but ultimately decided these documents were no match for a solid culture and lean, well-functioning organization. To document and memorialize the cultural values, a set of recitals was developed as a basis for constructing a long-term incentive program.

What they did develop was a set of corporate values and their intended effect. Here's what the process started with:

- Customer Focused: ↓ politics   = ↑ performance
- Strong Brands: ↓ push   = ↑ pull
- Innovation: ↓ status quo   = ↑ disruptive technology
- Continual Improvement: ↓ rework   = ↑ quality
- Social Responsibility: ↓ waste   = ↑ environment
- Cost Mindful: ↓ costs   = ↑ value
- Simple & Lean: ↓ complexity = ↑ efficiency
- Respectful: ↓ jerks   = ↑ team
- Compliance & Safety First: ↓ accidents   = ↑ awareness

This was not a verbose statement of values, but very informative and effective! The company's values were constantly and persuasively communicated to all employees and were reviewed periodically with everyone's input. Although the original values have evolved to fit current needs, the cultural values of The Wine Group are essentially the same as they were from the outset when Art's team became the owners.

Art is convinced that the recitals and the list of corporate cultural values would not have been successful if they were not sold to the organization by management "walking the talk." And they were: the founders encouraged entrepreneurial efforts among the team and The Wine Group became an early, but rarely first, adopter of industry trends. The company strived to be a learning organization and thus accepted failure if it led to progress. They never punished failure but encouraged taking calculated risks. They continually sought internal progress and studied the industry for new product and acquisition opportunities.[13]

Company Culture Creates or Destroys

Now, I'm not advocating a simplistic "Doing the right thing guarantees success and doing the wrong thing guarantees failure." Unfortunately, we have plenty of examples to the contrary. My point, rather, is that Principled Entrepreneurs create a culture not just for the sake of profit, but ultimately for the sake of a sustainable business: providing goods and services that are truly good and truly serve, created through the excellence of the company's employees. I am amazed that the generally accepted definitions of a founder's or CEO's job do not include building the corporate culture, and the fact that this culture must necessarily be underlined with personal behavior.[14]

My friend Paul Zak,[15] author of *The Moral Molecule*,[16] did extensive research into what helps groups behave in ways that foster collaboration and trust and what hurts those prospects. He points out that the two core ingredients in the formation of a group are: 1) an objective the group wants to pursue together and 2) a high level of trust among the group members. He points out that while objectives vary, trust seems to be one aspect of creating a group that could be studied and fairly well compared across all groups equally. His team has done exactly that. Paul and his team have researched trust on teams for more than twelve years. They have come to call trust an "economic lubricant" because it became so abundantly clear in their research that without it, groups—and the economy, which is a really big group—would cease to function. Apparently, our brain produces oxytocin when we experience trust and collaboration. Oxytocin produces a feeling of well-being and happiness. That feeling creates a virtuous cycle: I like it if you trust me, so I trust you back, which deepens your trust in me, and so on. Zak was able to show how company culture is a key protagonist in trust: it can either create or destroy it. And that when trust diminishes or is destroyed, along with it goes the company's performance. He calls on leaders to be "neuromanagers"—to cause oxytocin production in the team. We do this by doing what we say, by living constantly by our declared values.

When this aim is not just something we say, but something we live by, it is imitated by others in the company. The more authentic we are, the more we attract employees who share our values. Such employees—at all levels of the company[17]—become our competitive advantage. They do what they do out of inner conviction, not because they're told to do it. They become the greatest assets and advocates for our success because such employees in turn communicate through their own actions to customers, who go on to communicate to the broader market. Ultimately, this authenticity becomes your "real" brand. The character of your company. This is the making of a performance culture.

How Art Attracted People into a Performance Culture

People who perform well at their job should flourish in the company. Excellence must be noticed and rewarded. Creating a culture based on adding value takes care of a couple of issues. Most importantly, it kills office politics, because people who thrive in a highly political environment rather than thriving on the work itself gradually leave on their own accord. Slowly but effectively, the right team collects—in a way, self-selecting itself—around the newly developing cultural values. A healthy company culture almost automatically attracts the right people and repels the wrong ones by clearly and loudly stating and living out the important values: excellence, performance, and value.

Art approached building this type of culture not with decrees but, again, by example. When he was still at Coke New York and it acquired Mogen David, a struggling wine company, Art was asked to integrate it into their operations. To do so, he moved to Chicago for a time to be at their offices every day. There were immediate cuts to expenses, but mostly he set the tone of *how* and *when* to work. For instance, "Two-Martini Lunches" were out.

Though Art believed very much in the importance of marketing, he felt that some of Mogen David's marketing programs and plans were ineffective and inefficient and so he cut them out. Mogen David's franchise brands were in steep decline, and yet many key members of the team were flying off to Europe to explore low-leverage opportunities like importing Greek wines. "Greek wines?!" Art would say. Boondoggles like this and marketing for marketing's sake were not his style. The first priority was to evaluate the marketing team and dramatically realign priorities. Concurrently, he was doing the same with the production facilities, where he hoped to find like-minded employees. Lynn McShane, The Wine Group's VP of Sales, likewise moved to Chicago to manage the merger of the two sales forces. Everything in their power was done to clearly signal, explain, and model The Wine Group culture and values to the new team.

Art's actions, as clear leadership often does, in effect divided the company he was integrating into two distinct camps. Some rebelled. Others who felt unfulfilled and unchallenged by the old way, those who wanted something more, rose to the occasion and took responsibility and accountability for pursuing excellence. The clarity was useful: Art found his people.

Lou D'Ambrosio was one of them. He worked at headquarters in California, but Lynn Bates, The Wine Group's Chief Operating Officer, asked him to go visit the Mogen David Chicago facility to understand their financial issues. After sizing up the Chicago facility, Lou took it upon himself to visit the production facility in Upstate New York where he found a very efficient production facility capable of absorbing the entire production of the Chicago winery. *Lou was a guy who lived out our Wine Group Culture*, Art thought to himself. And as a result he was able to take initiative and bring solutions, not problems, to the table. By merging all production into the New York facility, the company saved $2.00 per case—millions of dollars per year. Shortly after this move, Lou was promoted to senior vice president of production services.

Dick Alessi became another one of "Art's people." Working in the Mogen David Westfield winery, he tirelessly encouraged and motivated the employees of the small outlet despite their being treated as third-class citizens by headquarters in Chicago. Under Alessi's leadership, that satellite winery produced a quality product and had excellent staff. After the merging of the two production facilities, Dick was promoted to general manager of the Mogen David Wineries.

These two leaders self-selected into The Wine Group management team that turned Mogen David from an inefficient operation into a valuable part of The Wine Group's portfolio. Their values perfectly fit the culture of The Wine Group, and they became close associates and trusted sources of advice and counsel for the company.

There are many other examples that illustrate how talent was unearthed at The Wine Group, but it might be more accurate to say that the talent found The Wine Group. What attracted people to this team is to a large extent Art's unapologetic vision and values. It is very important that a leader not mince words.[18] People tend to gravitate to a cause that aligns with their own values, but without clear articulation of principles, this self-selecting process may not happen. "Art's people," together, they formed the team that would fulfill Art's vision of creating the US "wine for everyone." They were a team of creators with a culture of excellence.

Art did everything in his power to enable the excellence of others. Just as with Dick and Lou, he would give talented and committed team members every available chance to learn and grow. He would encourage risk taking (within sensible limits, of course) and never punish failure. He was tolerant of mistakes and failures—be it the spoiled vermouth or a failed new product—as long as team members were pursuing excellence, their own and therefore the company's.

The building of a team like this may seem effortless, but it is actually very tough to achieve. It requires radical honesty. A company with politics and a "no offense" and "no conflict" culture cannot do it. Imagine how much tough feedback an athlete needs to become ready to compete at the Olympics. A tough-love kind of coach is what enables such achievements—someone who believes in you but is relentlessly pushing you to perform at your full potential. Such a coach is not afraid of conflict, and won't tell you only what you want to hear. He or she is only afraid of your not living up to your potential.

This kind of tough-love coach is not simply a critic. The coach can claim the additional quality of having a stake in a positive outcome. The trouble with the critic (as opposed to the coach) is that their benefit usually has nothing to do with your flourishing. Their objectives have nothing to do with your development or your excellence.

When someone's benefit in dealing with you is obscure, there is usually a problem. A win-win outcome will only result by chance, because your own benefit is not really part of the equation. That is what happens when a company is highly political. It's a place where two different games are being played at once: the game of doing what the company does, which would be objectively judged by merit, and the game of politics, of creating criteria, influence, and benefits that have nothing to do with what the company actually does. Unfortunately, culture is the culprit when politicking takes hold of a company.

Art worked in a few politics-ridden companies in his early career and was thoroughly put off. It was one of the core convictions he brought to The Wine Group: no company politics! He made it clear that "politics cripples performance."

He felt that playing politics "smothered" excellence. To Art, it was clear that company politics and company performance were like a seesaw. When politics is up, performance is down. People who brought solutions and had high performance would excel under Art's leadership, and those who "played politics" would self-select and find work elsewhere.

Imagine running a company like that. Being a tough coach who believes in each team member's potential for excellence rather than a political manager who tries to orchestrate peace and conformity. That's Art. It's not always comfortable, but it is exciting, deeply meaningful, and rewarding on all levels: personal, financial, societal, and spiritual.

The bottom line of Pillar 3 is that you should actively create your corporate culture, signal it to the world as loud and clear as you can, and then screen your team not only for skill and experience, but also for culture, character, how they see and interpret the world around them, and how they react to it.[19]

Living Pillar 3: Culture Eats Strategy for Breakfast

1. How can you increase vision and decrease prescription on your team or in your company?
2. Ask the constituents of your company: "What values do you feel this company stands for? What words, attributes, and feelings come to mind when you think of us?" Then ask them *why*. Evaluate the results and compare them to your own list. Make an action plan for the next twelve months, consisting of continuous small and large actions that embody the virtues you want and counteract the ones you don't.
3. How did you, your team, and company react the last time there was a "vermouth" kind of mistake? How can your next reaction become more like that of The Wine Group?
4. Create a list of ten cultural values. Start with your own personal values, then create the list for your team and/or company. Discuss those values with your colleagues to agree on a final list.

5. Schedule a meeting to brainstorm what it would take for your team to create a culture of excellence. Put together a path to that reality in no more than five steps undertaken in one year.

6. If your company or team is privately held, create a set of company recitals for current and future owners. Define how each of you can live out and embody them every day in the large as well as the small actions and decisions. If your company is public, make a list for your management within the leeway provided by your company's bylaws. Bring these recitals up for discussion with your board.

7. How can you celebrate the right kind of failure better? How can you encourage the right kind of debate and conflict within your team? Ask the team members, and implement the best suggestions. Measure the effects of failing and debating better and make corrective adjustments regularly.

8. How can you increase trust among your team? Suggest three ways to your team as a starting point to brainstorm a final list of actions you will take.

9. Who is on your team and why? Do they flourish? Would you hire them again today? If not, how can you help them fit in, or how can you help them find the place where they can flourish? What is their character? Do they share the company values? Do they fit into a team complementarity with their talents and skills? How can you be less of a critic and more of a coach for them?

6

Pillar 4: Principled Entrepreneurs Always Seek to Create Win-Win Solutions

*The most important single central fact about a free market
is that no exchange takes place unless both parties benefit.*
—Milton Friedman

The more your customers are satisfied with your product or service, the more loyal they become. The more profitable a customer is, the more committed a business is to them. If they're both free to find each other, prosperity ensues because they transact only if they both profit from it.

How can Pillar 4—the claim that Principled Entrepreneurs always seek to create a win-win proposition—be implemented in a company or a team? The answer is that a proper free market transaction happens only when the buyer and seller are free to engage with each other or not. The more we can promote this kind of complementarity, the more value the products and services we provide add, and the larger the economy grows. This is not only one of the paths to human progress, it is also the only path to widespread prosperity.

Iqbal Quadir was born in Bangladesh and traveled an unlikely path to study at a US university and eventually become a venture capitalist in New York City. He lived the American Dream that so many all around the world yearn for.

One day in 1993, during a power outage, his productivity plummeted because he was cut off from his computer network. Iqbal had an epiphany. He realized that his connectivity in many ways was his key asset, his "ticket" to work inside his company and, by extension, play in the larger economy. It was necessary both for identity and productivity. Sitting idle reminded him of home and childhood. *No wonder the productivity back home in Bangladesh is lower!* he thought. *Without a network, one is much less than what he or she can be in the economy.*

This was the genesis of his new dream: bring cell phone service to the people in Bangladesh so that their phones could connect them to each other and allow them to form networks of the economy. Think about it: Bangladesh was a virtually untapped market of tens of millions of people.

Very soon, he was pulled back to reality. There was no infrastructure for cell phones in low-income areas. Many people living in these areas couldn't afford the service fees, much less a phone, he was told when he first pitched his idea to potential investors.

But Iqbal would not let go of his dream. He compared the ownership of a cell phone for many in Bangladesh to the ownership of a car in the US: most people cannot afford to pay for it up front, but having a car enables them to make the necessary money to pay it off over time. Similarly, cell phones would include people in the market economy who had previously been excluded, integrate them into networks of productivity and exchange, give them an online identity, and allow them to compete in the market. In short, if they had phones in their hands, they could earn more, which would give them the ability to pay for their phone service. Iqbal would often say, "Connectivity is productivity!"

It took four years to convince Telenor, Grameen Bank, and several other partners to join him in founding Grameenphone. Experts kept telling him that his efforts would prove futile. The path to market indeed proved difficult—the communities he wanted to reach out to were so deeply off the beaten (market) path that Iqbal had to build his own cell towers as well as a distribution and sales network to serve them. "Experts told me that we must first focus on primary needs. In a poor country, food, clothing, shelter, medicine—these are much more important than some high-tech digital phones," he remembers.

Iqbal had a different intuition: "We don't have to be the big brothers who decide whether the poor should buy food or shelter or water. They know perfectly well what to do—all they need is the opportunity to act. They already are motivated to earn more; they only need the opportunity to do so." Serving these communities with phone service is not charity, but a real investment in their future opportunities and success. Iqbal proved all the naysayers wrong, knowing that, as he told me, "the ingredients were there for success, including the people's desire to advance their lives . . . the only thing missing was someone to start cooking and the dish would be ready soon thereafter."

With more than 77 million subscribers (as of September 2020), Grameenphone is the largest mobile phone operator in Bangladesh, profitably generating over $1.6 billion in annual revenue.

Grameenphone gave one of the most disadvantaged workforces in the world a way to access the productivity tools produced in developed markets.

This was indeed no charity investment. "Telenor, of Norway—a country of 5 million people, now has 200 million subscribers in Asia. I dare say, Bangladesh actually provides more money, you can call it 'aid,' to Norway. Hundreds of millions of dollars of dividends are going back to them every year—much, much more money than the aid Norway ever provided to Bangladesh. That's the way it should be. This mutual respect, mutual gain, and mutual transformation are possible between the first world and the third world following a healthy formula of advancing mutual economic interests, giving rise to inclusive growth."

In 2006, Iqbal began to support his younger brother, Kamal, who then set his mind on taking the idea one step further to integrate more people of Bangladesh into the world economy. Kamal started a cell phone–based platform where customers can buy and sell their goods, skills, and time. CellBazaar is an emerging-market mobile commerce platform that allowed farmers to get current market prices for their produce and cut out profit-absorbing middlemen, enables artisans to offer products beyond their local street market, and empowers laborers to find the best-paying jobs. Its greatest achievement may be to turn consumers into person-centered producers.

CellBazaar quickly thrived and acquired millions of users. Before long, several competitors appeared on the market. As they say, imitation is the sincerest form of flattery.

Kamal then sold CellBazaar to Telenor, the main investor in Grameenphone, so the two brothers could focus on their next opportunity.

Iqbal describes their innovation strategy as simply "solving problems" for people. When they identify a problem that many people need to solve, they realize that there is a market for that solution. People get economically empowered by adopting the solution, and a part of that economic empowerment translates into an ability to pay. This means that the businessperson providing the solution can have a win-win arrangement with those who adopt the solution.

One large problem—perhaps the largest—is safely making financial transactions with other people who may be at a distance. Now that people can talk over a distance, they naturally may wish to send money to each other. The brothers also saw that there are many ways people can send money to each other in the West, and thought it would benefit people if they could create a mobile money network. Thus, they conceived of their third company, bKash: banking for the unbanked. Kamal organized the company and runs it in Bangladesh and Iqbal supports it from Boston, where he now lives. Today, 55 million Bangladeshis rely on their services, making bKash the leading mobile financial service company in Bangladesh, with 75 percent market share. Their customers can open an account for free, and the average transaction size is about $20.

The Great Lie: Business Is a Zero-Sum Game

As much as Iqbal and Kamal's story exemplifies the way free markets actually work, and yet the misunderstanding, or rather misrepresentation, persists that the free market is a zero-sum game: someone has to lose for someone else to win. In ten years of teaching at university, twenty years in the private sector, and ten years in economic development, I've been astonished at how this misperception permeates all three sectors.[1]

This prejudice—I actually call it a lie because it's so obviously wrong to anyone looking at the facts—lies deep in our culture and is conveyed and reinforced in every imaginable way. I only recently found out that the game of Monopoly was actually meant to discourage people from certain aspects of the free market economy. The game's creator, Elizabeth Magie, who lived in the same Prince George's County, right outside Washington, DC, that I do today, was a follower of economist Henry George[2] and wanted to promote his economic and political views with the game. George argued that land ownership was prone to fall to the rich and would be used to exploit the poor. Thus, if landowners could be taxed to an extent that would prevent them from financially benefiting from their real estate, such exploitation could be prevented.

A zero-sum game (literally!) was the perfect way to show this economic "truth"—that land ownership will eventually lead to one (or a few) person(s) owning all of it and driving others to their ruin—to the public at large. Thus, Monopoly, initially called "The Landlord's Game," was born.[3] The game, according to Magie's stated goal, was meant to demonstrate the evils of accruing vast sums of wealth at the expense of others. What she, and countless others beside her then and now, failed to see is that any transaction leaves both parties better off. If I rent a flat, I have to pay rent for it, but I also get the value of having a place to live from it. Free market transactions always create two winners and are inherently *not* a zero-sum game. A firebrand against the railroad and steel and oil monopolists of her time,[4] Magie noticed the consolidation and, like everybody else, was worried about the power of these companies. In their worry, they failed to notice that these very same "monopolists" drove consumer prices down and, in effect, built the infrastructure for the American Dream.

It's no surprise that "The Landlord's Game" became very popular in left-wing circles and around many college campuses around the US during the early 1900s. Though Elizabeth Magie—or Lizzie, as she was called—probably followed Henry George's belief that intellectual property was akin to real estate and would only bring poverty to the masses, she nonetheless filed for a patent for her game in 1904. She did not pursue a commercial production of the game but encouraged people to copy the game and make their own versions of it, eventually selling her patent to a game company for $500, or about $15,000 today. Little did she know that Monopoly would eventually become one of the most-sold board games in history. A certain Charles Darrow, who was taught a Quaker-adapted version of "The Landlord's Game," made some further improvements to the rules and looks of the game and approached the same game company to which Magie had sold her original rights to give the game another go in 1935. Lizzie never received more than her $500 for the famous game she invented. The company today doesn't even recognize her as the creator.

Thus, a game that was meant to teach a falsehood about the free market—that property rights, both physical and intellectual, are evil and prevent social mobility—served in hindsight as an example of how property rights are indeed a path to the American Dream. Lizzie's negative view of copyrights hurt her and the game. Only after someone took Monopoly and applied a copyright to it did both the consumer and the seller benefit from the game she invented.

I doubt that this story—or any other, for that matter—can change the mind of some. But I hope it gives readers a reason to reflect. It is a very important aspect of Principled Entrepreneurship to understand the fallacies underlying the zero-sum view of business and the anti–free market worldview.

The first fallacy of that worldview is the materialist myth—the false belief that the economy is a zero-sum game and that the wealth that is created by businesses in the economy is like a pizza: if someone gets a bigger slice, someone else would necessarily get a smaller one. The misunderstanding in the "economy as a pizza" analogy is in comparing the economy to *one pizza*. It's more like a pizzeria. As more orders come in, more pizzas are created in response to the demand.

The second fallacy of the zero-sum view is the greed myth. It holds that the free market and business in general operate by greed and that, by definition, doing business makes one selfish and miserly because it requires you to *take* from others. Without denying that individuals can and do behave greedily, it is not the market system that creates greed. Here again, the underlying assumption of scarcity is false. In order to create financial wealth, you have to create value. Value is a function of customer satisfaction, and customer satisfaction is a result of other-directedness and openness. The free market as a mechanism requires exactly the antithesis of self-centeredness. That is why an independent business service always beats the service you get at the DMV.

This mischaracterization of the free market has found its way even into the thinking of entrepreneurs and business leaders—the core idea being that a company is in a win-or-lose battle with its competitors, and the company can't rest until all competitors are defeated. In this view, launching a company or a product is like going to war; it's an existential fight. This is a conflict-based view of the world—back to the zero-sum game.

Perhaps the worst and most damaging effect of this zero-sum view of the economy is that it may give good people like you the idea to actually pursue zero-sum transactions in the economy with a clear conscience. If these are the rules of the game, why feel bad, right? *It's not personal,* you say, *it's just business. It's a dog-eat-dog world,* you reason to yourself, as you cheat your customers, employees, or investors. The zero-sum myth about business allows otherwise moral people to inflict great pain and injustice while thinking that they're just playing the game as it's meant to be played.

Principled Entrepreneurship Benefits Everyone

Our current system aims to produce *a free and competitive market economy.* For simplicity's sake, we call it capitalism. This is not the best name for it, but that's a topic for another time. Our economic system is not perfect, but let's take stock of some of its important achievements.

First, access to global markets is generally a good thing for all countries. Exports and imports have greatly improved the living standards of every country on Earth and this progress wouldn't exist without capitalism. Both sides win when we trade, especially when we trade free and fair. (Think of the Grameen Phone example.)

Second, the vast majority of humanity lived in poverty for thousands of years. Thanks to capitalism, the number of people living in abject poverty is, for the first time in human history, down to around 10 percent. And for the first time ever, we have a realistic chance of bringing that down to 0 percent. Think of it: Not one person in the world need be in abject poverty! Everyone wins when we create value in the private sector.[5]

A third positive result of the current system is that an increasing majority of countries are led by rule of law. Human rights and freedom of conscience are more respected and observed than they've been at any time in human history. Competitive commerce, because it is trust-based, allows justice and prosperity to emerge and win.

Fourth and finally, human health and longevity are also at all-time highs—notwithstanding the recent COVID-19 crisis. The prosperity that spreads with free markets simultaneously makes for a healthier humanity.[6]

These positive developments are clearly the result of our competitive free market system because the advances mostly happened since the 1980s during which time there was little competition from other economic systems on offer. This is a fact often disregarded by the "business is a zero-sum activity" argument. There is clear evidence that the approach of the last forty years has had tremendously positive results.

That is not to say that every problem has been solved, but no system has brought about more inclusion, or lifted more people out of abject poverty more rapidly, than the free market system. If we look at the outcome so far, we can easily see that the general trend of the free market is the creation of win-win solutions on all levels.

How Should We Define *Winning?*

When considering what a good economic system looks like, what a good company should do, or how we should work, it pays to first define what we mean by "winning." And when trying to define winning, I think we need to first look at the *why* of it all. Principled Entrepreneurship holds that the goal of work, business, and therefore the economy is human excellence and flourishing—creating goods that are truly good and providing services that truly serve.

By using our human effort and ingenuity to find profitable solutions for legitimate customer needs, we achieve several key benefits that only work and business can provide. We do not just make more, but we become more. Our excellence as individuals is enhanced by our collaboration and competition within a team, a company, an industry—the world market. We progress and humanity advances through our business achievements. The value we create expands the money supply, and that, in turn, allows us to include others in our networks of productivity and exchange so they can also flourish in the same way. That is what we call prosperity. That is the contribution of work to human flourishing. We do well if everyone has access to this opportunity, and we thrive if all who are able to access it actually do so. If we have an environment where businesses, the workforce, the customer, and society at large are better off because of the work that's being done in companies, we call it a win-win solution. This is what we aspire to with an economic system.

Defining what winning means for ourselves affects the way we see the world, what happens, and how we react. It becomes our mental model. Because this is not a science but an art, no one can create this mental model for us—it's something we can only do ourselves and something that is shaped by our life situation and experience. But the Principled Entrepreneur understands that developing our mental model, our attitude in and toward life, can and should be done intentionally. Throughout the rest of this chapter, I provide a variety of concepts and insights that help in developing a Principled Entrepreneur's mindset and worldview.

Business Is Not Like War

Launching a company is an exciting and exhilarating exercise. The first time I did it, I missed a major lesson: it's not just about the product that you launch, but the company. It's easy to focus on what it takes to launch this product, get it into the sales channel, do the marketing, ensure production, and so on and forget that, from now on, this is the core function of your company. You're not just doing this once; you're establishing your work pattern, even the culture of the company. One aspect of launching a company is to determine and put into practice how we interact with one other, with the market, and with the world.

The first time I participated in starting a company, I followed, as did my colleagues, the common war analogy to the market.[7] Launching a product is like going to war. It's a war against one's competitors and we don't rest until the enemy has been defeated. We took on the conflict-based view of the world described above. A zero-sum game was being played; us versus them! What we missed in this approach is that our competitors should not really be our focus. The customer ought to be our focus—and maybe love would be a better analogy than war for that relationship.

This kind of conflict view of the world is a great distraction from Principled Entrepreneurship. It's also fundamentally non-economic. Capital and labor, instead of being intrinsically opposed to each other as Marx saw it, are actually mutually complementary. There will never be capital that doesn't need labor and vice versa. This is a both/and rather than an either/or. This either/or mentality, this us-versus-them approach, which I would ascribe to Marx, has infiltrated much of our worldview, at every level. It's poisoned the relationship between government regulators and citizens, teachers and pupils, managers and workers. I believe that this is a deeply flawed view. God created the world not as adversarial but with beautiful complementarities.

In view of us as human persons who were created with equal dignity, there can be and often are differences among us that we can all perceive. That is because equality doesn't necessarily mean sameness. Between us exists a beautiful complementarity, where each contributes their own gifts, and our collaboration results in a kind of flourishing that no one person could not achieve on their own. The same is true for the

economic sphere. Our economy, or should I say the free market economy, is not a zero-sum game but depends on win-win collaborations.
As a matter of fact, it is these voluntary win-win collaborations between
market participants that create new value, new money, and therefore
prosperity. When we all participate in complementary ways, if we each
insist on win-win exchanges, the results will exceed our wildest expectations. It's not us versus them. It's only us together. This is what connects
all the stories you've read in this book. It's the fundamental approach to
collaboration that The Wine Group, Victorinox, and Michelin share.

Principled Business Promotes a Complementary World

I believe that business in a free market is by definition a win-win situation. I'm free to sell to you or not and you are free to buy from me
or not. If a deal happens, it's a win-win. Otherwise, people would not
participate in the transaction. When Iqbal offered cell phone service in
the slums of Bangladesh, it wasn't just him as provider who was better
off. Everyone with a cell phone as a result of the transaction came away
with a productivity tool that was worth immeasurably more to them
than what they paid for it.

Is that a good or a bad thing? Most people view business as amoral
or immoral; I choose to see it as moral. It is the antithesis of selfishness.
It rejects that either/or approach; instead, it chooses the both/and solution. The secret of the free market economy are the win-win transactions it encourages.

Instead of a win-lose mentality, business must always take a win-win
approach—to other companies in your industry and to your employees.
The adversarial approach is a great distraction from Principled Entrepreneurship and has poisoned business relationships on all levels.

It does not have to be this way. And it shouldn't.

Art Ciocca always tried to understand his employees, competitors,
and investors. I write "tried to understand" because this is an approach,
a mental model, not a fixed method. Let's take labor relations as an

example of how he did this. Some locations of his company were union-ized and some were not. The Franzia location had a worker's union, but several other locations did not. It didn't really matter to Art. He treated all employees with the same respect across the board. There were some obstacles and differences, but they could always be settled. He recalls never having been approached with any issues regarding pay—by unionized or non-unionized employees—because The Wine Group paid a reasonable and fair wage. "Most negotiations with the union were about work rules," Art told me, "and I did negotiate hard for those because they affected plant efficiency. We were the most cost-efficient producer in the industry . . . but I can honestly say that we have never been dealt a card by the union that we could not deal with. It's all about the relationship—don't make it adversarial. Keep it productive!"

The Wine Group also needed seasonal farm workers, and they also never unionized. It's not because unions weren't interested in doing so, but because Art proactively engaged with them. He always applied the same process: sit down and listen, then figure out a win-win solution.

He also applied this approach to the sales channel. He partnered with small, young, and "hungry" wholesalers when they tried to estab-lish themselves in the market, gain some scale, or balance their offerings or synergize with the supplier. The Wine Group helped them with this, even if it meant taking back product or giving the wholesaler some wig-gle room on the terms—something few other wine producers did for them. Wholesaler relationships are often a power-based relationship: whoever has the market power dictates the terms. It easily turns into a win-lose game.

The Wine Group treated its distribution channels as though they were part of the company and created win-win relationships by working together and helping one another. They would find ways to partner with wholesalers rather than to just "use" them. They would actually invest in them by developing special products to fill voids in their portfolio and offering special pricing in return for driving sales in areas that were mutually beneficial. The Wine Group specifically built up several key wholesale relationships that they wanted to maintain for a long time, thereby building up much loyalty and goodwill. These friendships very much benefited them in the long term—one of these wholesalers helped The Wine Group financially during a tough time, refused to take on a competing product line, and remained patient when the company was bringing new products to market that needed some time to be perfected. As a result, both the wholesalers and The Wine Group prospered. The point here is that this both/and approach works on all levels. You can apply it in your family, at school, and in your business. It's a way to approach others, a way to perceive and solve problems, a way to find and pursue opportunities. It's the path to the kind of win-win solutions that give the free market its liberating force.

In fact, the free market economy is the only path to sustainable prosperity. There has not and will never be another way to create long-term and lasting opportunities and prosperity for all. The results of the past two hundred years speak for themselves.

Choosing a World of Abundance over a World of Scarcity

Win-win and both/and solutions fit into the worldview of abundance, not the worldview of scarcity. I call them worldviews because it is the belief that causes the result. The best entrepreneurs I've met in my life "believed" their vision into reality.[8] For some reason, our culture loves to focus on scarcity and negativity. That might be a result of our fallen nature, which makes belief more difficult than resignation. We tend to find scarcity more plausible than abundance.

But it doesn't have to be this way. Every human activity is an opportunity to bear fruit and is a continual invitation to exercise the human freedom to create abundance, even if our fear is always ready to undermine it and create scarcity.

An economy built on human ingenuity and imagination is perpetually abundant. It is often feared that there is no way to continue with economic growth. But that is not true. We will always come up with new ideas, and will always find ways to add value for each other. Entrepreneurship is essentially focusing on making or achieving more with less. This takes many, many forms, but we always measure a key aspect of it—the added value—in terms of money. Ultimately, the abundance that's created takes the form of the new services and products that are being offered. An economy based on the scarcity mentality functions in the opposite way. Such a system would necessarily have to focus on wealth redistribution rather than wealth creation, and on win-lose transactions that inhibit social mobility and general prosperity.

So, is a successful economy all about creating and having ever more? Do we all become consumerists in such an economy? No. The core of the economy is to create value for others. In that process, we are sometimes the creator and sometimes the consumer. Both are needed to create prosperity. There is nothing inherently wrong with wanting to have more material goods, but there is something morally wrong (and, ultimately, economically destructive) about imagining that having more is being more. The mission to create wealth that stems from a worldview of abundance is challenged by the call to generosity. The two go hand in hand.

The Difference Between Selfishness and Self-Interest

"It is not from the benevolence of the butcher, the brewer, or the baker that we expect our dinner, but from their regard to their own self-interest. We address ourselves not to their humanity but to their self-love, and never talk to them of our own necessities, but of their advantages."[9] This famous statement from Adam Smith gave rise to the iconic caricature of the selfish businessperson. But he intended this observation to mean something quite different from the way it is often taken today, thanks to a misperception of what's meant by "self-interest."

One of the reasons we tend to expect a zero-sum game is because we mistake self-interest for selfishness or self-centeredness. The two could not be more different. Self-interest is what's needed to engage in any sustainable business in a free market. It calls for two parties to agree on a deal that's good for both of them, a win-win (or positive-sum) solution that gives them both the same value in an exchange. That is how value is generated: whenever a free, voluntary transaction is made at a price that is above what it cost the producer or provider to generate it. The difference—we can call it profit—is new money. That's the miracle of the market-based economy. This system never runs out of steam because we always find new value in an exchange.

In the market economy, an offer of assistance is usually initiated by an entrepreneur or businessperson. They are the ones who ask, "How may I help you?" and then proceed to find an ingenious way to satisfy that need in a way that creates more value than what they had to put into the solution. Be it the creation of affordable table wine, bringing cell phones to the people in Bangladesh, or making car tires, business is an inherently other-directed activity—a service to humanity, a truly noble vocation.

How can it then be described as selfishness?

Because of how it's being talked about. "When you spend your days giving, giving, giving and leaving nothing left for yourself, you aren't winning in business,"[10] is the observation of a young entrepreneur in a *Forbes* article where she proceeds to provide six ways being selfish can make you successful. She goes on to actually give some very good advice, but it's all based on this very flawed understanding of self-interest. You see, selfishness and self-interest *are not the same thing*.

Selfishness is defined as "devoted to or caring only for oneself; concerned primarily with one's own interests, benefits, welfare, etc., *regardless of others*, characterized by or manifesting concern or care only for oneself."[11] Selfish behavior creates win-lose transactions. Think of standing in line at the DMV, or being placed on hold on the phone with the IRS.[12]

You either do it their way, or you're not getting what you need—fit their needs or go without. There are selfish people in every profession, including business. It's just that if the economy is based on competition and free market principles, the selfish businessperson necessarily goes out of business eventually—and probably sooner rather than later.

Where selfishness disregards others, self-interest, by contrast, takes others into account on the way to finding mutually beneficial solutions. This is the actual behavior that we see in a free market economy. Self-interest is objectively rational behavior that is beyond mere desire or self-regard. If you're happy with the solution and that makes you come back as a satisfied customer, I will benefit from having a repeat customer that allows my business to prosper. It's in my self-interest to make you a happy customer, just as Adam Smith explained.

The win-win nature of the free market economy enables individuals to do well by doing good. I would go so far as to say that this kind of other-directedness is one of the key virtues of Principled Entrepreneurs. Through their efforts, there is a tremendous amount of motivation and moral purpose in free market transactions.

I think the real contention here is that the free market places the judgment of people's real interest with them, rather than delegating it to the government or another bureaucratic organization. It seems to be paradoxically tempting for us today to abdicate individual judgment to "experts." The issue often being ignored here is that we want to yield decision making to them—whether government regulators or any other form of expert—who are not immune to selfish behavior themselves any more than the average citizen and businessperson.

Business Is "Co-opetition"

Did you ever notice that in some industries, all the big competitors are actually located in the same place? Like the car industry in Detroit, or high tech in Silicon Valley, or the movie industry in Hollywood and the insurance industry in Hartford. Figure 3 shows a map created by Professor Michael Porter with some of the many such clusters of companies focusing on the same industry. Why do similar companies sit on top of each other like that? And it's not the case only on a global or national level. Even within cities, car dealerships line up next to each other and insurance companies have their local headquarters right around the corner. Would it not be easier for them to compete with each other if they spread out? Away from each other?

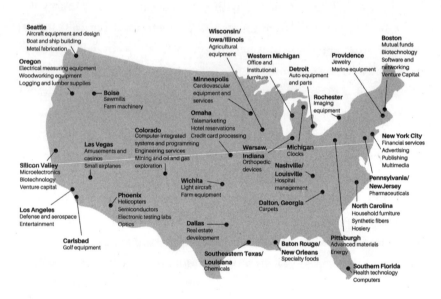

Figure 3: A Selection of US Industry Clusters

Michael Porter[13] discovered in his research during the late '80s that groups of similar and related firms actually group together in defined geographic areas that share common markets, technologies, worker skill needs, and are often linked by buyer-seller relationships. Porter discovered that the success of a company depends both on internal and external factors. Its internal culture, processes, and insight can make or break it. But so can the immediate business environment.

It is difficult to find a geographic location that offers specialized suppliers as well as employees that the company needs, a particular infrastructure that the location provides, specialized university research centers that focus on the industry, and the scientists who are educated there all in one place. Therefore, either by attraction to the place or because of interest in helping to build or perfect it, competitors in one industry find it to be mutually beneficial, rather than damaging, to coexist in close proximity. Porter thus discovered what he called the cluster theory.

"Clusters promote both competition and cooperation. Rivals compete intensely to win and retain customers. Without vigorous competition, a cluster will fail. Yet there is also cooperation, much of it vertical, involving companies in related industries and local institutions. Competition can coexist with cooperation because they occur on different dimensions and among different players."[14]

One of the first industry clusters he examined was—you guessed it—the California wine industry.

"The California wine cluster is a good example," Porter wrote back in 1998. "It includes 680 commercial wineries as well as several thousand independent wine grape growers. An extensive complement of industries supporting both the winemaking and grape growing exists, including suppliers of grape stock, irrigation and harvesting equipment, barrels, and labels; specialized public relations and advertising firms; and numerous wine publications aimed at consumer and trade audiences. A host of local institutions is involved with wine, such as the world-renowned viticulture and enology program at the University of California at Davis, the Wine Institute, and special committees of the California Senate and Assembly. The cluster also enjoys weaker linkages to other California clusters in agriculture, food and restaurants, and wine country tourism" (Figure 4).

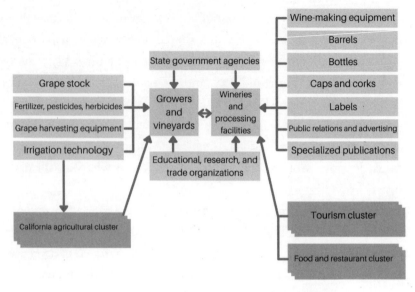

Figure 4: The Anatomy of the California Wine Cluster

Porter noted that even though we might be more aware of the large-company clusters, it is actually the startups and small companies that benefit most from being a part of a cluster. Just think of the startup scene in Boston or Silicon Valley. This poses a paradox: in a super-connected world that seems to "shrink" by the day, the physical location of companies continues to make a big difference, and the more complex our economy becomes, Porter predicts, the more important location will become.

The cluster theory is a kind of spontaneous order that comes about through all players in an industry acting in their own self-interest. A great by-product of self-interest is that we do not see our competitors exclusively as such, but that we find ways to cooperate with our competitors for the benefit of us and them. The wine industry is a good example. It should come as no surprise that when it comes to sales and marketing the industry is extremely competitive. That's actually good news for everyone. There is nothing better than good, fair, and honest competition to sharpen focus and make everyone better off—especially wine consumers worldwide.

Let me be clear—the positive competition I'm describing does not include cronyism or rigging the system to gain an unfair advantage. In the wine industry example, while companies compete on sales and marketing, other parts of the industry are collegial and cooperative with viticulture, enology, and plant production around the world. There are countless examples of the world's best UC Davis–trained viticulturists and enologists traveling the world to help distant wine companies make better wine. California winemakers believed it was good for the industry when everyone was selling the best wine possible everywhere. Art tells the story of traveling to Australia at the invitation of Australia winemakers to learn firsthand about bag-in-a-box wine production.

Obviously, every entrepreneur wants to succeed and flourish. But that objective does not demand you having to annihilate every other company in your industry. Beating your competitors should not be your focus; instead, focus on how to better satisfy your customers and your company will prosper. Your success also doesn't require that you deal wretchedly with your employees or investors. When your employees flourish in what they do and your investors get a good, long-term return, your company has the ultimate competitive advantage. Whenever they face a dichotomy of an either/or choice, Principled Entrepreneurs create a both/and solution.

Doing What You *Ought* to Do, Not Just What You *Feel Like* Doing

Iqbal and Kamal's experiences in Bangladesh demonstrate that, contrary to popular belief, those people we often think of as "dominated" by the international market are actually being excluded from it. The

Quadir brothers' genius has been to create profitable companies that focus on expanding access to networks of productivity and exchange. They didn't wait for change; they acted while the institutional system remained the same. They recognized the human dignity in millions of people living in poverty, offered them access to the market, and those people themselves seized the opportunity to flourish and pursue prosperity. Their story is my favorite example of new wealth creation.

What's different about Iqbal's approach from many others I've seen is that it focuses on market-based solutions specifically focused on the individual person's opportunity to grow and flourish in a competitive market. It is also a vehement rejection of the zero-sum view of business. Iqbal's proactive approach is focused on the solution rather than the problem, and wealth creation rather than poverty.

The basics of the economy, in every form of economic system, remain the same: there are networks of productivity and exchange that are critical to enable individuals must be able to participate in if they are to reach their potential and to attain prosperity. Increasingly, these networks are decentralized and inclusive, controlled more by individuals through ability and opportunity.

Our challenge is not to pre-define the "next stage" toward prosperity and human flourishing, but rather to be ready to do our part to make it work. The economy of the next several decades depends in large part on each of our individual abilities and our character. What will we do with this newfound empowerment and freedom? As we all become individual protagonists in the economy, with the powers that used to be wielded only by nobility, we now have to face the same test they did: with great power comes great responsibility.

The core issues of solidarity and subsidiarity—that is, the ideas of our human connectedness and interdependence as well as the respect for everyone's dignity and right to self-determination—do not go away; they just rest with every one of us now. That is one of the great benefits of the free market.

We surely need institutional systems that enable, even foster, virtuous behavior. This is what the separation of powers in government, the rule of law, property rights, and freedom of contract are all about. But any system promoting freedom is ultimately unable to last without its participants' virtues and talents.

Will we allow others to enter into our circle of productivity? Will we allow others to enter and use the free market as we do? Or will we put up barriers to our network of productivity? Will we invite others into our circle of exchange? Will we provide the less fortunate an opportunity to fully flourish? Will we create win-win solutions?

What our economic and social progress needs most today is not a departure from the free market, but the application of personal virtue in all aspects of life: personal, family, work, and civic. It's a topic that gets little attention, but personal virtue is critical to the continuation of the win-win economy. Everyone in the US today, with respect to such things as communications, food security, and health care—lives better than King Louis XIV or John D. Rockefeller.[15] While in the past it was the great king or leader on whose magnanimity the masses relied, we have now entered into a time where this magnanimity becomes our very own opportunity and responsibility. To achieve this, personal virtue and character will become the most critical aspect of general prosperity. Progress throughout history has been achieved when those who are in power respond virtuously. More are empowered today than ever before. The trend is encouraging, and we seem to be on the right track. But we have a long way to go.

There is a constant "battle" for the freedom of the individual. In the name of protecting freedom, big government-business oligarchies sometimes threaten to take away self-determination.[16] But this amounts to no more than win-lose solutions. True development can happen only if the individual person's possibilities and potential are actualized. This cannot happen in a vacuum, for man is a social animal. Human flourishing is dependent on the freedom and exercise of the free will of each individual in our society. While we cannot want for others what they don't want for themselves, we ought to offer them the opportunity to apply their talents and will. Or, in other words, we ought to include them in our networks of productivity and exchange.

John Henry Newman once said that we attain heaven by "using this world well." In this new stage of development, more and more of us are empowered to do that than ever before. The task we face is very personal yet has the potential to have a global impact. The responsibility is with each of us. In this regard, true freedom is not fulfilled in doing what I feel like doing, but in doing what I ought to do. In this lies the opportunity and challenge of our future. Will we act like Iqbal and Kamal Quadir and use our ingenuity to expand networks of productivity and exchange and create win-win solutions, or will we act selfishly and use our economic power to expand a win-lose economy of exclusion? Doing what we ought to do is to use our freedom and excellence to create solutions for everyone. The great secret we have revealed from our history is that man's principal resource is man himself.

Living Pillar 4: Principled Entrepreneurs Always Seek to Create Win-Win Solutions

1. What product or service could you bring to a new market or market segment, especially at the bottom of the pyramid, in your town, your country, or the world?
2. Are you a good representative of the free market system? Is your company a good example of and for it? Have a team discussion and explore five ways that you can become a better free market participant and representative. (The question being: How can we resist the spread of crony capitalism?)

3. How can you teach/explain to new audiences that business is a win-win proposition and a force for good? How could you counteract the materialist view with an example from your life? How could you counteract the greed myth with an example from your life?

4. Help others see that things are getting better. Collect and share good news with others about the state of the world and humanity. On social media, email lists, company news . . . spread good news.

5. Brainstorm ways to turn adversarial situations into complimentary solutions.

6. Describe the ways that each stakeholder of your company, team, or family is complementary to/with each other. Share your observations with the team and build up the document with the new information/feedback you get from them. Team members will find it edifying to give and receive this kind of thought. Look for and ask for actionable insight.

7. Brainstorm ideas about where you can create abundance where there is currently a scarcity mindset. That is, find places to create win-win solutions where there are win-lose solutions. CarMax is a great case study in this. They took the used car buying transaction as an example of a win-lose experience for the consumer and fixed all the issues that consumers mentioned in terms of how this is a "lose" situation for them, and then they created a win-win business plan and became one of the largest, most profitable, and most fun car dealers to work for in the US.

8. What parts of your vocabulary have to change—and how—to help you and others adopt an abundance mindset?

9. Make a visual representation of your industry cluster with your team. Find areas or relationships that are weak or broken.

144 | The Art of Principled Entrepreneurship

How can you help strengthen or create them? Is there a business opportunity you can pursue in that space?

10. In terms of what your company does and how it does it, what does success look like for your employees? For your customers? For your managers? For your founders? For your investors? For your community?

7

Pillar 5: Always Think Like an Entrepreneur

Entrepreneurs add more value and have more fun.
–Art Ciocca

Entrepreneurs are creators, not harvesters. Entrepreneurs focus on creating successful product portfolios where brands stand for superior value, and profitable organizations where the employees become the competitive advantage.

Why does Pillar 5 encourage us to always think like an entrepreneur? Because Principled Entrepreneurship is a mindset more than a theory. Entrepreneurship is never done; it's always only becoming. This chapter shows how we can remain a creator in mind even if we at times have to harvest certain parts of our business.

When I asked Art about what motivates people to engage in entrepreneurship and business, he told me that, looking back at his experience, he found that there are really two kinds of people:

> There is a kind of a continuum with creators at one end and harvesters at the other end. I think that what determines where you are on this line is a function of what your value system is. The self-centered, what's-in-it-for-me kind of attitude is on one extreme. That kind of short-term focus is what I would call the harvester's mentality.
>
> I have found that such individuals usually think that the answer to everything is wealth; that the journey itself doesn't matter and that other people really don't matter either. It's all about making a lot of money and doing so right now. Creators, on the other hand, are not solely focused on material things. I know, in the beginning, I certainly wasn't. I was kind of a frugal guy growing up. I didn't have a lot of needs. I gravitated toward something more important than financial well-being or money.
>
> I happened to love the industry I was in at the time—it was the wine industry. I saw the potential. I wanted to be part of something bigger than me. I wanted to be part of a successful venture. I was trained as a marketing guy. I was trained to build, to grow right from the outset.
>
> I think my experience in the Navy kind of taught me to lead people, to help them grow, to contribute to something more important and bigger than they were. And that's what I wanted for myself. So I think I always had kind of a growth mentality right from the outset. I don't know when that develops and doesn't develop, but it proved to be the right mentality for me because there was so much satisfaction in it and it was so much fun.

I was never in it to make money. I was in it to build something bigger and more important than I was, or than any of us are. And that's what motivated me the whole way.

Be a Creator, Not a Harvester

Entrepreneurs are creators at heart; at its core, work is all about creation. As we have said repeatedly, business is inherently other-directed and driven by a sincere desire to add value by asking, "How may I help you?" That approach constantly expands not only consumer satisfaction and excellence at work, but also the economy. When companies serve others well, they generate a profit that represents a reward for work and a return on investment. The main decision after creating a return is—what to do with it. Once the proper "rewards" have been made in the form of wages, the question for the Principled Entrepreneur is whether to use their reward to reinvest in the company to innovate and create more, to train employees, buy new or additional equipment, increase customer outreach—or to harvest it and pull it out of the company.

There is no one-size-fits-all formula to tell the entrepreneur what to do. How could one possibly anticipate all the particularities of a company's situation? How could one predict the mix of issues they deal with internally, in the industry, and beyond? What is essential to making this kind of decision is a set of values and priorities—the Principled Entrepreneurship mindset—fortified by a well-trained will and good *character*.

As discussed in chapter five, the leader of a company has a tremendous influence on how the group behaves, how they "group think." Have you ever noticed how companies and teams reflect their leaders' personalities? Think of Apple under Steve Jobs, ServiceMaster under Bill Pollard, Whole Foods under John Mackey. Each organization much more readily reflected its leader's behavior than some set of rules written in the HR manual.

That is especially so in terms of fundamental beliefs and values with regard to the ultimate goal of work and the company. In any company, there come decision points where you have to choose between two masters. This tends to be a choice between short-term money-making and something that requires long-term focus, like a commitment to the overall team or any other form of excellence. These types of choices can reveal a creator's or a harvester's mindset.

Creators focus on generating value, looking forward, and thinking of the next way the team or company can grow in excellence and create more value for customers. They focus on opportunities to initiate new activities.

Harvesters focus on extracting the value created. They end the cycle. They focus on the endgame of redistributing the benefits gained from the activity. The creator-harvester continuum that Art talks about is a kind of lens each one of us sees the world through. Harvesting or creating is primarily a personal value: seeking to *plant* or to *extract* in everything we do.

That does not mean that a creator never harvests. There is a "time to plant, and a time to pluck up that which is planted." But a good farmer harvests with great care for the land and an eye toward growing the next season's crop. It is the same in a business. Sometimes it's necessary to decide to sell a company, or to make a balance sheet–centered decision. Other times you ought to reinvest your profits into the company, or to take a balance sheet hit and use cash to bolster your brand.

When Art faced the disaster of the spoiled vermouth, he had to decide between two options: destroy the faulty product and face a significant hit to the balance sheet but maintain the quality standard, or sell the compromised product (which was perfectly safe to consume) and realize a positive financial outcome (but take a hit with respect to quality and morale).

These are moments when no business book is going to tell you what to do. All the frameworks and processes it describes might be necessary in a successful business, but even engaging in all of them together is not sufficient for you to create an excellent company. For that, it's your deeply held personal values that need to come into play. They show whether your ultimate value is to *create* or to *harvest*. The moments where you make decisions based on your values make an indelible mark on the company. These are the crucial moments when company character is formed because all employees, investors, and customers are *watching* you and will in one way or another mimic your behavior and, ultimately, your values.

The entrepreneur's *creator* value is thus transferred to the company, as in the case of The Wine Group. What to do with spoiled vermouth was a big decision, but every company and every entrepreneur has to answer this question every day: Do you ultimately seek to *create* or to *harvest?*

Always Thinking Like an Entrepreneur Enables More Clarity and Better Decision Making

Art Ciocca's story of The Wine Group is one example showcasing a Principled Entrepreneur applying each of the five pillars. His story shows how the mindset of a team can lead to long-term value creation, how it can make for fulfilling careers for individuals and innovation and excellence in an industry. And how it can create a most valued brand with customers.

The promise of this book is that the pursuit of Principled Entrepreneurship is the engine for continued prosperity and is the most effective way to ensure that everyone in our society can indeed enjoy life, liberty, and the pursuit of happiness. A vision like this is always built from the bottom up if we want it to include everyone and have it be sustainable. And the key ingredients in this story are creativity and freedom.

After success in business, it becomes tempting to take shortcuts to implement one's vision by top-down decree and one-size-fits-all declarations. History and the day's news are rich with examples of governments and companies trying to do that. These moves are often not ill-intentioned, but nonetheless they do not tend to work out in the long run, and usually create a lot of unnecessary misery and unhappiness. These grand solutions are appealing because the other way is tedious and complex: convincing others of what's the best thing to do and allowing them space to apply their will to become the cause of change. If only everyone just did what I told them to do! Right?

Unfortunately, the top-down or authoritarian approach to governance tends to undermine the workforce in the long run. It frustrates creativity and engenders a kind of learned helplessness. Working with people's freedom requires a lot of patience, but in the long term it gives everyone space to develop their gifts and inspires more people to think like entrepreneurs.

Whether it's in business, government, or society in general, the Principled Entrepreneurship mindset can lead the way for how to celebrate competition and build companies and societies that offer opportunity and excellence for everyone, not just for those who have already "made it." This is critical to our future as a society, because if we do not pursue this dream of life, liberty, and happiness for *all*, we will be forced eventually to live the opposite, which means the nightmare of tyranny and oppression.

The faith in this plurality as well as individuality of excellence is the Principled Entrepreneurship approach's ultimate strength, but it is also the reason why it at first appears easier to go against it—that is, to stop being a Principled Entrepreneur. It's risky and messy to allow these bottom-up solutions to take shape. Yet the pursuit of excellence as a society and of a business consists of finding ways to challenge everyone to find and develop their personal gifts and use them in a way that complements those around them, including those they work with, their neighbors, and their friends.

This kind of kaleidoscope of strengths creates the most successful and resilient groups, but is also very difficult to achieve because it demands that everyone commit their will to the pursuit of both personal excellence and collaboration in finding just the right balance or rhythm to make the group work by the contribution of everyone's individual excellence, not only their own.

This kind of teamwork is challenging on all sides—for those in management who have decision power and for those on the team who do not have the same power but need to have faith and embrace the risk to pursue their excellence. It requires us to go beyond the us-versus-them approach. It's the work of life, maybe the most important thing we do in life. And because it deals with individuals, there is no one size fits all—there's only a way to think about things, and principles to embrace that enable and maintain entrepreneurship.

Do you see why Principled Entrepreneurship is more of a mental model than a framework of business, more an art than a science? It's difficult to put Principled Entrepreneurship into words. On the one hand, because it's hard to express, it's little written about. On the other hand, when people do venture to write about running companies, Principled Entrepreneurs find many of the step-by-step management manuals comical. There is no "color by numbers" approach to human excellence. Such approaches cannot work because they cannot possibly anticipate the specific mix of humanity that any particular business deals with. Each business is different. Its people, its customers, its locality, its industry, its competitors and cooperators—all of these aspects make a business so beautifully unpredictable. These variables can be optimized only through risk taking and faith within a framework of wisdom and good character. This is the expertise of the Principled Entrepreneur. Human flourishing needs entrepreneurship—Principled Entrepreneurship—and its success depends not only on us becoming such entrepreneurs but, even more importantly, remaining so.

Keeping Your Company
Entrepreneurial Takes Planning

Always thinking like an entrepreneur is core for the Principled Entre-preneur. But this does not only apply to your own thinking and acting; it also applies to the company you lead. The two are somewhat inter-twined as we've seen, but I think it's still easier to stay entrepreneurial in your own life than keeping that up in a company in the long term.

"At some point around my twenty-fifth year as CEO, I believed I reached the point of diminishing returns in terms of learning and con-tributing. I sensed some of my original partners were in the same boat. We had succeeded beyond our wildest expectations, we had lived for the business for over two decades, and we were no longer behaving like entrepreneurs," Art told me. I was amazed to hear that Art felt at some point that he was losing his zeal for the business. But it's quite under-standable. He had seen the same issues over and over again. Some of the members of his original team had moved on. Sales had slowed, and there were not many exciting opportunities in the works. Others were tired, too, and no one was stepping up to fill the void. It was time for some new blood.

There is a time in the life of every CEO when he or she is too close to the everyday goings-on of the company to have a fresh perspective. "It's times like this when it pays to have good friends, confidants, or advisors with perspective who can help you see more clearly what you're missing," Art explains.

The diagnosis and admonition Art received from his advisors was that he'd failed to groom a successor from within. "I learned the hard way that succession planning is a vital area that must be managed, reviewed, and evaluated on an ongoing basis." Now that The Wine Group needed new ideas and new strength, no one was ready.

Art was a quick study and learned that the CEO, advisory board, and, when necessary, outsiders ought to constantly monitor and promote potential successors within the company. It is far better to have a long-term succession plan and gradually upgrade it over time than to allow the organization to coast and rest on its laurels. No one is smart enough to do it all on their own. Everyone needs help and perspective, especially entrepreneurs or CEOs who have been in place for a long time. Art took his new insight to heart.

"I decided to find a suitable successor so I could hand over the leadership of The Wine Group. I realized that this meant that my ownership role was winding down as well and I had a sense of responsibility to offer similar opportunities for others to experience that same exciting journey of living the American Dream as I had."

As a result of the failure to bring along an insider, the company was forced to hire from the outside. Hiring from outside the company is a risk because there is always the chance for a cultural mismatch. "Of course, we tried to hire for character and values before talent, but there is always that risk until you see the individual in action," Art explained.

Establishing the Creator Company

Art needed to codify the Principled Entrepreneurship mindset into The Wine Group without creating a rigid or forceful environment to enable future generations of leaders to have the same opportunities to practice Principled Entrepreneurship as the previous generation had. Creating this atmosphere required imagination and flexibility.

The Wine Group's corporate recitals, which the company formulated shortly after becoming independent, provided strong incentives for management to add value and growth to the company. At that time, they also put a strong *disincentive* into the corporate bylaws for failure to discharge the stewardship responsibilities as intended.

The core concern that was addressed and preempted by this feature was the potential of harvester thinking. The agreement specifically states: the only circumstance under which the company may be sold is if it fails financially and can no longer be operated as a freestanding private company. In that event, only minimal proceeds from any sale may accrue to the owner-managers under whose watch the company deteriorated. All additional proceeds go to charity. This mechanism was erected as a safeguard installed to keep future management teams focused on fulfilling their stewardship roles, and thinking like creators.

I can't think of a stronger signal of the importance of creating value for customers and promoting the excellence of employees than to tell owners that there's no other way to generate a personal return for them. The sentiment of this clause reminds me of the explorer Hernán Cortés, who, upon discovering the New World in 1519 and facing great dangers in disembarking and exploring the area, destroyed his ships upon arrival to send a clear message to his men: there is no turning back.[1] I love how this makes the purpose of the business clear beyond any doubt.

Art's team did all that but eventually realized that by failing to groom the next generation, they weren't applying their creator mindset to the most important aspect of the company: the future leadership.

Planning for the Next Wave of Creators

Once Art noticed the need for succession planning, he made sure that the corporate recitals would be revised to include a call for a continual focus on succession planning. Since grooming your successor does not come naturally to 90 percent of us, he introduced the practice that the management team has to engage an outside consultant on a long-term basis to act as a sounding board when recruiting new senior owners or managers, and to assist in grooming future owners and managers. The board's compensation committee was obliged to annually review all senior manager profiles and evaluations and brief the board on the findings, highlighting promising new talent. A special focus was to be put on the board discussion around finding the next generation of senior executives.

That's a great solution. But I think the most innovative and brilliant solution was the other way Art's team thought of to ensure everyone would *be* and *hire* people with a creator mindset. Unlike a public company where stocks and stock options are often monetized in the days or months following retirement or leaving the company, their model made quality succession planning an inherent priority for senior managers and executives. It was set up so that The Wine Group senior executives have monetized only a small portion of their equity (10 to 30 percent) prior to leaving the company (or retiring) and are therefore dependent on their successors to continue creating value that could fund or support their predecessors' equity redemptions over multiple years.

With a smile Art said, "What I love most is the long-term nature of this model because it provides a strong alignment of interests between previous, current, and future generations of owners/managers. The model rivets attention on the quality of your successors."

This completely prevents "scorched earth policy" behavior on the one hand and the buddy system (handing over the reins not to the best qualified but to the best friend candidate) on the other.[2] This policy has a profoundly positive effect on company culture, creates incentives to provide true win-win solutions inside and outside of the company, and ensures that the company always remains entrepreneurial.

The Great Opportunity

When I asked Art what his message was to the young students I teach, he didn't hesitate: "Always think like an entrepreneur. Always, and in all ways. You can't be one unless you first think like one. The good news is that you can always think like an entrepreneur—whether you manage a small team in your first job or if you're a CEO. Thinking like an entrepreneur is the first step in becoming one. You have to learn to walk before you can learn to run. Start today. There's no time like the present!"

His words reflect his hope in the future, but they also reflect his realization that we have been facing an increasing crisis surrounding the American Dream over the past forty years, with startups slowly declining and today being at a record low.[3]

Fewer people want to be entrepreneurs now because it feels too risky. Entrepreneurial thinking in general is diminishing. We are trained to be risk averse all the way from kindergarten to new employee training. The regulations and paperwork involved in starting and running a small business are increasingly onerous, such that being an entrepreneur is starting to look like a money-losing proposition. Why would anyone want to do that? Well, there's change in the air, and the moment is right!

Every challenge we face is an opportunity in disguise. The COVID-19 pandemic and the subsequent economic downturn is a case in point: While the stock market didn't show it during the crisis itself, the novel coronavirus has severely impacted our business landscape. It was akin to a fire in a forest: many big trees (Hertz, Macy's, JCrew, Neiman Marcus, JCPenney, Brooks Brothers, Lord & Taylor, Friendly's, L'Occitane, Virgin Atlantic, Remington, Cirque du Soleil, Chuck E. Cheese, Pier 1 Imports, Gold's Gym, and many others) were destroyed, many of them never to reappear. The devastation was even worse for small businesses. Anyone without solid reserves or a quick pivot went under. Many people lost what they once considered secure jobs. The suffering the pandemic brought about did not happen only in hospital rooms. There were countless people who lost their livelihoods and worried about how they could put food on the table the next day.[4]

But as with every crisis, it was time constrained. The other side of a crisis is like the other side of that fire going through the forest: there's lots of room for new growth and room for new ideas. This is prime territory for Principled Entrepreneurs. Just think of all the new space created in so many industries by the disappearance of these large companies. The opportunities for innovation and growth are immense. Principled Entrepreneurs are the ones who will take rational risk (faith), are other-directed (empathy), and have vision, optimism (that the world can be better), and the creativity and can-do attitude needed to move our society forward and give the next generations the same chance at prosperity and peace as we had in the last forty years.

There is a wonderful opportunity to shift our attention away from our fascination with the almost gambler-vibe of the financial markets and back to our actual creative work. It's a shift that moves away from the impersonal, spectator-like involvement in the economy to a direct, creative participation. More and more people are doing this and it noticeably elevates not only their sense of self and personal excellence, but also their overall happiness. Making your work the "point" of what you do, not just the means to generate the desired result, is transformative.

My work with "maker" companies is especially inspiring, but I also see a lot of startups and "acquisition" entrepreneurs who create tremendous value by bringing together the reverence for the existing craftsmanship in a company and "the internet of things" of the technology era to create amazing products and services, and solutions to problems.

What is very encouraging is that entrepreneurship numbers are up among many of the groups that were traditionally excluded from networks of productivity and exchange, who were not given a fair chance at social mobility in the US: women, African Americans and Latinos,[5] and people over fifty years[6] of age who struggle to be hired. The hope that the next generation will be better off than the last is still alive.[7]

I believe we are about to witness a resurgence of entrepreneurship, a revitalization of the American Dream. After forty years of unprecedented prosperity and relative peace, we mustn't kill the goose that lays the golden eggs by allowing the decline of the very system that makes these goods possible. It is time for our generation to discover that true prosperity doesn't come from a government program, is not manageable like a classroom, and will never happen "as planned." No, the American Dream depends on a few simple principles—a mindset that ultimately puts the human person at the center of our concern in society and business. Let's not wait to make that long-overdue move. The choice is not between crony capitalism and the state-run economy. The choice is for freedom and responsibility. The time for Principled Entrepreneurship is now!

And by the way, many, if not most, Principled Entrepreneurs are not currently in a startup effort, and they're not necessarily CEOs of big companies either. That's because, as we've seen repeatedly, Principled Entrepreneurship is a mental model, a way of thinking about work, business, the economy, and life.

A key aspect of the principle "always think like an entrepreneur" is that everyone can start to take a proprietary interest or think like a creator. That's what entrepreneurs do. There is magic in thinking this way. It enables you to see issues more clearly and, as a result, develop good new ideas and find better solutions. This is valuable advice for everyone, especially those early in their careers. "There is no better way to prepare for an entrepreneurial career than to practice it on someone else's nickel," as Art likes to say. Meaning: start thinking like an entrepreneur while you're in someone else's employ. Don't wait until you're out on your own.

Be a Principled Entrepreneur starting today, and never stop having the mindset of a creator—it will serve you well in whatever you do! The key is to embrace change with innovative action: dare to dream, do not be afraid to take risks, have faith, and always make things more valuable than they were when you found them. In their book *The Innovator's DNA*, Clayton Christensen and Hal Gregersen write that the thing that distinguishes entrepreneurs from everyone else is that they make aligning thinking and acting a habit. They're not just entrepreneurs when they focus on building a company. They always think and act that way. Experimentation at any level of your career has risks, but so does the opposite. Risk is part of the equation of life in either action or inaction. But as a Principled Entrepreneur you are willing to take those risks when pursuing your vision. Failure is only bad if you do not learn from it. Don't wonder, "Can I do it?" Ask, "How can I do it?" Focus on what you want, not what you fear, and you will always think like an entrepreneur!

Living Pillar 5: Always Think Like an Entrepreneur

1. Where are you on the harvester/creator continuum? Once you have your answer, ask three friends who know your work. Then reconcile their feedback to come up with an objective answer. What changes in thinking and acting can you undertake to move toward a creator mindset?

2. What is the greatest value you have ever created with your work? Describe that experience—how did it feel and how did it work out? Reflect on the lessons you learned from that and make a plan to create the life/work situation to make it happen again.

3. What three changes can you implement in your life and for your team during the next three months to move yourself and the team further toward the creator side of the continuum? Think in terms of the "Cortés burning the return ride" kind of initiative that Art took by writing The Wine Group investor agreement.

4. Think of the last "bottom up" initiative or solution on your team. What worked? What did not? Make a plan to take action accordingly to enable such efforts to occur and succeed again.

5. What is your succession plan? Would your team/organization be ready to continue if you could not do your work next year?

Is your current succession structure rewarding harvesters or creators? Make a creator-focused plan and start to identify and groom several possible successors for your job. Create a system that keeps you accountable for this, something like creating a succession planning committee on the board that you regularly report to or committing to do so with a mentor or friend.

6. If your company has a harvester-leaning incentive system and you cannot change that, think of steps that you can take or changes you can introduce to decrease a management team's incentive or temptation to pursue short-term profit with a scorched-earth kind of approach.

7. Brainstorm some ideas of how your team can attract, screen, and retain creators and repel habitual harvesters.

8. How would someone with a Principled Entrepreneurship mindset act in your situation? What risks would that person take? What security would they insist on? What would be their next action? You have to play the role until you take on the identity.

9. What are the temptations and factors that make you not always think like a Principled Entrepreneur? Examine them closely and discuss them with good mentors and friends. Then, make a plan to address them over the next six months.

10. Keep a list of opportunities you see where someone could add value for consumers. Set some time aside every couple of weeks or months to evaluate if this could be an opportunity for you to create that value. If it is, determine what the first step would be toward validating that value proposition and initiate it within one week.

11. What maker-skill would you love to develop? Think of things like cooking, coding, woodwork, electronics, design, and so on. Do some research on what kinds of courses are offered in your area where you can get practical experience. Commit to taking

one such course every year and to experiment/play with that skill during the rest of that year.

12. Brainstorm a side hustle for yourself. If you were guaranteed success in that project, what kind of company would you start? Now figure out how you would scale that to a side hustle startup.

13. Identify a non-business activity or area of your life where you can create value by thinking and acting like a Principled Entrepreneur. Start a SkunkWorks project to pursue it for several months. Then review the progress and decide if it warrants further effort. If it does, make a plan for it. If not, start over.

8

Inspiring and Motivating
the Next Generation

I started this book off by telling you the story of how Art Ciocca and I
lamented the state of entrepreneurship education, how we felt that it
did not give students a good understanding of the free market and did
not adequately prepare the next generation to take full advantage of the
opportunities that lay ahead. We were not happy with it; we felt that the
state of our business education endangered the American Dream, and
we tried to do something about it.

That was over ten years ago. In the meantime, I have found out it's
one thing to try to convince a group of liberal-arts professors that business is a force for good. It's another to create a curriculum that actually
reflects that. And it's a different thing altogether to daily motivate and
inspire future business leaders and entrepreneurs to make use of business in a way that perpetuates the American Dream.[1]

After a career in business and being critical of how higher education
and business schools teach on the topic, joining The Catholic University of America made me part of a team that had the rare privilege of

designing a business school from scratch. It fell to me and my team to define the Principled Entrepreneurship part of it.

I teach Principled Entrepreneurship because I believe that school should not only teach theory and business frameworks but also help students in their search for human excellence, what I usually refer to as happiness.[2] I like to point out to the students that there are a few basic laws that govern this quest—not in the prescriptive way but in an enlightening way. One of these laws is that happiness is a derivative of meaning. If we understand the "why" behind the things we do, then we can do any "what" and figure out any "how." If we understand the "why" in work and the economy—and if that reason reaches beyond your wallet or balance sheet—then your career is a path to fulfillment and happiness, and you will easily, and happily, figure out a "how." I'm amazed that many business schools teach only the "how" and give no guidance or help to the student in finding their "why." This is a significant disservice. It misses the whole point of receiving a business education: to prepare to pursue our excellence through a career in business. Those activities are not what we do *aside from living*. They are an integral part of life.

In this chapter, I will explain in some detail how we teach Principled Entrepreneurship at the Ciocca Center for Principled Entrepreneurship at The Catholic University of America. I don't do this with the intent of telling others what to do, or to insinuate that it has to be done exclusively this way, or that this teaching and learning must take place at an institution. Art Ciocca's story is a great example of how Principled Entrepreneurship is taught and passed on within a company. The point is that Principled Entrepreneurship needs to be taught in the boardroom, the office, the shop floor, and business school. I foresee a future where higher education ceases to be a finite, four-year sprint during which students memorize facts and theories about something they've never done before and will forget before they start their first job. What we need is lifelong learning. We need to develop a university that's at your side when you need her most. A mix of a really smart friend, a chiropractor, and a gym membership: you call on them when you have a specific question, a big problem, or you want to stay fit over time. The four-year university degree has to be turned into the foundation of a lifelong learning process where one is at times student and at other times teacher, where ideas are explored and tested and various fields of knowledge are encouraged to intersect and flourish. While this is the long-term vision and we are pursuing that with various efforts and experiments like our "Lunch & Learn" or "Venture Lab" programs, I am excited to teach—or, as I'd rather say, inspire and encourage our students on their path of Principled Entrepreneurship. My intent is to show that Principled Entrepreneurship can be "taught," and to share our learning so far in this regard. We make constant strides toward doing this more effectively and we always learn as much as our students do during each one of these courses. And as in all things, we also want to remain entrepreneurial as we do this work. Therefore, I welcome your engagement and any feedback you might have so that we can together find ever more excellent ways to pass on these Principled Entrepreneurship pillars that enable those who come after us to pursue the American Dream as effectively and enthusiastically as we've had the privilege to do. Please visit business.catholic.edu to reach me.

What Is Entrepreneurship and Can It Be Taught?

It's difficult to teach an art. Perhaps the most one can do is describe Principled Entrepreneurship and the let students gravitate to or away from it.
—Art Ciocca

When I'm asked the classic question whether or not entrepreneurship—or Principled Entrepreneurship, in our case—can be taught, I always hesitate to answer because I'm not sure the questioner has the time to hear the full answer. I usually give the short answer, which is "No . . . and yes . . . and it depends."

Entrepreneurship is often defined as "the activity of making money by starting or running businesses, especially when this involves taking financial risks; the ability to do this."[3] With this definition, the answer to whether it can be taught would be no. The ability to start a company and having the nerves to handle the financial risk is a natural talent. Not everyone has the disposition to handle that kind of uncertainty and risk. Teaching it would be unnecessary and impossible.

I would suggest, however, that the Oxford definition of entrepreneurship provides only half of what is involved and is a bit wrongheaded. In my experience, entrepreneurs are actually not much more risk-tolerant than the average person. It's just that they perceive an opportunity, they see a solution that others don't, and so, to them, the success of their business is far more certain than to an outsider, someone who doesn't see or understand the opportunity they see. In that sense, they don't necessarily take more risks than others. Or rather, their risk taking is real, but is balanced by the possibilities they see. If we saw what they saw, any one of us would and does do what an entrepreneur does. We all act on something we feel certain about. The question is, are we trained to do so in order to create value? Not all ideas create value, and not everyone who starts or leads a business is an entrepreneur.

In fact, entrepreneurs don't all start or lead companies, as we said in the previous chapter. In my experience, *entrepreneurs are people who do more with less.* Principled Entrepreneurs do this toward a specific aim. They are disruptors or change agents who improve the system positively. They might have an insight they recognize and—whether they run a company, manage a team, or are an employee somewhere in a large organization—they act on that insight in a way to improve things around them. They make the world a better place by creating value for others through human excellence. In this sense, entrepreneurship can and ought to be taught.

We can teach students how to gather information, how to generate original insights, how to create customer value through human ingenuity, and how to develop the conviction and confidence to follow through. After all, as we've said, entrepreneurship is more an attitude than an aptitude, an application of our free will—the most human of all aspects of our nature. And the exercise of our free will does not have to be taught per se, because everyone has it. But dedicated instruction can help us strengthen the entrepreneurial attitude and teach us how to harness our wills consistently for human excellence. Learning requires, however, that the student be an active participant and not just a mere spectator on the journey.[4] So it depends on the student whether or not entrepreneurship can be taught.

In the final analysis, yes, entrepreneurship can be taught, but it's akin to teaching someone to play the piano. It is most effective with people who have a natural talent to begin with. At most US schools, entrepreneurship education has been done very poorly. In his book *Burn the Business Plan*, Carl Schramm cites Syracuse University professor Mike D'Eredita, an Olympic rowing coach and accomplished entrepreneur: "If we trained our Olympic athletes like we train our entrepreneurs, America would never win even a bronze medal." Schramm goes on in the book to describe ten lessons for aspiring entrepreneurs and their teachers to keep in mind as they teach entrepreneurship. He illustrates each of his points with role models,[5] and throughout he insists that action based on right thinking is more important than a beautifully written business plan.

Entrepreneurship is a method and a mindset, more than a mere process. Therefore, entrepreneurship education has to pay adequate attention not just to the theory of entrepreneurship, but to the nature of the human person and the purpose of the market economy. This is where education of Principled Entrepreneurs has to start: right thinking leading to the right action. Teaching Principled Entrepreneurship is absolutely possible. It entails learning the fundamentals of human dignity, value creation, and the free market economy. It involves a balance of theory and praxis. It takes the student on a journey of self-discovery, self-control, and self-actualization. In this field of study, no one is simply the teacher; we are all students of Principled Entrepreneurship because it is never done. The path is the goal.

Only Knowledge, Skill, and Attitude Can Be Taught

When I first started teaching, a colleague who had been doing it for decades told me that a teacher can teach only three things: skill, knowledge, and attitude. Skill is the ability to do specific things well, to gain proficiency in various tasks. Knowledge entails understanding and memorizing information that allows the student to develop pattern recognition and analyze situations accurately. Attitude is shorthand for having character—to have the right attitude toward things and developing the habit of doing what ought to be done[6] rather than what you feel like doing. It's employing your education, skill, and knowledge for good. The goal of a good education is to teach all three. A great education builds the student's character so she can pursue skill and knowledge to do good for the rest of her life.

What I have learned over the roughly ten years of teaching at a university is that the US educational system does some of this very well but could improve on the whole. Business schools tend to teach as if we are training office drones. We're highly focused on teaching knowledge and skill but neglect teaching the right attitude. We ask students to memorize, remember, and regurgitate. We make them imitate our actions, repeat tasks, and think inside the box. In doing so, we prepare them the way their great-grandparents were prepared for their careers during the

Industrial Revolution.[7] It's a time-tested process that worked well in the past. But the future of business is not going to be like the past. This is why a focus on teaching attitude is more important than ever before.

Teaching Students to Effectively Exercise Their Will

The task-focused economy is over. In the evolution of work, machines accomplish mundane and thoughtless factory tasks better than any human. Artificial intelligence will soon do the same in the office. And that is a good thing. The future of work lies in the value of the human person—not as a cog, not as a means to an end, but as a creator of value. Good and motivated employees who want to pursue personal and team excellence are the ultimate capital.

This kind of motivation requires freedom. No one can want for you. Either you want to be engaged and want to give your best or you don't. No one but yourself can force you to do that. You need to exercise your will to do it. Your free will. That freedom is the future of the economy, for better or for worse.

There has been a trend toward the freedom and excellence of each individual person since the beginning of humanity. Freedom, at least in terms of democracy, has expanded from most of humanity being enslaved in autocratic states to the majority of us living in one-person, one-vote democracies and the rule of law being applied to each person more or less equally ever since the early 2000s.[8] We're not perfect and never will be. But we have made tremendous strides toward treating each person better. Freedom is not something that *is*, it is always only *becoming*. If we're lax, if we don't proactively promote and exercise our freedom, we move backward.

Education is connected to both civics and economics. To continue the move toward civil liberty and equality, we not only have to be well aware of history and philosophy, but we also have to be able to apply the insights gained to our own lives by making tough choices and then sticking to them. We have to be able to use our free will effectively.

The opportunity I see in how we educate today is that our approach does not yet reflect this change. We are still set up to educate people to succeed in a land- and financial-capital economy, where uniformity and conformity were valued. School is not set up to train the next generation to creatively use their free will in the service of human excellence. It doesn't have to be that way. An education in Principled Entrepreneurship has to help the student develop a strong, free will.

At the Ciocca Center, what we add to all this is that we aim to create a community of learners through what we do. It is critical to put the person at the center of this undertaking, as it is in any other. Our success does not lie in the average outcome. It lies in each individual life we touch, in each Principled Entrepreneur we inspire. In each person who learns to pursue their excellence and with and through that excellence creates value for others.

What to Teach

Attitude (The Principled Entrepreneurship Mindset)

Teaching "attitude" is a bit more difficult and subjective than teaching math and science. But it is nonetheless a critical component of a good education for any profession.

Think of a job opening for a sales team manager in your company or on your team. Let's say that you are asked to ensure that this position is filled by the very best person. Make a list of requirements, a list of what you wish the job applicant would have to offer the company and the new team.

I've done this exercise many times with a live audience, often with corporate management teams. Every time, the result is the same: the list

ends up consisting of 20 percent specific skill requirements and 80 percent attitude issues. In short, we all hire character over skill. But business
school, in preparing the next generation of team members for us, often
teaches only skill. That's a problem. But it doesn't have to be this way.

Skill (Will, Discernment, Decision Making, Praxis)

Aristotle wrote, "What we have to learn to do, we learn by doing." Business schools exist to teach business. But do they teach how to *do* business? In my experience, many of them teach it in theory, not in practice.[9]
It's a bit like teaching someone to swim on dry land. We talk about
business, we read about business, we role-play business scenarios in the
classroom. What's needed is for students of entrepreneurship to learn by
doing with the help of faculty theoreticians and practitioners—ideally,
some of whom are both.

I believe the best way to learn to be a Principled Entrepreneur is to
start a company[10] or spearhead an effort that adds value to customers.
At the Ciocca Center, we ask each student to start a company—however
small the effort[11]—so that we can get them into the pool to begin learning to swim. Students, of course, need to learn the various business skills
such as accounting, finance, strategy, and so on. But experiential learning is also necessary.

Well-educated students will also have learned to make good life
decisions, not just business decisions. I think it's essential that students
are taught to discern well when making career and life decisions. Once
they're in the midst of their careers, their life decisions will have a potentially major impact on the business they run or work for. Making good
life and business decisions—practicing good discernment—is a skill. A
good business school teaches students that skill.

Knowledge (Liberal Arts, Business Theory, and Self-Knowledge)

"Know thyself!" is the great admonition attributed to Plato.

All actionable knowledge starts with knowing oneself. It is imperative that Principled Entrepreneurship students live Plato's admonition. Our courses at the Ciocca Center all contain some elements of self-knowledge within the curriculum. Business school is a good time to grow as a person, to get to know yourself on a deeper level so you can make appropriate, helpful, and effective plans to become the person God made you to be.

Just as it is important for people in society in general to understand the reason for their own existence, it is important for everyone in our society to understand the reason for our civic system, for what we do, how we do it, and why we do it. It is imperative that businesspeople in general and entrepreneurs in particular understand how and why the free market system is the best system for the prosperity of humanity. If we don't know that, we will lose it.

A good business education will leave the student with a full understanding and appreciation of the free market economy. In our program, students are required to take classes on entrepreneurship history, economic theory, and human anthropology.

In creating a person-centered company, it stands to reason that some sustained reflection on the nature of the human person is important for helping students succeed as Principled Entrepreneurs in their future careers. That's why we devote an entire course to exploring the human person from several perspectives.

The course begins by developing a philosophical understanding of human nature, starting with different views. *Is the human person simply a body, a physio-chemical entity (materialism)? Or a soul trapped for a time in the cage of a body (dualism)? Or a self-sufficient being (individualism)? Or a single-minded pleasure-seeker (hedonism)?* These ideas are then contrasted with an understanding of the human being as an intimate union of body and soul, who exists and thrives only as a communal being, and whose fulfillment includes knowing and loving truth, beauty, and goodness.

We turn to a variety of thinkers who develop the idea of the human person—from Plato and Aristotle, to St. Thomas Aquinas, to several contemporary figures, including Martin Luther King Jr., psychiatrist and Holocaust survivor Viktor Frankl, philosopher and theologian Michael Novak, and Pope St. John Paul II. In the final weeks of the course, students hear from guest speakers who relate their own experience of the challenges of living a person-centered approach in business.

The primary goal is for students to grasp how the fundamental understanding of the human person has important practical implications in business and economic life. We want students to reflect on how all the other elements of business theory and practice are ordered well in light of the truth about the human person. Students gain a deeper grasp of what it means to say that "the person is at the center of business" and are encouraged to develop alertness to concrete ways of applying these insights in their own personal and professional lives.

We explain three things in detail that are critical prerequisites for Principled Entrepreneurship to flourish:

1. Human anthropology and work: As Adam Smith remarked, we don't see dogs engage in production and trade. Humans have the capacity to create, and do create all the time. In fact, humans' highest calling is to become co-creator with God whereby the human and the divine will work together to participate in the divine plan of creation. In top-down approaches to business, humans are seen as a means to an end and work thus becomes less important than capital—in fact, work itself loses its true meaning.

2. The "entrepreneurial element"[12] shows that without that kind of unpredictable X factor or wild-card ingredient to the economy, the richness of human societies, and the complexities of the market system, cannot be fully explained. In traditional

economics, the human person is seen as an optimizer of information, not a creator of information and knowledge.

3. Social cooperation under the division of labor is not simply human beings agreeing to work together, it is also human persons being transformed through the act of working together to achieve a higher goal. Principled Entrepreneurship is fundamentally the idea that the organizations we create are also made for the fulfillment of the human person partaking in them, and not just for production. Hence human organizations have several goals, the most important of which is human flourishing, or eudaimonia.

Students study economist Israel Kirzner's theory, as well as many other authors such as Joseph Schumpeter and William Baumol. The theory part is meant to teach the complexities behind the idea of entrepreneurship so that students have a deep view of the concept. Markets are complex systems that include many institutions that can help or hinder entrepreneurship. Students study, for instance, the evolution of the venture capital industry and how the internet has impacted the financing of ventures in the last twenty years.

If students don't have this knowledge and digest, synthesize, and internalize it—forming it into part of their personal "why" for doing business—they cannot be good Principled Entrepreneurs because their actions won't come from a sound framework of thought. Without a good understanding of human nature and the market economy, we end up looking to the government for solutions to poverty and progress. Those are costly misunderstandings, and a good education in Principled Entrepreneurship can prevent that.

Using a Trading Game to Gauge Happiness

One way that we help students internalize the value of trade and value is through a simple game. It is a slight but impactful variation of a popular exercise that also exemplifies the value of open markets and the "subjectiveness" of value.

The "trading game" gives each participant a bag with a "goodie" inside. For this game, get some small items, half of them that would appeal to the students and the other half that would appeal to an adult woman, a mother of the students or group you are doing the exercise with. Have the group form a circle and give each student about three to five items in their bag. The gifts should be of roughly the same monetary value, and it would be useful if some of the items "go together." A pocket mirror and lipstick or a comb would be a good idea, and make sure the items are distributed among different bags.

Once every student has a bag, tell them that you just gave them a couple of gifts for themselves and their mom and that they should check it out. Ask them how happy they are with the gift for their mom on a scale of one to ten. Write it down and compute the total points of "happiness" in the room. Then allow students to trade gifts with the person on either their left or right. After that, compute the new number of happiness in the room. Finally, allow more time for anyone to trade with anyone else. The final number of happiness will show that the more we engage in trade, the more we get to choose what we find of value, the happier we are.

After the game, I ask the students to tell everyone what they got for themselves and for their mother, and why it makes them happy. Without fail, the students put major effort into finding gifts that will create happiness for their mother. Interestingly, this made both them, and presumably their mother, happier than they were before the trading took place.

A key aspect of reflecting on this exercise is that it puts the person in the center. Each person enjoys the process and the result, even more so when they plan to give the value they create with their trades to someone else. The longer you play, the more exchanges you have, the more value is generated in the room, the more joy the players have in making the exchanges. This shows that the path is actually as much, if not more, of the goal as the end. The process of making the trade and negotiating is actually as critical a part of the value creation as the creation of the product itself. Happiness is experienced as a result of both the creating and the trading. That is because value is created either way, and creating or increasing value is one of the things that makes us humans happy.

Students learn that as long as we are free to create, trade, and give to others, we create value. And as long as we create value through win-win solutions, we grow the economy and we create abundance. This concept is fundamental to the proper understanding of the free market economy and Principled Entrepreneurship. It is a shame that it is not more generally known.

How to Teach Principled Entrepreneurship

There are three key components to teaching Principled Entrepreneurship.

1. Discover who you are, create a vision for who you want to be, and develop a plan to get there

Creativity is highly correlated with self-knowledge,[13] and passion with purpose.[14] If we want to help students prepare for their lives as Principled Entrepreneurs, we have to move from trying to tell them what to do to helping them find their identity, values, desires, and passion, and then help them figure out a way to create new value from those that generate an economic return. Only then will the work we do on a daily basis no longer just be a way to make a living, but become a way of life. A vocation. A path to human excellence and happiness.

In the foundational course we call "Vocation of Business," we help each student explore their personality, dreams, and identity. Through various exercises, they create a list of the top values they have and describe how they intend to manifest these in life. Each student learns about mission statements and creates their very own after careful research and deliberation. They determine what virtues they need to cultivate to best support this mission. They go through what's called the MCODE[15] exercise to find out what their core motivations are and how that applies to their work. They are encouraged to explore and find their personal learning style.

What many students don't initially understand is that virtues manifest themselves and are trained in even the smallest everyday acts. Training in virtue is akin to going to the gym. It takes the constant exercise of our will. Virtues are like a section of a workout routine. They start out as an aspirational activity, like wishing we could get out of bed when the alarm rings the first time. We won't succeed right away; it's one step forward and two back. Unless we apply our free will, we would give into our lower desires and give up. But as we stick with it, forgive ourselves for past failures, recommit, and never give up, the activity slowly becomes a habit. We eventually do it without even thinking about it. Once we achieve that, we can focus on the next such activity, the next virtue to pursue.

I ask each student to choose three virtues to which they aspire and practice them on a daily basis for an entire semester. Their reflection write-ups after this period of "training" always amaze and inspire me. Virtues are so easily acquired,[16] and become so powerful when we possess them. The students often point out that they found it remarkable how these habits come about through small but consistent effort, yet how amazed they are at how far they've come in just three months.

Altogether, the virtues we possess add up to our character. As people, we are creatures of habit. How we see, how we think, how we act—even how we feel. All of these areas are opportunities for intentionality, for applying our will, for training in virtue and development of firm character.

What this means for Principled Entrepreneurs is that we live in a hopeful reality. Every human being has the ability to grow in their perfection, in their excellence, and it's easier than most people think.

Principled Entrepreneurs believe in humanity. Principled Entrepreneurs always see the human person—and that starts with ourselves—as the solution, the opportunity, the hope. Never the problem. I believe it is absolutely imperative to teach this to aspiring entrepreneurs, to add this to their arsenal of virtues.

Discovering our personal vocation is actually the toughest thing for any one of us to figure out. It requires faith, insight, wisdom, experimentation, and determination. It is a very difficult process—much more difficult and complicated than memorizing facts and completing processes step-by-step. As a matter of fact, it is so difficult to do that I suspect a majority of people don't do it and never find out what their actual vocation is. They never put the core of their energy into envisioning and becoming the best version of themselves. They go through life without knowing who they really are. You can't be a Principled Entrepreneur without first discovering who you want to be.

2. Discover and develop your aptitudes, creativity, and strengths

When was the last time you lost track of time when you worked on something? The kind of experience we call "being in the zone."[17] It happens when we are so fully absorbed in an activity, so enthralled, that we have such a high level of energized focus and fulfillment that it transcends time. Was your experience related to what you do for work?

Most people I meet don't experience flow in work, and I think any college or university curriculum should find a way not only to teach students about flow, but create situations for them to experience and replicate it and help them discover ways to find a career that allows them to experience flow on a regular basis.

At the Ciocca Center, we go about helping our students find their "zone" by having them try out a lot of different things. Through the various courses we offer the student, we ask them to do a wide range of business-related activities that they have never done before. The "first business" experience of the "Vocation of Business" class taps into creative and online activities and the definition of customer-centered value propositions. The Small Business Lab requires that students get hands-on experience in a variety of businesses, both established ones as well as startups that we work with. They're taught to quickly study the competitive landscape, analyze the opportunities, manage the financial aspects of the business, develop strategies, and engage in team work to sell the new vision both inside and outside of the company. The theory courses combine research, presentations, and debates. The Principled Entrepreneurship course has a heavy focus on creativity, innovation, and communication. The guided studies and internship programs give the students more practical experience in a variety of industry sectors and growth stages. Altogether, the students' education is designed to expose them to all aspects of business and give them plenty of extended hands-on experience.

Throughout this process, students are guided to think about their experience and analyze it from a perspective of growth in personal excellence and service: What value can I add? That context helps them to notice when they experience flow and gives them the support and confidence to make career decisions consistent with their true vocation.

3. Discover and develop how to apply the previous two points to create value for others, and learn to put failure in the service of the pursuit of excellence.

At Catholic University's Busch School of Business, our freshmen business students' first assignment in the Vocation of Business course is to start their own company. Specifically, students are asked to start a special interest social media account. By exploring what they have to offer others in terms of their unique interest or expertise, they create a social media effort that explains and explores this topic and recommends various products along the way. Through this three-month-long exercise, students internalize the most rudimentary but essential question of business: "How may I help you?" They are at once customer centered and self-aware.

These blogs are then monetized in part through strategies such as affiliate marketing. As an affiliate of websites like Amazon, the student earns a bonus each time someone buys through one of their links. Thus, each student creates their own "small business" during the first semester of their freshman year. The hurdle I have to overcome with them is the same every year: fear of failure, especially in the context of a class. I have come to believe that students and aspiring entrepreneurs need to have permission to make mistakes.[18] I like to tell my students that no one is an overnight success. Rather, we fail into success, as long as we make each failure a learning opportunity.

This simple exercise of creating their "first business" serves better than any lecture I could give or any book I could recommend to have someone experience the true purpose and motivation of business. Business is not selfish but inherently *other directed*. A business has to offer a product or service that its target customers are willing to buy. Business starts with putting myself in the other person's shoes to see the world from his or her perspective. That is the substantive difference between selfishness and self-interest. You can learn empathy only by "doing it," that is, by practicing satisfying customer needs and creating value for clients.[19] That is a key focus of our class: teaching the students to work from the customer backward. We want them to learn that a value is added when we create real value for others from our excellence.

And learn they do! Every time I teach the course, I am astonished at the marvelous expertise, experience, and knowledge the students have to offer. Their blogs range from how to raise chickens to where to buy the best makeup, and from starting an art collection to finding the ideal community service. The variety of topics reflects the students' wonderful individuality and how that personal uniqueness can add value to society.

What's not surprising is that many students find that the experience of starting something new, "from scratch," is not their "thing," that the focus on thinking up, preparing, and launching a product or service is not satisfying and rewarding. Through their experience, they realize that they're not this kind of entrepreneur. That's actually a great outcome. It's part of the intention of this class: find your talents and pursue your excellence.

A part of what we are able to provide students is the "permission" to pursue work in line with their interests and talents rather than having to fit into the schema provided by external expectations. I find that this kind of freedom is welcomed by them and provides the students tremendous vigor in their next steps. Some have felt motivated to study accounting, finance, marketing, or whatever their talent was, and pursue that completely, because they now knew what they did and didn't like. They knew their talents, and that knowledge and freedom enabled them to pursue those talents.

Others do like the experience but fail at their first business for some reason. We guide these students at the end of the course with a lecture about failure and success. During that class session, we work together to explore how we can reflect on failure and learn valuable lessons from it. How we can proactively draw conclusions and form hypotheses that will guide our next effort. We teach the students how to learn from failure, and expose them to the truth that Principled Entrepreneurs don't just succeed. They fail into success.

The bottom line of teaching Principled Entrepreneurship is to help students apply their talents to create value and prosperity. If we are successful at that, we have fulfilled the value proposition that business education holds.

. . . And Don't Forget Creativity!

In conventional schools, it sometimes seems to me we are literally teaching the creativity out of our students. As far back as 1968, researchers told us that our education system was not just out of tune with the needs of the evolving economy, but that it actually was detrimental to key aspects of student performance. In a simple test of creativity, five-year-olds scored at 98 percent while the average adult scored 2 percent. The fact that schooling had something to do with it was indicated by the result that ten-year-olds came in at 30 percent and fifteen-year-olds at 12 percent. [20] The longer we attend school, the less creative we become. It's as if you would teach a great artist to the point when all they can do is paint by numbers. No more original masterpieces!

The trouble is not that there is no room for rigorous testing and evaluation, for math and science. The problem is that we have to first be imaginative if we want to invent something new—find new approaches, brainstorm better solutions. It is a matter of right order; I don't say we need one and not the other. This is a classic both/and situation. The rigor of examination and testing comes after the creative process. If the focus on testing overtakes the focus on exploration and wonder, it will destroy creativity.

Creative thinking is found at the intersection of technical knowledge, creativity, skills, motivation, and contemplation.[21] And it thrives in an environment of constant observation, action, feedback, and competition. It behooves companies and schools to create the conditions for these four human traits and the environment of keen observation and constructive feedback to be developed if we want innovation and creativity in our workforce.

The great book *The Innovator's DNA* by Dyer, Gregersen, and Christensen clearly lays out several key habits of great entrepreneurs:

They learn through observation, a skill almost never taught in school. Entrepreneurial thinkers must deeply know and understand their potential customers in order to see those unseen opportunities, those gaps and vacancies in the marketplace. They are always watching people and how they behave, what interests and engages them, what does not. They are students of human behavior. They understand that demography, geography, history, psychology, and sociology are every bit as important as marketing and finance.[22]

Gary Hoover adds:

Virtually all breakthroughs come from taking two things that everyone else sees every day and combining them in a new way. Combine taxicabs with the world of freelancers and you get Uber. Take that idea and combine it with Marriott and you get Airbnb. One of the most successful businesses my friends and I started was Bookstop, which combined the concepts behind Waldenbooks (then the nation's biggest bookseller) and Toys R Us (also a huge success at the time with its big selections and low prices).[23]

This is how students become innovators, creators. We need to provide an entrepreneurship education that reflects that.

In our Principled Entrepreneurship class, students are asked to innovate a product or service by the end of the semester. Through a series of experiences and projects, they are taught what Christensen, Gregersen, Hoover, and so many have pointed out: to create requires being still and observing, to contemplate before jumping into action. Students learn to receive and turn critical feedback into positive change. All this makes them better creators, which is the key goal of teaching Principled Entrepreneurship.

Teaching Principled Entrepreneurship Helps Students Find and Form Their Life Story

Role Models

To live up to our excellence in a world that tends toward mediocrity, we need role models and mentors to inspire and support us. No one does this alone.

That's why, in the course of our entrepreneurship education, we match each student with a specific mentor. We teach the student how to take advantage of having a mentor—how to build a proactive, inspiring, and productive relationship with them. I believe that having a role model is one of the key powers of personal change, the fuel of much of our willpower. If we see others whom we admire, whom we look up to, do something really well, it makes us see it as desirable and also attainable. We can dream only of what we know, or a derivative of what we know. To expand our dreams, we need to meet people who break our mold, people who went beyond what we imagined possible, and who do things differently than we expected. This makes us better dreamers, and therefore more successful entrepreneurs.

Students also study some stories of Principled Entrepreneurs. One of the key lessons they learn in reading about other entrepreneurs is that it is something of an art, and requires both prudence and instinct. Entrepreneurship as a field of study is relatively new—as late as the early 1980s, business schools did not offer any courses in it, even though by that time, Steve Jobs and Bill Gates were already well along in establishing their respective companies. Art started running Coke NY's wine company in 1975 and led the management buyout in 1981. And that's not even mentioning the great entrepreneurs such as Ford, Hewlett and Packard, Eastman, and so many others from whom there is much to learn. This timeline reveals an important truth: it was not teaching entrepreneurship that brought about great entrepreneurs but the other way around. We try to honor that process in what and how we teach.

The reason why it is so critical to have role models is because when we truly identify with them, their story becomes our story. Like an acquired taste, we absorb the role model's example into our own life as a running commentary, our story's narrative. And the story you tell yourself *is* the life you live.

Board of Advisors

We also ask the students to create a "board of advisors" for themselves—a group of role models who inspire them. Each student is asked to research and "appoint" a group of people to sit on the personal board of their life: specific persons that the student will go to for guidance. These personal boards of advisors work essentially the same way company boards do.

"If you could have your dream team of advisors for your life, who would you put on that board?" I like to ask the students. They put together a board that consists of three members that they can actually talk with and reach out to for feedback and three that are *virtual*, that is to say they can be historic figures and authors that the student can only reach by reading what they wrote or what they inspired. We encourage our students to really consult that board of advisors whenever they're making serious decisions. Of course, there is a limitation to the corporate board analogy, but the project drives home a key point: take your life as seriously—no, more seriously—than you take any company or business that you start or work for. What's taught at the average business school tends to imply to the students that their best efforts are to be given to the company and their own development comes second. That is of course not true. A great company needs great people. And the employees, even the founder, don't exist for the business, but the other way around. We have to teach Principled Entrepreneurs never to forget that.

Teachers and professors, for their part, must never forget that their contribution to forming Principled Entrepreneurs is only the beginning. Business schools can be tempted to become self-centered to the point that we forget that our contribution is a mere fraction of what a person learns throughout their career. What we consider to be the objective methods, rules, and fashions of management, finance, and marketing theory change so frequently that they might be out of use when one of our students gets into the industry. What doesn't change are the values and attitudes of Principled Entrepreneurship. They're hard to teach because they're the "soft" side of business. Hard to define, implement, and measure. But they are what make all the difference in a person's career and a company's long-term success. And we do well to remember that—just as in a company or a startup—they are more caught than taught. Therefore, professors and teachers who live Principled Entrepreneurship are more effective than those who only talk about it.

9

Start Today!

The story of the team at The Wine Group is classic because the wine business is a great metaphor for business and entrepreneurship in general. That is to some extent because we all feel a certain familiarity with the subjects of making and consuming wine, even if we have never done so. It's more relatable than a software or pharmaceutical company, for example. But in its essence, it is the same story that has repeated itself many times over the past one hundred years: a group of committed friends can bond together, work very hard, and create a successful company that adds value for society as well as for everyone else involved in it.

We make good wine because people enjoy it. Wine is made through human ingenuity. When we make wine, we practice a craft and become fulfilled through the work itself. The best winemakers don't measure themselves by only a particular year's vintage, but by the long-term health and quality of the overall company. The good vigneron is a creator, sower, and planner who has a vision and care for the vineyard beyond one generation. To the good vintner, the craft of winemaking is a path that is inseparable from the final product. Because of the commitment to the craft, making wine is a personal endeavor. The bad vigneron is an exploiter of the vineyard, focused only on one harvest and taking no pride in craftsmanship, spending no focus on the consumer, no care for the sales channel, no care for the reputation of the company. Such winemakers are depleting the soil, hurting the vines, and exploiting the process, the whole company, and those who work in it. If you were the owner of a vineyard, who would you want in charge?

The answer is logical and easy to understand. Yet we struggle when we look at doing business in this way. I hope this book has convinced you that the core reason for business and work—of the economy—is the flourishing and prospering of the human person.

Principled Entrepreneurship is the art of focusing business on the human person, creating value for consumers and profitability for the investor. It requires wisdom and skill precisely because of that: humanity in all its amazing plurality and diversity cannot be managed with a one-size-fits-all approach to achieve this unique balance. No, Principled Entrepreneurship requires a nuanced, situational approach to business that takes into account every individual person and situation. It is the art of finding just the right solution or innovation to create value for customers through the ingenuity of the individuals involved in one's company. That is, in my opinion, the approach to business as it's meant to, and ultimately, ought to be. The five pillars of entrepreneurial thinking laid out in this book define the approach of creating competitive businesses that are good *and* profitable.

Principled Entrepreneurship is a "both/and" approach. We are too often told that we have to choose between earning a profit and truly doing good. Such dichotomies, especially as they relate to work and business, are often not true. Instead, to recap:

- We can have values and create value.
- We can have a long-term mindset and react to momentary market situations.

- We can make a profit and have everyone else involved in our business be better off as well.
- We can focus on growing our business and help our employees grow and contribute to society.
- We can pursue our personal excellence while simultaneously helping others pursue theirs. In fact, the excellence resulting from collaboration exceeds the cumulative individual excellence.

Making this work depends on a mindset—a creator's mindset that sees the human person as the solution, not the problem, and sees a business's first and most important task as creating value for customers. A Principled Entrepreneur's mindset is not only focused solely on the results, but also on the path that gets us there. It is a mindset that doesn't try to evade responsibility for finding solutions and accountability for their outcome; it seeks it. Principled Entrepreneurs don't see failure or less-than-perfect success as a final result, but as a learning opportunity to pick up again and aim to do better.

This Principled Entrepreneurship mindset is required and good for not only those who start or run companies. It is mine and Art's hope that by reading this book, you are inspired to put these Principled Entrepreneurship pillars into action in whatever position or job you're in. Take an ownership mentality, find win-win solutions, and take responsibility for the outcome. It makes the difference between making a living and making a life. When you adopt a Principled Entrepreneurship mindset, you start to see problems as opportunities to create value for others, learn from failure to pursue excellence, and see the world as a place of complementarity and possibility. The mindset will not only make you a better entrepreneur; it will also make you a happier person.

As this book went to press, the COVID-19 pandemic was raging and threatening health and the economy, causing many contemporaries to go into "hiding." Many established companies, as we discussed in chapter 7 on Pillar 5, "Always Think Like an Entrepreneur," went out of business, and several industries came to a standstill. The space this creates for Principled Entrepreneurs is hard to overestimate. "I think it's one of those kinds of opportunities that only comes around once every lifetime," Art told me as we discussed the topic. "There are seismic changes taking place in the economy and society, and while this makes some run for the woods, Principled Entrepreneurs know that change spells opportunity." And early numbers seem to confirm what Art is predicting. We were already seeing entrepreneurs become very proactive a few months into the pandemic. There was a surge in new business applications in 2020, and it has not let up. John Haltiwanger, professor of economics at the University of Maryland who studies these trends, notes that "seven of the highest months ever in the data [of new business applications] are between July 2020 and now."[1]

The promising trend in these "pandemic startups" is that they started during the pandemic but their businesses address issues that were present long before the COVID-19 shutdowns and anticipated the restructuring that would follow it. Haltiwanger points out that a third of these businesses are "non-store retailers" and their ancillaries, a creative destruction that Amazon started long ago. But they represent a cross section of the economy: professional, scientific, technical services, and so on. What they have in common is that they embrace the opportunity to do business differently. They capitalize on an inflection point that might not come around again in the foreseeable future. Many of these innovative businesses are virtual and attract great talents that are not happy at their current jobs—a trend we discussed several times in this book. How? Well, probably every one of these businesses does it differently. That's the point of Principled Entrepreneurship.

Art Ciocca's story manifests the Principled Entrepreneurship mindset so completely and beautifully that I believe the story itself speaks more strongly than any of the other words in this book. Throughout my friendship with Art—in what I have learned about his story and his thought process during our hundreds of hours of interviews, and especially in the experience of laboring to write this book with his help—I have come to realize that Principled Entrepreneurship is not about *what* you are, but *who* you are. More important than all our success in business or our accumulation of wealth is the richness of our principles and how we live them out. Art is not a man driven by ambition to power; he is a man driven by principles and values. Art and his team at The Wine Group were driven by a worthy set of principles and values that set them apart. They did not see their work or their customers as a means to an end. They envisioned their work as a creative act that created value for others, and as a path to the joy and satisfaction that comes with knowing you have done something well. It is the focus on finding meaning in that creative path—that individual and team participation in God's creative power—that makes us more fully human, gives our lives transcendent meaning, and makes us deeply happy.

During the writing of this book, Art's health deteriorated considerably, but you wouldn't have noticed it from the intensity and enthusiasm of his collaboration. Art is a quintessential creator, an entrepreneur in all ways. He consistently looks for opportunities to explore, to build, to make things better. He does not settle for easy solutions, his only ambition being a desire for excellence. When he would read a new chapter or edit, he'd say with a twinkle in his eyes, "I'm really starting to like this. How about . . . ?" That bit of encouragement is his way to continually improve, without squashing the effort to date. It's how he encourages his collaborators to reach for the next level. I personally experienced how motivating this small piece of encouragement is, and I hope you can attest to the positive results of that challenge after having read this book.

Which brings us full circle. Guarino Di Giacinto was convinced he had achieved the American Dream when he came ashore from Italy and was able to make a good living for his family as a blacksmith. His grandson, Art Ciocca achieved the American Dream by taking over a fledgling wine company and, with his team, turning it into one of the most successful companies in the field. The critical element of Principled Entrepreneurship is not the owning or even starting of a company—but the mindset. Grandpa Guarino's declaration that, "Here in America, you can achieve anything!" is a spot-on slogan for the Principled Entrepreneurship mindset. Every generation has to deal with the particular challenges and complexities of their time in history, and therefore "living the American Dream" looks different for each generation, even every individual. What it has in common for everyone, though, is the goal of living up to our personal potential in finding ways to add value for others, and the right to enjoy the fruits of our work. This is how Principled Entrepreneurship and the American Dream are connected. The former describes the path and the latter the goal.

As we reached the end of our collaboration for this book, I traveled to San Francisco to review the final manuscript with Art. I asked him what he thought was the greatest insight he had gained from the process. Without hesitation, he answered, "I realized that I started to think and act like an entrepreneur long before I actually became one. Principled Entrepreneurship is not about your position in a company—it's about how you think about the company and your work. Don't wait to become a Principled Entrepreneur. Start today!"

Acknowledgments

A big thank-you to all who participated in the evolution of *The Art of Principled Entrepreneurship*, and the readers who offered valuable feedback on the evolving manuscript: Andrew Abela, Elizabeth Alton, Michael Berolzheimer, Dan Braga, Luke Burgis, Tim Busch, Lee Carosi-Dunn, Grady Connolly, Dino Cortopassi, William Cueto, Suzanne Dans, Dina Dwyer, Kevin Gentry, Andy Gilett, Dan Hesse, Brian Hooks, Bill Jesse, Steve McClatchy, John McNerney, Max Messmer, Michael Matheson Miller, Ruth Mills, Candace Mottice, Madeleine Naleski, Chris Norris, John Poreba, Amy Proulx, Iqbal Quadir, Gretchen Reiter, Mark Renella, Jay Richards, Frederic Sautet, Gonzalo Schwarz, Elizabeth Shaw, Robert Smelick, Phil Sotok, Brandon Vaidyanathan, Magatte Wade, Brian Walsh, and Paul Zak.

With gratitude to all the students of my Vocation of Business and Principled Entrepreneurship classes over the past ten years—you are awesome and a deep inspiration. I learn so much more from you than I am ever able to teach you.

Thank you to Art Ciocca and Charles Koch who inspired Principled Entrepreneurship and supported my writing with much grace, patience, and unwavering support. I am deeply indebted to Carlyse Ciocca who contributed to the stories and interviews and supported this endeavor all the way through. Without her and Art's input and inspiration, I could never have crafted the stories in this book. They inspired them, but any errors or omissions are entirely my responsibility. Art Ciocca passed away two days before this book went to print. Working with and learning from him during the two years of writing *The Art of Principled Entrepreneurship* was one of the great privileges of my life. May he rest in peace.

Special thanks to Katie Dickman for her brilliant editing, and to Brigid Pearson for this book's beautiful cover. Thanks also to my wonderful literary agent, Leah Spiro, and Matt Holt at BenBella who believed in and helped make this project a reality.

In deep gratitude also to my collaborators at the Art & Carlyse Ciocca Center for Principled Entrepreneurship and my colleagues at the Busch School of The Catholic University of America. I wrote this book in the first person singular, using "I" when in fact pretty much all the learning and development of the approach of Principled Entrepreneurship was accomplished by a plurality. A special thanks to my collaborator Rebecca Teti, whose honest feedback and valuable suggestions made a world of a difference. Any errors and oversights in this book, however, are mine.

To my friends Scot Landry, Bob Allard, Jan-Hein Cremers, and Karl Wirth. The idea of asking Art to "serve" as the story for this book came from you—and with it, the title. It's hard to put into words how much I appreciate you individually, as well as your support and advice.

And finally, to my fantastic wife, Michelle: Thank you for your love, guidance, wisdom, patience, and humor. It's simple: without you, this book would not exist.

Recommended Reading

Great Books That Talk About or Apply Pillar 1: The Economy Exists for People, Not People for the Economy

* *The 22 Immutable Laws of Marketing: Violate Them at Your Own Risk!* by Al Ries & Jack Trout.[1] If there is only one marketing book you ever read, then let it be this one. Ries and Trout distill marketing into twenty-two "laws" that stay true to focusing your business on the customer and creating a company brand based on virtue and excellence. It is simply a classic.
* *Wealth of Persons: Economics with a Human Face* by John McNerney.[2] This book takes you on a journey to discover that entrepreneurs don't engage in only creating and selling products and services but they create human interaction. McNerney explores the idea that an economy of communion could be built around this idea. A great contribution to and execution of Pillar 1 of Principled Entrepreneurship: the economy exists for people, not people for business.
* *Dream No Little Dreams* by Clayton Mathile.[3] An inspiring story of a Principled Entrepreneur who bought a very small dog

food company from a pet nutritionist and turned it into the famous Iams company. Clayton's story very much reminds me of Art Ciocca's, which goes to show that many of the great Principled Entrepreneurs have a similar path.

- *Living in Color* by Mike Shaughnessy and John Haugh.[4] Another team of Principled Entrepreneurs with a very inspiring story about starting a company by simply addressing a customer need. Mike and John started off actually trying to convince their employer to give its customers a product they were asking for. When the company refused, they built a company that would live by customer satisfaction and changed the history of the plastics industry worldwide. I use this book regularly in my class and am proud to call Mike a personal friend.

- *Value Proposition Design: How to Create Products and Services Customers Want* by Alexander Osterwalder.[5] This book focuses on the key aspect of any business transaction: the value proposition. It is the part of our business that is often considered an afterthought instead of making it the starting point. Osterwalder is one of the best authors in this field and his book is intuitive and actionable.

- *The Pope & the CEO: John Paul II's Leadership Lessons to a Young Swiss Guard* by Andreas Widmer.[6] This one is my own story of Principled Entrepreneurship and how my path has been influenced by an unlikely business mentor: Pope John Paul II.

Great Books That Talk About or Apply Pillar 2: To Work Is to Create; To Create Is to Be Human

- *Shop Class as Soulcraft: An Inquiry into the Value of Work* by Matthew Crawford.[7] The *University of Chicago Magazine* wrote that the book "welds philosophy and motorcycle repair, celebrating manual work and the competency, self-reliance, and knowledge it fosters." The book helps us see work—and not just intellectual work but especially physical work—as what it is: a path to human excellence. The book gives much food for thought because Crawford knows business, academia, and the repair shop, and can help us see each one more clearly. In the end, he admonishes us to seek more meaning and less money if we truly want to find freedom and happiness.

- *Now, Discover Your Strengths: The Revolutionary Gallup Program That Shows You How to Develop Your Unique Talents and Strengths.*[8] A key aspect of creating teams is to know each person's strengths. I found that the Strengthsfinder framework is a great tool to help Principled Entrepreneurs assemble effective teams.

- *The Human Advantage* by Jay Richards.[9] While many fear for the future of work, Richards explains in this book how we will never run out of work. Value creation is intrinsically connected to humanity. No machine will ever take away our creativity and our virtue—the two core components of value creation.

- *Getting Work Right: Labor and Leisure in a Fragmented World* by Michael Naughton.[10] A superb Catholic discussion about work, business, and vocation. Very interesting and enlightening for anyone. I love Michael's thinking and writing. He has a gift for explaining profound and complex issues in a very understandable way. A true teacher!

- *The War of Art* by Steven Pressfield.[11] This book is straightforward and provokes highly actionable insights. Since the first objective of work is to create, all work is deeply related to art. This is why a book aimed originally at artists can be such a blessing for entrepreneurs, especially Principled Entrepreneurs.

- *And Why Not? An interview of François Michelin* by Ivan Levai and Yves Messarovitch.[12] I read this book when it first came out and was deeply inspired by the insights and stories François Michelin conveyed. Stories from Principled Entrepreneurs that feature products we all have a great familiarity with make the insights that much easier to generate and see.
- *Good Profit: How Creating Value for Others Built One of the World's Most Successful Companies* by Charles Koch.[13] I found this book one of the most effective management books I've ever read. It's clear, focused, and easily understandable. And the underlying value in everything is the unmeasurable, incomparable resource that the human person is. This is a management theory that keeps people—be it customers or employees—at the center of concern.

Great Books That Talk About or Apply Pillar 3: Culture Eats Strategy for Breakfast

- *Trust Factor: The Science of Creating High-Performance Companies* by Paul J. Zak.[14] Paul explains how the human brain reacts to experience and environment (like company culture) by producing chemicals that affect trust. In great detail, he explains what kinds of employee interactions increase trust and how to bring that same effect to your customers. A fascinating read with lots of practical advice for managing high-performance and excellent teams.
- *Getting Ahead: A Family's Journey from Italian Serfdom to American Success* by Dino Cortopassi.[15] Art Ciocca introduced me to Dino, a member of The Wine Group's original board of directors, so we could talk about the company. What happened next is best experienced by reading his book. Dino

is a force of nature, a Principled Entrepreneur par excellence and a brilliant thinker. I was hoping to include some of his stories in this book . . . but there are so many and they are so deep that they deserve their own book. And, well, this is it!

- *The Five Dysfunctions of a Team: A Leadership Fable* by Pat Lencioni.[16] Pat has a great gift of noticing patterns, and for this book he applied it to analyze what makes teams dysfunctional and by extension what makes successful teams work well. This is simply essential reading for anyone in a leadership role.
- *The $100 Startup: Reinvent the Way You Make a Living, Do What You Love, and Create a New Future* by Chris Guillebeau.[17] A veritable workbook to find and create win-win businesses. Guillebeau masterfully guides you through the process of creating your business by consciously changing your own (work) culture.

Great Books That Talk About or Apply Pillar 4: Principled Entrepreneurs Always Seek to Create Win-Win Solutions

- *Wanting: The Power of Mimetic Desire in Everyday Life* by Luke Burgis.[18] My colleague Luke describes in his latest book how our desire is actually learned. Instead of allowing these desires to be acquired haphazardly, Burgis describes how we can learn to desire the good of the other and thus seek win-win solutions in everything we do.
- *Love Your Enemies: How Decent People Can Save America from Our Culture of Contempt* by Arthur Brooks.[19] In this book, Arthur shows that competition is not the same as war, that there is not just one winner when we measure ourselves in excellence. Though often focusing on the political side of things, Brooks

describes the exact same concept that we need in business: when we compete well, we both become better. And as always, his humor makes this book a "one sitting" read.

- *Grit: The Power of Passion and Perseverance* by Angela Duckworth.[20] What this book describes is the "currency" of competition and success. It is the fuel of excellence. Grit is difficult to acquire—more difficult than money—but it's always a part of the win-win equation. Sometimes we do lose on the objective level. We lose the sale, our product is a dud, the company fails. On the subjective level, that is still not a loss if we don't want it to be. Duckworth's book is a win-win manual.
- *Abundance: The Future Is Better Than You Think* by Peter Diamantis.[21] I love Diamantis's always positive outlook. And he makes sure in this book that the reader knows he's not just thinking about the glass being "half full," but he actually shows in great detail how the world is getting better, not worse. I don't agree with some of his conclusions, but his showing that we have a bright future ahead is contagious.

Great Books That Talk About or Apply Pillar 5: Always Think Like an Entrepreneur

- *The Complacent Class: The Self-Defeating Quest for the American Dream* by Tyler Cowen.[22] Cowen has a keen pattern recognition to pinpoint the issues and opportunities in our society. The bottom line is that if we don't have to compete, we become complacent. And complacency is the end of prosperity. This book will make you want to act.
- *Buy Then Build: How Acquisition Entrepreneurs Outsmart the Startup Game* by Walker Deibel.[23] What I love about this book is that it dispels the notion that all entrepreneurship is

about starting up a company. Franchising, acquisition, and being a hired manager of a team or a company all qualify as entrepreneurship and offer excellent opportunities for Principled Entrepreneurs. Deibel gives a play-by-play account of how to become an acquisition entrepreneur. Well done!

- *Burn the Business Plan. What Great Entrepreneurs Really Do* by Carl Schramm.[24] Carl is a master of Principled Entrepreneurship and his book is a guide to lead with right thought and right action. He cuts through the red tape of analysis paralysis and proposes a framework for fast-paced action and results.
- *Competition and Entrepreneurship* by Israel Kirzner, edited by Frederic Sautet.[25] This book is the textbook of our Theory of Entrepreneurship course. Kirzner describes this approach when he says, "I speak of the essentially entrepreneurial element in human action in terms of alertness to information, rather than its possession." This is "knowing where to look for knowledge." He sees alertness as the "ability to perceive new opportunities which others have not yet noticed."
- *Invention: A Life* by James Dyson.[26] This is a joy of a book to read. Dyson kind of reminds me of Art Ciocca in his stick-to-it-ness. He famously created 5,127 prototypes of the cyclonic vacuum cleaner before he figured it out. Art didn't have to do that many iterations of the WineTap, but it took the same kind of commitment to thinking like an entrepreneur and using failure only as a stepping-stone to success.

Endnotes

Principled Entrepreneurship: A Definition

1 Charles G. Koch, *Good Profit: How Creating Value for Others Built One of the World's Most Successful Companies* (Currency, 2015), 125.
2 Charles G. Koch, "Continually Transforming Koch Industries Through Virtuous Cycles of Mutual Benefit" (Koch Industries, 2020), https://www.kochind.com /KOCHInd-Dev/media/KochIND/Landing%20Pages/vcmb/Continually -Transforming-Koch-VCMBs-WEB.pdf.
3 "What is Market-Based Management?" Charles Koch Institute, https:// charleskochinstitute.org/market-based-management/.

1. A Model for Principled Entrepreneurship: Meet Art Ciocca

1 The only valid purpose for any enterprise, for profit or nonprofit, is to provide products and services to customers, to the public, or whatever market the organization serves.
   Gary Hoover, "The Ten Myths About Profits," Medium (Archbridge Notes, December 3, 2020), https://medium.com/archbridge-notes/the-ten-myths-about -profits-6b864c6963c5.
2 I'm sure you are wondering why I'm not defining "truly good" and "truly serve." It's because their meaning is something each one of us has to create ourselves. We are moral agents and, as such, it is up to us to develop or choose and then consistently keep to a moral code. Abdicating or delegating that responsibility is one of the things that I believe is one of the great temptations of our time.
3 "Aquinas once wrote that humans are made in the image of God but that since God is infinite He may be mirrored only through a virtually infinite number of humans." Michael Novak, *The Spirit of Democratic Capitalism* (New York: Simon and Schuster, 1983), 53.
4 Some might call this "stakeholders," but "constituents" is what Art calls this group: "At my company, The Wine Group, we create value for our consumers, our employees, our middlemen, people in our supply chain, and lastly owners. And we do it in that order because if you put owners first or anywhere else in this

lineup of things, you're prone to make very bad decisions for the company as a whole. So it's very important to understand this correctly."

5   Bruce D. Henderson, "The Origin of Strategy," *Harvard Business Review*—Ideas and Advice for Leaders (Harvard Business Publishing, 1989), https://hbr.org/1989 /11/the-origin-of-strategy.

6   Posted by Jim Burns, "To Understand Content Strategy, Start with What Is Strategy?," avitage.com (Avitage, November 9, 2017), https://avitage.com/ understand-what-is-strategy-to-formulate-content-strategy/.

7   Gallup conducts a study on worker engagement every year. While there are ups and downs in terms of the fully engaged and actively disengaged, the general trend is that two-thirds of US employees are disengaged: 2017 study results: https://www.gallup.com/workplace/231668/dismal-employee-engagement-sign-global-mismanagement.aspx; 2018 study results: https://news .gallup.com/poll/241649/employee-engagement-rise.aspx.

8   I speak here of a truly free market where no one manipulates or cheats . . . which is not what's happening in any of our systems today. Because that is an ideal, we have to put checks and balances in place to ensure that those who get cheated or manipulated—who are made to personally lose as a result of business, industry, or the economy—receive justice.

9   Economists don't agree on a specific definition of what entrepreneurship is or what entrepreneurs do. I believe that this is because entrepreneurship is an art—and as such does not lend itself to being measured by what economists use: predictable, scientific, replicable experiments. Entrepreneurs create by turning their ideas into reality—by creating. Jay W. Richards, "What Economists Know, Believe, and Debate," *Journal of Markets & Morality* 23, no. 1 (2020): 117–30.

10 Technically speaking, what The Wine Group did with its WineTap is an example of an internal creative destruction where a company develops a superior alternative and kills its own costly alternative . . . along with that of its competitors. The more common creative destruction happens when a new entrant in a field innovates and makes the existing competitors' product or service obsolete.

2. Principled Entrepreneurship and the Story of the American Dream

1   Other directedness, initiative, efficiency, faith, deferred gratification, collaboration . . . just to mention a few. We will discuss virtues and values more in the following chapters. My point here is simply to state that a competitive market that is open to everyone creates values that benefit society at large.

2   Intellectual property, or copyright, is described in Art 1, Sec 8, Clause 8 of the Constitution. The recognition of intellectual property indicates the focus of commerce and business in the new country, since the key part of "value add" for a customer is often derived from intellectual property by the inventor. Enshrining

that in the Constitution meant that the incentive for inventors and entrepreneurs to create value for customers was always going to be guaranteed.

3   Sarah Koch, "Immigrants, We Create Jobs," The Case Foundation, August 18, 2017, https://casefoundation.org/blog/immigrants-we-create-jobs/?gclid= CjwKCAiA25v_BRBNEiwAZb4-ZXicpFMU9pGHJoWUVzjZ7k COKesDGkk3aipdldU_gj4WzZbq4Lm3pxoCxB8QAvD_BwE.

4   "Facts & Data on Small Business and Entrepreneurship," SBE Council.org (Small Business & Entrepreneurship Council, 2018), https://sbecouncil.org/about-us/facts -and-data/.

5   "Small Businesses Have a Big Impact on the US Economy," AN.edu (American National University, November 28, 2015), https://an.edu/blog/small-businesses -have-a-big-impact-on-the-us-economy/.

6   Karen G. Mills and Brayden McCarthy, "The State of Small Business Lending: Credit Access During the Recovery and How Technology May Change the Game," Harvard Business School Working Paper, No. 15-004, July 2014, https:// www.hbs.edu/faculty/Pages/item.aspx?num=47695.

7   "Small Businesses Are the Backbone of the Economy," Better Accounting (Better Accounting, August 11, 2020), https://betteraccounting.com/small-businesses-are -the-backbone-of-the-economy/.

8   Economies of Scale refer to the cost advantage experienced by a firm when it increases its level of output. The advantage arises due to the inverse relationship between per-unit fixed cost and the quantity produced.

9   William D. Norhaus, "Schumpeterian Profits in the American Economy: Theory and Measurement," Working Paper No. 10433, April 2004, JEL No. O30, O31, O4, https://www.nber.org/system/files/working_papers/w10433/w10433.pdf.

10   Matt Nesvisky, "Who Gains from Innovation?," NBER (National Bureau of Economic Research, October 2004), https://www.nber.org/digest/oct04/who-gains -innovation.

11   Andy Kessler, "To Serve the Public, Seek Profits," Wall Street Journal, October 11, 2020, https://www.wsj.com/articles/to-serve-the-public-seek-profits-11602435735 ?st=g78rqo91hnu2pgm&reflink=desktopwebshare_permalink.

12   Small Enterprise Assistance Fund 2011 Development Impact Report: "For the 20 cases conducted to date, every dollar invested into frontier market SMEs has generated, on average, an additional $13 dollars in the local economy." These are investments SEAF makes in emerging, or "frontier," markets where the freedom of markets is not functioning effectively. I would assume that the return is even higher in developed markets where the system is closer to a free market. Stephanie Komsa, Katherine H. Wheeler, and Tanja Atanasova, "2011 Development Impact Report," seaf.com (Small Enterprise Assistance Funds, 2012), https:// www.seaf.com/wp-content/uploads/2011/03/2011-Development-Impact-Report -Impact-Beyond-Investment.pdf.

13 An interesting read on this topic is Gary Hamel and Michele Zanini, "A Few Unicorns Are No Substitute for a Competitive, Innovative Economy," *Harvard Business Review*, February 8, 2017, https://hbr.org/2017/02/a-few-unicorns-are-no -substitute-for-a-competitive-innovative-economy.

14 Meredith Wood, "Raising Capital for Startups: 8 Statistics That Will Surprise You," Fundera (Fundera Ledger, February 3, 2020), https://www.fundera.com /resources/startup-funding-statistics. Only 0.05 percent of startups raise venture capital.

15 Rana Foroohar, "American Capitalism's Great Crisis and How to Fix It," *Time*, May 12, 2016, https://time.com/4327419/american-capitalisms-great-crisis/.

16 An interesting read on this topic is Gary Hamel and Michele Zanini, "A Few Unicorns Are No Substitute for a Competitive, Innovative Economy," *Harvard Business Review*, February 8, 2017, https://hbr.org/2017/02/a-few-unicorns-are-no -substitute-for-a-competitive-innovative-economy.

17 Rana Foroohar, "American Capitalism's Great Crisis and How to Fix It," *Time*, May 12, 2016, https://time.com/4327419/american-capitalisms-great-crisis/.

18 Some researchers point out that this number should be more like 78 percent and that increased affluence makes this comparison not as indicative and valuable, but the same researchers still agree that there has been a decline. Luis Parrales and Gil Guerra, "Episode # 6 Transcript: Gonzalo Schwarz on Markets, Inequality, and Economic Opportunity," *Panorama Podcast*, October 18, 2020, https://www .panoramapodcast.org/transcripts/gonzalo-schwarz.

19 I use the term *successful* here in the way that Steven Covey used it: that outward success is not actually "success" if it is not the manifestation of inner mastery.

20 Traditionally, asking the "Who?" question focuses on the team in a physical way, seeking efficiency as Deming did. "What" focuses on figuring out what customers want and how to sell it to them, as Ries and Trout did so well. "How" is what Porter taught us through business strategy—and now the final question, which we found out is also the first one, is "Why?"

21 Associated Press, "Americans Are the Unhappiest They've Been in 50 Years, Poll Finds," NBCNews.com (NBCUniversal News Group, June 16, 2020), https://www .nbcnews.com/politics/politics-news/americans-are-unhappiest-they-ve-been-50 -years-poll-finds-n1231153.

22 Christopher Ingraham, "Analysis | Not Only Are Americans Becoming Less Happy - We're Experiencing More Pain Too," *Washington Post* (*The Washington Post*, December 6, 2017), https://www.washingtonpost.com/news/wonk/wp/2017 /12/06/not-only-are-americans-becoming-less-happy-were-experiencing-more -pain-too/.

23 Jim Harter, "4 Factors Driving Record-High Employee Engagement in U.S.," Gallup.com (Gallup, February 4, 2020), https://www.gallup.com/ workplace/284180/factors-driving-record-high-employee-engagement.aspx.

24   This is sometimes called "intrapreneurship," as when Meredith Sommers explains: "Intrapreneurship is acting like an entrepreneur within an established company. It's creating a new business or venture within an organization. Sometimes that business becomes a new section, or department, or even a subsidiary spin off." Meredith Somers, "Intrapreneurship, Explained," MIT Sloan School of Management, June 21, 2018, https://mitsloan.mit.edu/ideas -made-to-matter/intrapreneurship-explained.

25   Michael Michelini, "Buy Then Build: Book Review," *Mike's Blog*, July 29, 2020, https://mikesblog.com/buythenbuild/.

26   Recent research suggests that the success rate of franchises is about 8 percent higher than the independent business success rate. Others claim that it's much higher—but some of that data is challenging, and it's very difficult to compare some franchise businesses with others. In any case, a common quote one hears is that, "It's almost an inverse: In the first five years, one in ten independent businesses succeed and one in ten franchises fail. It's a remarkable difference." I think that even with this great variety of opinions, they all clearly suggest that the failure rate of franchises is significantly below individual startups. Carol Blitzer, "Franchise Owners Weather Turbulent Economic Times," Palo Alto Online, December 11, 2011, https://www.paloaltoonline.com/news/2011/12/11/small -franchise-owners-weather-turbulent-economic-times.

27   Katherine Gustaf, "What Percentage of Businesses Fail and How to Improve Your Chances of Success," ed. Allison Williams, LendingTree.com, August 7, 2020, https://www.lendingtree.com/business/small/failure-rate/.

28   Kerby Meyers, "Entrepreneurs of a Certain Age, in This Uncertain Time," Ewing Marion Kauffman Foundation, August 5, 2020, https://www.kauffman.org /currents/entrepreneurs-of-a-certain-age-uncertain-time/. Robert Fairlie, Sameeksha Desai, and A.J. Herrmann, "2018 National Report on Early-Stage Entrepreneurship," Ewing Marion Kauffman Foundation, September 2019, https://indicators.kauffman.org/wp-content/uploads/sites/2/2019 /09/National_Report_Sept_2019.pdf. This report explores every possible socioeconomic and other entrepreneur segment.

3. Pillar 1: The Economy Exists for People, Not People for the Economy

1   "US Wine Consumption," Wine Institute, 2021, https://wineinstitute.org/our -industry/statistics/us-wine-consumption/.

2   In this book, I focus only on the period of time during which Art ran The Wine Group, from 1975 to 2000. But even today, Franzia—The Wine Group's flagship brand—is still number one, eighteen years later. Emma Cranston, "These Are the 30 Most Popular Wine Brands in America," VinePair, December 18, 2020, https://vinepair.com/booze-news/30-most-popular-wine-brands-in-america/.

3   Jay W. Richards, "What Economists Know, Believe, and Debate," *Journal of Markets & Morality* 23, no. 1 (2020): 117–30. See my colleague Jay Richards's essay to see this and other concepts that are agreed on by economists.

4   "What Business Are You In?: Classic Advice from Theodore Levitt," *Harvard Business Review*, October 2006, https://hbr.org/2006/10/what-business-are-you-in -classic-advice-from-theodore-levitt.

5   I would say that wine was even stronger in Carlyse's background than in Art's: Around the turn of the twentieth century, an Italian immigrant named Giuseppe Franzia sent word to Italy that he needed a wife. It was a few years after the Gold Rush and Giuseppe, who had made a stake working as a truck farmer, wanted to settle down as a grape farmer in the Central Valley.

The girl who was supposed to set sail for San Francisco backed out at the last minute and sent her friend Teresa Carrera in her place. Teresa stood all of four feet, ten inches tall. She arrived in California and stepped off the ship ready to marry Giuseppe on the spot. Giuseppe bribed the local priest to marry them that day instead of waiting the required three weeks to post the bonds of matrimony. So they married and set off via horse and buggy for Giuseppe's farm.

Giuseppe had an eye for agriculturally rich land. Over the years, he managed to save enough money to buy eighty acres of incredibly fertile property in Ripon, California. Teresa and Giuseppe grew grapes there. She cooked three meals a day, bartered with neighbors, usually chickens in exchange for what she needed, and raised her five sons and two daughters.

Over the years, the family home in Ripon had become a favorite gathering place for many of the area's prominent Italian businessmen and early wine industry pioneers. They were drawn there by Teresa's fabulous pasta dishes, fresh homegrown vegetables, and delicious homemade wines. (During Prohibition, limited amounts of wine could be made for home consumption.) Among them were Ernest and Julio Gallo, Charlie Rossi, Abe Buchman, and the head of the Bank of Italy (which soon became Bank of America), A.P. Giannini.

In 1933, while Giuseppe was away in Italy, Prohibition was coming to an end. Teresa saw an opportunity to lessen the dependence of their family on the risks of shipping and selling their perishable grape crop each fall in eastern and midwestern markets. She knew that if she could build a winery to make and bottle wine, the family would have all year to sell it and bring in more money. With her vision for a family wine business clearly in mind, Teresa knew just where to go. She traveled by horse and buggy directly to A.P. Giannini's office in San Francisco and asked for a $10,000 loan, pledging the family farm as collateral.

With $10,000 in hand, she gave $5,000 to her five sons to start the Franzia Winery, and the other $5,000 she loaned to her son-in-law, Ernest Gallo. His venture became Ernest & Julio Gallo Winery.

When Giuseppe returned from Italy and learned what his wife had done, he threw a fit. He believed it was too risky and much too perilous for his family to sustain. He was a simple farmer whose goals started and ended with growing grapes. Little did he know that Teresa's entrepreneurial venture would have such a monumental impact.

This petite mail order bride from Italy started two of America's largest wine companies, all while her husband was away in Italy. What began as Franzia Vineyards at the turn of the century turned into a thriving company that has grown and evolved as a result of the hard work of everyone invested in its future.

Teresa Franzia is an inspiring and exemplary Principled Entrepreneur. She took a calculated risk based on her knowledge and experience, and because of that was able to live the American Dream (and capital to support it was somehow available).

Eighty years later, the famed but struggling Franzia Wineries were sold to Coca-Cola New York. They hired a Gallo-trained maverick to run it, Art Ciocca, who quickly built it up to a formidable competitor. When Coke NY wanted to sell the company again so they could focus on their core business, Art took the chance and led a management buyout. Soon after, the new head of the old Franiza wineries fell in love with a young woman he met at the tennis club. It was love at first sight. Then they found each other's story. The winery came full circle: Art Ciocca married Theresa's granddaughter Carlyse Franzia.

6   This is actually not what was being decided. The decision at the time was not whether or not the glass investment was a good or a bad investment. The decision was whether or not to chase after The Wine Group with clearly superior plastic packaging and a cost advantage in that product category. The investment in glass was a sunk cost as it pertained to this decision, and not pursuing the new packaging solution was a classic opportunity cost. This decision about new packaging wasn't going to bring the investment back or make it worth it. It ought to have had no bearing on this decision. But it did, because our desire to protect past effort, even if it has no bearing on the future, is so strong that we allow that emotion to cloud our decision as to what's most effective for the future. Many products and businesses have lost because they decided to protect a "sunk cost."

After investing so heavily in glass production, then having a plastic alternative to the glass bottles threaten that investment, the choices were classic: turn the page or double down. Gallo doubled down.

The example shows how the concepts of sunk cost and opportunity cost are often connected and interrelated and it pays off to examine all our decisions against those two biases.

7   Economies of scale refer to the cost advantage experienced by a firm when it increases its level of output. The advantage arises due to the inverse relationship between per-unit fixed cost and the quantity produced.

8   All the quotes by Carl Elsener are "lifted" and translated by me from the various video interviews I link here. https://de.myvadesigns.com/10-stainless-steel-spring-loaded-things-you-should-know-about-swiss-army-knife-706595.
Michael Heim, "Victorinox Kämpft Gegen Das Schweizerkreuz Aus China: HZ," handelszeitung.ch (Handelszeitung, February 7, 2017), https://www

.handelszeitung.ch/unternehmen/victorinox-kaempft-gegen-das-schweizerkreuz
-aus-china-1336469.
Studio71, ed., "Das Beste Unternehmen Der Welt! Warum Ist Es Bei
Mitarbeitern so Beliebt?," YouTube.com (Galileo, March 6, 2020), https://www
.youtube.com/watch?v=5PDOMsQ0ZUA.
Pino Aschwanden, "Reporter—Das Glück Der Arbeit—Warum Man Bei
Victorinox So Gerne Angestellt Ist," Play SRF (Play SRF, 2007), https://www.srf
.ch/play/tv/reporter/video/das-glueck-der-arbeit-warum-man-bei-victorinox
-so-gerne-angestellt-ist?urn=urn%3Asrf%3Avideo%3A6c4a63ce-7a76-4ecb-8c60
-696b68e1aad6.
Die grössten Schwyzer Arbeitgeber 2020, Amt für Wirtschaft, Kanton Schwyz, 7.
August 2020, abgerufen am 8. Oktober 2020 https://de.wikipedia.org/wiki
/Victorinox#:~:text=Das%20Unternehmen%20wurde%201884%20von,von%20
480%20Millionen%20Schweizer%20Franken.

9   Creative Commons, "First Swiss Army Knife from 1891, Produced by Wester &
Co Solingen/Germany," Wikipedia, June 6, 2009, https://en.wikipedia.org/wiki
/Victorinox#/media/File:Wester_&_Co_2.JPG.

10   Acier inoxydable.

11   *"Die Grössten Schwyzer Arbeitgeber 2021"* (Amt für Wirtschaft, Kanton
Schwyz,December 31, 2020), https://www.sz.ch/public/upload/assets/21205/Die
%20gr%C3%B6ssten%20Schwyzer%20Arbeitgeber.pdf.

12   We should never forget that work is *for* us, just as the economy is for us, not we
for it. If we treat the desk as an "altar"—meaning that we worship it rather than
it serving us—we reverse the natural order of things and that has tremendously
negative consequences. Derek Thompson explores that in his article "The
Religion of Workism Is Making Americans Miserable," Atlantic, February 24,
2019, https://www.theatlantic.com/ideas/archive/2019/02/religion-workism
-making-americans-miserable/583441/.

4. Pillar 2: To Work Is to Create; To Create Is to Be Human

1   A competitive advantage is an advantage or differentiator a company has that
cannot be easily imitated by competitors. Michael E. Porter and Victor E. Millar,
"How Information Gives You Competitive Advantage," *Harvard Business Review*,
July 1985, https://hbr.org/1985/07/how-information-gives-you-competitive
-advantage. Given the individuality of the human person—and the unlimited
possibility of human excellence—the greatest competitive advantage a company
can have is its team.

2   He actually did not say that it is the "only" social responsibility . . . and his essay
and position is much more nuanced and resonated than is usually portrayed.
Milton Friedman, "A Friedman Doctrine—the Social Responsibility of Business
Is to Increase Its Profits," *New York Times*, September 13, 1970, https://www

.nytimes.com/1970/09/13/archives/a-friedman-doctrine-the-social-responsibility-of
-business-is-to.html.

3   Profits are not the only important thing in a company, but they are essential. For
example, the large profits Procter & Gamble made by introducing a successful
detergent (Tide) in the 1940s enabled that company to fund the first toothpaste
with fluoride, Crest, and improvements in household paper products (Puffs,
Charmin, and Bounty). Boeing developed the finest and earliest successful
jet airliners with the profits it had made on military bombers. Unprofitable
companies cannot place "big bets" or risk millions on new ideas. Profitable
companies can.
Archbridge Institute, "Ten Myths About Profits, Part 2," Medium (Archbridge
Notes, December 9, 2020), https://medium.com/archbridge-notes/ten-myths
-about-profits-part-2-27869f0f7b3a.

4   A study by Bhandari and Javakhadze on Corporate Social Responsibility and
capital allocation efficiency states focusing on CSR strategies hurts companies
financially because they aren't devoting all their attention to investment
opportunities. In the long run, this lack of focus on increasing profits leads to
losses for company shareholders.
Avishek Bhandari and David Javakhadze, "Corporate Social Responsibility and
Capital Allocation Efficiency," *Journal of Corporate Finance* (Elsevier, April 2017),
https://www.sciencedirect.com/science/article/abs/pii/S0929119917300652.

5   Jason Fernando, "Corporate Social Responsibility (CSR)," Investopedia (Dotdash
Publishing, February 2, 2021), https://www.investopedia.com/terms/c/corp-social
-responsibility.asp.

6   Also a classical definition of friendship.

7   There's a beautiful story that Carlos Rey tells in the epilogue of the book
Purpose-Driven Organizations about how business school taught him Friedman's
mantra about shareholder value with the result that he decided against a career
in business. And that he found his way back to a meaningful career in business
after the sage advice of Mother Teresa in Calcutta to "put love into everything
you do!"
Carlos Rey, Miquel Bastons, and Phil Sotok, in *Purpose-Driven Organizations:
Management Ideas for a Better World* (Cham: Springer International Publishing,
2019), 131.

8   Whole Foods is now part of Amazon, so that "love" preamble of their
management principles has since been lost—but here's an article that discusses it:
Sigal Barsade and Olivia A. O'Neill, "Employees Who Feel Love Perform Better,"
Harvard Business Review, January 13, 2014, https://hbr.org/2014/01/employees-who
-feel-love-perform-better.

9   Sigal Barsade and Olivia A. O'Neill, "Employees Who Feel Love Perform
Better," *Harvard Business Review*, January 13, 2014, https://hbr.org/2014/01/
employees-who-feel-love-perform-better.

10 I want to be very clear about an aspect of this that could be misunderstood: When I say "work" I don't just mean paid work—which is actually the point that follows in the next paragraph. I mean "to create something of value—a service or a product." That value often does not get compensated with money, nor is it always taking part in the setting of the economy. Taking care of an elderly parent, of kids, managing a family, tending the garden, mentoring people . . . that all counts as "work" even though it is not "paid" in the traditional sense.

11 Tomas Chamorro-Premuzic, "Does Money Really Affect Motivation? A Review of the Research," *Harvard Business Review*, April 10, 2013, https://hbr.org/2013/04 /does-money-really-affect-motiv.

12 A. M. Cargon, *Administrative Science Quarterly* 63, no. 2 (2020): 323–69.

13 Fr. Giussani once commented that "Work . . . must assist and be in function of the truth and happiness to which everyone personally aspires," and that "in this sense . . . the aim of work is not the work itself, rather it is man." Luigi Giussani, "Human Work: Speeches by Msgr. Luigi Giussani" [Supplement to] Page 20 *CL Magazine*, Davis, CA: Communion & Liberation, [s.d.]. [Translation].

14 I'd like to make sure it is understood that I assume in all I write about work that I do so in the context of a balanced life. Workaholism or workism is not healthy. I do not suggest that all we ought to do is work. But I write about work, and so I limit my comments on it. By no means do I downplay the other aspects of a well-balanced life, like family, friends, leisure, civic engagement, and so on. I hope that's obvious.

15 Jay W. Richards, *The Human Advantage: The Future of American Work in an Age of Smart Machines* (New York: Crown Publishing Group, 2018), 66.

16 It's also fair to mention that Tim's book never "meant" to say that you should really work for only fifteen hours a week, but he promoted the idea that you could become much more productive and put into four hours what you now put into forty hours, and then have time for more creative things. I actually quite like the *The 4 Hour Workweek* book and other works by Tim Ferris. Here's the article on how much he actually works: "The Myth of the 4-Hour Work Week" by Scott at Live Your Legend, February 15, 2012, ttps://liveyourlegend.net/the-myth-of-the -4-hour-work-week/.

17 In 1957, an article in the *New York Times* predicted that because of work becoming automated, we would no longer find our identity as being an architect, or plumber, or accountant, but instead identify ourselves by our hobbies, such as stamp collector, golfer, or scrapbooker. I do agree that we ought not to make our work or job the end-all-be-all of our identity, but with the right attitude toward it (i.e., that it is not just a means to an end but a way to pursue our excellence), the work we do represents a vitally important aspect of our persona. "Union Leader Urges Spur to Automation; Union Chief Here Asks Automation,"

https://timesmachine.nytimes.com/timesmachine/1957/09/22/issue.html?action
=click&contentCollection=Archives&module=ArticleEndCTA&region
=ArchiveBody&pgtype=article.

18 Jenny Marlar, "The Emotional Cost of Underemployment," Gallup.com, March 9, 2010, https://news.gallup.com/poll/126518/emotional-cost-underemployment.aspx.

19 Even before the pandemic, roughly one in ten workers wanted to log more hours. Annie Lowrey, "The Underemployment Crisis," *Atlantic*, August 6, 2020, https://www.theatlantic.com/ideas/archive/2020/08/underemployment-crisis/614989/.

20 A February 2019 Harris poll found that roughly half of younger Americans would "prefer living in a socialist country," https://www.city-journal.org/end-insider -privileges-of-socialism-to-fix-american-capitalism.

21 Brittany Hunter, "Millennials Love Free Markets, but Don't Understand Them," Mises.org (Mises Institute, August 24, 2016), https://mises.org/wire/millennials -love-free-markets-dont-understand-them.

22 John Bitzan and Clay Routledge, "College Kids Don't Understand Socialism or Capitalism. Our Research Proves It: Opinion," *Newsweek*, July 12, 2021, https:// www.newsweek.com/college-kids-dont-understand-socialism-capitalism-our -research-proves-it-opinion-1608876?fbclid=IwAR0IHrKPJv8P4djFoRchwTy14 QJv-BsZjArFZuWTW0c9qWe-Qm5TScPL0d0.

23 Gonzalo Schwarz, "American Dream 2020 Snapshot," Archbridge Institute, October 19, 2020, https://www.archbridgeinstitute.org/wp-content/uploads/2020 /10/AI-AmericanDream2020Snapshot.pdf. This is a very informative essay that shows that the "dream" is made up of much more than "money." The key aspect of it, however, is the access to social mobility (full disclosure: I'm on the board of Archbridge).

24 Max Weber wrote that "the pursuit of wealth, divested of its metaphysical significance, today tends to be associated with purely elemental passions, which at times virtually turn into a sporting contest." Max Weber, *Protestant Ethic and the Spirit of Capitalism* (New York: Penguin Publishing, 2002), 313.

25 John McNerny, "The Business of Business: Recapturing the Personalist Perspective," *Business, Faith, and the Economy of Communion*, edited by Andrew Gustafson and Celeste Harvey, *Journal of Religion & Society Supplement* 22 (2020): 107–21, http://moses.creighton.edu/JRS/toc/SS22.html.

26 James Currier, "Your Life Is Driven by Network Effects," nfx.com, July 12, 2021, https://www.nfx.com/post/your-life-network-effects/.
In his article James Currier makes several suggestions to optimize our network in beneficial ways. Think of it not as controlling "spontaneous order" but choosing in which "flock of birds" you fly so that you are taking part in their spontaneous order process.

27 Always within the rules of the "game"—legal, fair, and benevolent. I would argue that spontaneous order can actually not happen unless there are rules that we all abide by. These rules are like the guiding rails for the order to spontaneously take

shape around. It's like a sports event—totally spontaneous, unpredictable as to who will win. But order will emerge as long as everyone plays their best . . . and by the rules.

28 "Most people do not listen with the intent to understand; they listen with the intent to reply." Stephen Covey—an article that teaches to listen with empathy. Stephen R. Covey, James C. Collins, and Sean Covey, *The 7 Habits of Highly Effective People: Powerful Lessons in Personal Change* (New York: Simon & Schuster, 2020), "Habit 5: Seek First to Understand, Then to Be Understood," https://www .franklincovey.com/habit-5/.

29 Stephanie Vozza, "How to Spot a Potentially Toxic Hire During a Job Interview," *Fast Company*, October 22, 2020, https://www.fastcompany.com/90566299/how-to -spot-a-toxic-person-during-a-job-interview.

30 Art explains this at length in interviews with Nadia Nasr for the Santa Clara University special collection on the history of the wine industry in California. Archives & Special Collections, Santa Clara University Library Arthur A. Ciocca, "Profile of Art Ciocca—Values and Lessons from a Career in Business" Collection. Series II: Lectures and articles, 1981–2015, interview and write-up by Nadia Nasr, February 18, 2018.

31 On the most fundamental level, profit is a signal that something has been done to a resource that increases value. Inversely, loss is a signal that something has been done to a resource that decreases value.

32 Mark J. Perry, "The General Public Thinks the Average Company Makes a 36% Profit Margin, Which Is About 5X Too High, Part II," American Enterprise Institute, January 15, 2018, https://www.aei.org/carpe-diem/the-public-thinks-the -average-company-makes-a-36-profit-margin-which-is-about-5x-too-high-part-ii/.

33 The values and incentives that are operating in firms that focus only on short-term monetary incentives are ill considered. They actually contradict, or don't follow, some of the most basic economic insights. Namely that humans act purposely to achieve extrinsic as well as intrinsic incentives and that our actions cannot be reduced to mere self-interest. Jay W. Richards, "What Economists Know, Believe, and Debate," *Journal of Markets & Morality* 23, no. 1 (2020): 117–30. Points 1, 2, on the list of "Thirty Truths" and disagreement bullet #7 on what economists debate.

34 "A Quote by Dalai Lama XIV," Goodreads.com, accessed August 6, 2021, https://www.goodreads.com/quotes/885801-the-dalai-lama-when-asked-what -surprised-him-most-about.

35 It is important to follow Wilhelm Roepke's advice here, when he called for "a new humanism that we should adopt a philosophy which, while rendering unto the market the things that belong to the market, also renders unto the spirit what belongs to it." My colleague John McNerney explains this quote in more detail in his book *Wealth of Persons.*

36   Currier, "Your Life Is Driven by Network Effects." In the article, he makes
several suggestions to optimize our network in beneficial ways. Think of it not as
controlling "spontaneous order" but to choose in which "flock of birds" you fly so
that you are taking part in their spontaneous order process.

5. Pillar 3: Culture Eats Strategy for Breakfast

1   Shannon Mullen O'Keefe, "How Do You Say 'Success' in Strengths?," Gallup,
September 20, 2020, https://www.gallup.com/cliftonstrengths/en/320447/say
-success-strengths.aspx.
Business leaders who invest in building cultures where people are positioned to
do what they do best every day see up to 19 percent increased sales, 29 percent
increased profits, 59 percent fewer safety incidents, and 72 percent lower turnover
(in high-turnover organizations).

2   Brandon Vaidyanathan, "What Creates Unhealthy Organizational Cultures?," The
Catholic University of America, accessed August 7, 2021, https://www.catholic
.edu/research/big-questions/what-creates-unhealthy-organizational-cultures.html.
He describes "slogans," or scripts as he calls them, as factors of bad culture and
points out that they can be changed through personal modeling.

3   Culture cannot only be created but also evolved or changed. I focus on the
creation of culture because it's the original process. But many entrepreneurs don't
get to initiate the corporate culture, but to change an existing one. Art Ciocca
did that when he and his management team bought the company from Coke NY.
The Hartford, a two-hundred-year-old insurer, transformed its corporate culture
successfully after the '08 financial crisis. They used the same steps and approaches
that I describe in how to create culture. "Changing a Culture Is the Hardest Task
of Leadership," by Liam McGee, chairman at The Hartford, February 18, 2014,
https://www.scribd.com/document/314782162/Changing-a-Culture-is-the
-Hardest-Task-of-Leadership.

4   Carlos Rey, Miquel Bastons, and Phil Sotok, *Purpose-Driven Organizations:
Management Ideas for a Better World* (Cham: Springer International Publishing,
2019), 11.
"Like the way classical management logic prompted the division of labor, and
the neoclassical logic prompted the development of organizational alignment,
perhaps a new organizational theory will form, one that guides the development
of the new logic of purpose within the organizations."

5   A mental model as I use it is how we attach meaning to our actions based on our
underlying intentions and reasoning. All our actions are in a sense first deliberated
by us and we consider why we take an action, what the action means, and what
we expect the result of the action to be. This is to say that as much of our actions
depend on our internal beliefs, values and expectations (mental models) as it does

on the "abstract" nature of any given action. Mental models help us act in the world, make sense of the world, and experience our place in it.

6   Several readers of the manuscript pointed out that it's hard to imagine what "else" there would be than a focus on the long-term success of the business. The answer is: a lot. Starting with company politics. It's a kind of mental model with regard to what your ultimate focus is—excellence or the advancement of your career or wealth. Managers can make short-term decisions that benefit a few at the detriment, even the demise, of the long-term success of the company. And corporate politics create a set of objectives that neither advance excellence, the company, nor anyone involved in it—except a chosen few.

7   Carlos Rey, Miquel Bastons, and Phil Sotok, in *Purpose-Driven Organizations: Management Ideas for a Better World* (Cham: Springer International Publishing, 2019), 98.

8   Jim Harter, "4 Factors Driving Record-High Employee Engagement in U.S.," Gallup, February 4, 2020, https://www.gallup.com/workplace/284180/factors -driving-record-high-employee-engagement.aspx.

9   Chris Argyris, "Teaching Smart People How to Learn," *Harvard Business Review*, 1991, https://hbr.org/1991/05/teaching-smart-people-how-to-learn. The author writes that leaders "need to reflect crucially on their own behavior, identify the ways they often inadvertently contribute to the organization's problems, and then change how they act."

10   Jonathan Malesic, "How to Save Americans from the Hell of Work," *New Republic*, March 4, 2019, https://newrepublic.com/article/153205/save-americans-hell-work.

11   Ron Carucci, "How Corporate Values Get Hijacked and Misused," *Harvard Business Review*, May 29, 2017, https://hbr.org/2017/05/how-corporate-values-get -hijacked-and-misused.

12   "The 2021 Edelman Trust Barometer" (Daniel J. Edelman Holdings, Inc., 2021), p. 19. The 2021 Edelman Trust Barometer found that CEOs as a group are currently the "most trusted" societal leaders, with 48 percent trust, a 3 percent loss since last year. (Note that the groupings being compared are government leaders, religious leaders, journalists, and CEOs, and the general leaning toward all is "mistrust.") Apparently, people's "own" CEOs are doing much better in terms of how much we trust them (here the leaning is toward "trust"). It's been at 63 percent for two years. So, clearly, many CEOs have done the hard work of identifying and living out their personal and corporate values at work.

13   There are two fundamental approaches to growth: little by little or giant leaps. This is true in life as it is in business: there are things that best progress by finding small improvements every day and seeking incremental improvements, 10 percent at a time—small but consistent progress that adds up tremendously over time. This is the Kaizen approach. When Art Ciocca first took over the company leadership when The Wine Group was still owned by Coke New York, he focused on process and productivity improvement. Step-by-step, he went through the

entire business and worked with his team to find ways to make all crooked lines straight. It took years to get there, but eventually he had a company that was super efficient and effective. Getting there took thousands of small steps in the same direction. It was the Kaizen approach. Then there are the inflection points of change: finding a new way of doing something, acquiring a new product line or company, a fundamental change in an approach can dramatically change the outcome. This is the "moonshot" mindset. Such changes don't simply make progress, they move the goalposts; they change the game. This is called the 10x approach, as in having a ten times better result at once. Not a 10 percent, but a 1,000 perecent improvement. Now. Knowing the difference and deciding which of the two to use in any given situation is a critical part of the art of Principled Entrepreneurship.

14   McKinsey & Co defined as recently as 2019 the six elements for CEO excellence as 1. Personal Working Norms—"Do what only you can do"; 2. Corporate Strategy—"Focus on beating the odds"; 3. Organizational Alignment—"Manage performance and health"; 4. Team and Processes—"Put dynamics ahead of mechanics"; 5. Board engagement—"Help directors help the business"; and 6. External Stakeholders—"Center on the long-term *why*."
Carolyn Dewar, Martin Hirt, and Scott Keller, "The Mindsets and Practices of Excellent Ceos," McKinsey & Company, October 25, 2019, https://www.mckinsey.com/business-functions/strategy-and-corporate-finance/our-insights/the-mindsets-and-practices-of-excellent-ceos#.

15   Paul J. Zak, "Paul J. Zak," pauljzak.com, accessed August 9, 2021, https://pauljzak.com/about/.

16   Paul J. Zak, *The Moral Molecule: The Source of Love and Prosperity* (New York: Dutton, 2013).

17   Behnam Tabrizi, "The Key to Change Is Middle Management," *Harvard Business Review*, October 27, 2014, https://hbr.org/2014/10/the-key-to-change-is-middle-management. Behnam Tabrizi found in his research that real change in a company cannot happen if the leaders don't get mid-level management buy-in and involvement. That's two or more levels below the CEO. What Tabrizi found is that this "buy-in" is dependent on several aspects and conditions—but first and foremost it is for the team to have values that overlap with theirs.

18   Michael Hyatt, "How a Shift in Your Vocabulary Can Instantly Change Your Attitude," Michael Hyatt & Co., February 26, 2016, https://michaelhyatt.com/how-a-shift-in-your-vocabulary-can-instantly-change-your-attitude/.

19   This is sometimes called behavioral-based interviewing.

6. Pillar 4: Principled Entrepreneurs Always Seek to Create Win-Win Solutions

1   Richards, *The Human Advantage*, 2018. This is astonishing especially since it is not challenged by economists that the free market creates comparative advantages that mutual exchange is beneficial to both parties—that is, creates win-win solutions.

2   Paul Putz, "Summer Book List: Henry George (and George Norris) and the Crisis of Inequality," Summer Book List: Henry George (and George Norris) and the Crisis of Inequality, July 2, 2015, http://peputz.blogspot.com/2015/07/henry-george-and-george-norris-and.html. George was actually not anti-capitalism, but he questioned private land ownership, intellectual property, and privately owned companies that dominate a market—monopolies.

3   The *Guardian* published an informative article about Elizabeth Magie. Mary Pilon, "The Secret History of Monopoly: The Capitalist Board Game's Leftwing Origins," *Guardian*, April 11, 2015, https://www.theguardian.com/lifeandstyle/2015/apr/11/secret-history-monopoly-capitalist-game-leftwing-origins.

4   Mary Pilon, "Monopoly Was Designed to Teach the 99% About Income Inequality," Smithsonian Institution, January 2015, https://www.smithsonianmag.com/arts-culture/monopoly-was-designed-teach-99-about-income-inequality-180953630/.

5   A flourishing and competitive private sector is an essential component of the common good of our society. It sets the stage for everyone to benefit from equal opportunity yet allows for varied outcomes. The challenge is to avoid cronyism, cheating, and overregulation that stifles competition and access for all. This is not easy and is something every generation has to ensure and act out anew, but it is the only path to equality and prosperity—to the American Dream.

6   Max Roser, Esteban Ortiz-Ospina, and Hannah Ritchie, "Life Expectancy," Our World in Data, October 2019, https://ourworldindata.org/life-expectancy. Just a very high-level measure such as worldwide life expectancy has increased by roughly thirty years over the past one hundred years.

7   Eric Barker, "Sun Tzu's Art of War: How Ancient Strategy Can Lead to Modern Success," *Time*, June 2, 2014, https://time.com/2801517/sun-tzus-art-of-war-how-ancient-strategy-can-lead-to-modern-success/.

8   William James, "The Will to Believe," The Project Gutenberg E-text of The Will to Believe, by William James, May 8, 2009, https://www.gutenberg.org/files/26659/26659-h/26659-h.htm. Originally written by William James in 1896. One important point James makes is about how certain beliefs must precede the achievement of certain goals. For example, if you've never run a marathon before, you first have to believe that finishing the marathon is really possible in order to go on and actually do it—obviously if you don't believe it's possible, you won't even try in the first place!

9   Adam Smith, "An Inquiry into the Nature and Causes of the Wealth of Nations," *The Glasgow Edition of the Works and Correspondence of Adam Smith, Vol. 2: An Inquiry into the Nature and Causes of the Wealth of Nations, Vol. 1*, January 1776, https://doi .org/10.1093/oseo/instance.00043218.

10   Stephanie Burns, "6 Ways Being Selfish Can Make You Successful," *Forbes*, March 12, 2020, https://www.forbes.com/sites/stephanieburns/2020/03/12/6-ways -being-selfish-can-make-you-successful/?sh=77ef5beb5538.

11   "Selfish Definition & Meaning," Dictionary.com, accessed August 9, 2021, https://www.dictionary.com/browse/selfishness.

12   So is the IRS and the DMV selfish, you ask? Well, the part that is selfish is the lack of alternatives, the lack of competition. The opposite of selfishness is self-interest—or as I like to call it "other directedness." This requires continually seeking to create win-win transactions. Our human nature tending toward complacency and selfishness, we stop trying to be other-directed the minute we are not under competitive pressure to do so. There are of course "selfish" organizations in any line of work, but because government offices have no competition, I call them "selfish" by design. I don't mean to say that individuals who work there are specifically selfish. But I am suggesting that we should have as little as possible done by this kind of system.

13   Michael E. Porter, "Clusters and the New Economics of Competition," *Harvard Business Review*, 1998, https://hbr.org/1998/11/clusters-and-the-new-economics-of- competition. The examples and charts I use to describe cluster theory all come from this 1998 *Harvard Business Review* article, which also outlines this theory in great detail.

14   Porter, "Clusters and the New Economics of Competition." *Harvard Business Review*, 1998, https://hbr.org/1998/11/clusters-and-the-new-economics-of -competition.

15   Richard W. Rahn, "Louis XIV, John Rockefeller Had Harder Life Than Common Man Today," *Washington Times*, December 22, 2014, https://www .washingtontimes.com/news/2014/dec/22/richard-rahn-loux-xiv-john-rockefeller -had-harder-/.

16   Glaeser, "How to Fix American Capitalism," https://www.city-journal.org/ end-insider-privileges-of-socialism-to-fix-american-capitalism. One of the most egregious ways that the government favors insiders is occupational licensing, typically presented as a way to protect consumers. Economists Morris Kleiner and Alan Krueger documented that, in the late 1950s, less than 5 percent of American workers needed some form of occupational license. Licensing in fields with a real public-health impact—pharmacy, say—may protect some consumers, but it's hard to see why the person selling you flowers or your eyeglass frames needs certification. Cutting hair is one of the more regulated occupations across the United States.

7. Pillar 5: Always Think Like an Entrepreneur

1   Paul Wagorn, "Burn the Ships," IdeaConnection, April 11, 2014, https://www
.ideaconnection.com/blog/open+innovation/open-innovation-commitment.html.
Cortés may have actually sunk rather than burned his ship, but that doesn't make
a difference to the point I'd like to make.

2   Tsun-yan Hsieh and Stephen Bear, "Managing CEO Transitions," *McKinsey
Quarterly*, 1994, Number 2, https://www.mckinsey.com/~/media/McKinsey
/Business%20Functions/Strategy%20and%20Corporate%20Finance/Our%20
Insights/Managing%20CEO%20transitions/Managing-CEO-transitions.ashx.

3   Victor W. Hwang, "Entrepreneurship Should Be a Priority for Covid-19
Recovery," Inc.com (Mansueto Ventures, September 23, 2020), https://www.inc
.com/victor-w-hwang/entrepreneurship-should-be-prioritized-amid-covid-19.html.

4   "The 2021 Edelman Trust Barometer" (Daniel J. Edelman Holdings, Inc., 2021),
14. According to the 2021 Edelman Trust Barometer, job loss has risen to the
number one concern and fear of people around the world. Higher than climate
change, cyberattacks, loss of freedom—and by a long shot higher than their fear
of actually contracting the COVID-19 virus.

5   Ricketts, "Opinion | in Praise of Today's Entrepreneurs," https://www.wsj.com/
articles/in-praise-of-todays-entrepreneurs-11572909118. In addition it is also
heartening to see that entrepreneurs in developing markets are slowly given more
access to our networks of productivity and exchange: Robbie Whelan, "Why
Goldman Sachs Is Interested in a Small Bike Shop in Mexico," *Wall Street Journal*,
March 14, 2019, https://www.wsj.com/articles/why-goldman-sachs-is-interested-i
n-a-small-bike-shop-in-mexico-11552555801.https://www.wsj.com/
articles/why-goldman-sachs-is-interested-in-a-small-bike-shop-in-mexico-
11552555801#:~:text=This%20year%2C%20Goldman%20Sachs%20
plans,equipment%20leases%20for%20Mexican%20customers.&text=That%20
can%20make%20it%20difficult,they%20tend%20to%20stay%20small.

6   William (Marty) Martin, "Entrepreneurship at Any Age," IntechOpen,
December 22, 2020, https://www.intechopen.com/chapters/73987.

7   Schwarz, "American Dream 2020 Snapshot," 7.

8. Inspiring and Motivating the Next Generation

1   I found that the most effective thing I can do when it comes to Principled
Entrepreneurship is actually not to teach in the traditional sense of the word but
rather to inspire and motivate. That is what's needed and it's what I found bears
the right, and most fruit.

2   Not to confuse "happiness" with pleasure. The latter can seem like happiness, but
pleasure lacks meaning and is fleeting. Real happiness, in contrast, is meaningful,
stable, and persistent. Pleasure is optional in human life, happiness is a must. For

most people, happiness is substantially a derivative from a stable mind engaged in meaningful work and a meaningful life.

3   "Entrepreneurship," entrepreneurship noun—Definition, pictures, pronunciation and usage notes | Oxford Advanced Learner's Dictionary at OxfordLearnersDictionaries.com, accessed August 9, 2021, https://www .oxfordlearnersdictionaries.com/us/definition/english/entrepreneurship.

4   We try to incorporate Newman's thought into our approach to education. Check out this essay by my colleague John McNerney on this topic: John McNerny, "Heart Speaks to Heart: Saint John Henry Newman's Educational Ideals," The Institute for Human Ecology, December 2020, https://ihe.catholic.edu/heart -speaks-to-heart-st-john-henry-newmans-educational-ideals/.

5   Schramm himself is a great Principled Entrepreneur. Having started several companies, he also did amazing work when he led the Kaufman Foundation, building it up to the leading expert group on entrepreneurship in the US and now teaching business at Syracuse University. An entrepreneur's entrepreneur! I am humbled to call him a friend.

6   I believe that if our "why" for what we do includes our personal and other people's excellence and flourishing, the temptation to cheat or find shortcuts decreases tremendously. Therefore, we do not treat "business ethos" separately in our entrepreneurship courses, but integrate it into the core of everything we teach.

7   Audrey Watters, "The Invented History of 'The Factory Model of Education,'" Hack Education, April 25, 2015, http://hackeducation.com/2015/04/25/factory -model#:˜:text=Here%20he%20is%20in%202012,system%20in%20the%20late%20 1700s.

8   Max Roser, "Democracy," Our World in Data (Global Change Data Lab, June 2019), https://ourworldindata.org/democracy.

9   I can't help but think that a business teacher who's never had the responsibility for a profit and loss statement will not "know" anything about how the economy is a positive-sum game. Someone who's principle experience with budgeting is in academia—as in most other "nonprofit companies"—lives from donations and fixed revenues, and their budgets are a zero-sum game for at least a year at a time.

10   It is a part of our freshmen *The Vocation of Business* class and we call this the "First Business" project

11   At the Ciocca Center, we ask students to start some form of an online affiliate marketing effort. This is easy to do, doesn't cost anything, and focuses on the core of the "How may I help you?" part of business. Once a student gets a feeling for that other-directedness, they will be well on their way to mastering the rest of business.

12   Frederic Sautet, "Is a Market Process Theory Purely Based on the Logic of Choice Really Impossible?" Posted: March 29, 2017, https://oll.libertyfund.org /page/liberty-matters-peter-boettke-israel-kirzner-competition-entrepreneurship #lm-kirzner_response3.

13 Mike Colagrossi, "Can Creativity Be Taught?," Big Think, October 12, 2018, https://bigthink.com/personal-growth/can-creativity-be-taught?rebelltitem=4 #rebelltitem4.

14 Karl Moore, "The Great Power of Connecting Passion with Purpose," *Forbes*, January 19, 2015, https://www.forbes.com/sites/karlmoore/2015/01/19/the-great -power-of-connecting-passion-with-purpose/?sh=53e871298784.

15 My friend and Ciocca Center colleague Luke Burgis, in his book *Unrepeatable*, writes about our personal "core motivation," that is our aim in working and collaborating with others. What he means is that we are all driven by various desires in terms of our work. Making a living is one of them, but by no means the most deterministic. There is often a misunderstanding of motivation; you've heard people say that someone is not "motivated," which is often a codeword for being lazy. That kind of understanding of motivation is negative—it suggests that you don't enjoy the task and therefore prefer not to do it, or avoid it. To fix the situation where my team member is not "motivated," I use either authority or incentives. I "bend their will," so to speak. This is because that understanding is a flat understanding of motivation, a purely utilitarian view of work—of the extrinsic motivators—that focuses exclusively on the outcome, on getting the job done. A positive understanding of the concept looks at the deeper meaning—the intrinsic and even transcendent aspects of the work itself. It looks at the *why* of the job. It's not the task that matters, it's what *accomplishing* the task means to you that truly matters. Understanding your core motivational drives can help you identify the kinds of environments in which you are more likely to thrive, and those which might unnecessarily drain you.

Luke and his coauthor describe a process of storytelling in which a person shares stories about times in their life when they felt especially satisfied with a project, proud of an achievement, and found themselves in the zone. They ask a series of questions about each of these stories that help identify what specifically it was about those achievements that was so satisfying—what it was about them, in particular, that was so fulfilling to that person. There are twenty-seven core motivational "themes" that they describe in total. The assessment they use, called the MCODE (short for The Motivation Code), finds patterns in the core motivation that runs throughout a person's stories of achievement, and helps a person identify their top five core motivational themes. This is [tremendously] valuable self-discovery, because how we are fundamentally motivated provides some insight into how we find meaning in our work.

When coupled with the entire team, the core motivations approach becomes a very powerful tool in finding common cause. I have used this approach to structure complementary teams that have a common bond based on their core motivations. You can learn more about MCODE at motivationcode.com. You can see all twenty-seven motivational drivers in the sample report they offer: https://www.story.solutions/motivation-code-mcode.

16   I say "easily" because it takes very little effort each time we practice them. The
     "hard" part is to resist the temptation to stop practicing them.

17   Being "in the zone" is a term that connotes "losing track of time" because one
     is so engrossed in what one is doing. Some call that state "flow." Mystics call it
     "ecstasy," and artists call it "rapture."

18   IBM's great Louis R. Mobley who built the IBM Executive School described
     six principles, or rather insights, that are necessary for creativity. One of them is
     having the permission to be wrong. Read this great article by my friend August
     Turak in *Forbes* on creativity at work in which he explains all six principles and
     more: August Turak, "Can Creativity Be Taught?," *Forbes*, May 22, 2011, https://
     www.forbes.com/sites/augustturak/2011/05/22/can-creativity-be-taught/?sh
     =5e2b28b61abb.

19   An article that suggests various ways to practice and learn empathy: "Empathy:
     The Single Best Way to Get Unstuck," Medium, November 5, 2015, https://
     medium.com/@unstuck/empathy-the-single-best-way-to-get-unstuck-fba35f5ffb85.

20   George Land, "The Failure of Success," YouTube, February 16, 2011, https://
     www.youtube.com/watch?v=ZfKMq-rYtnc.

21   T.M. Amabile, "How to Kill Creativity," *Harvard Business Review*, 1998, https://
     hbr.org/1998/09/how-to-kill-creativity.

22   Jeffrey M. Dyer, Hal B. Gregersen, Clayton M. Christensen, Jeff Dyer,
     The Innovator's DNA: Mastering the Five Skills of Disruptive Innovators. United
     Kingdom: Harvard Business Press, 2011.

23   Gary Hoover, "Entrepreneurial Thinking Made Easy," Hoovers World (Gary
     Hoover, January 4, 2021), https://hooversworld.com/entrepreneurial-thinking
     -made-easy/.

9. Start Today!

1   John Haltiwanger, "John Haltiwanger: American Entrepreneurs during the
    Pandemic," AEI (American Enterprise Institute, July 29, 2021), https://www.aei
    .org/podcast/john-haltiwanger-american-entrepreneurs-during-the-pandemic/.

Recommended Reading

1   Al Ries and Jack Trout, *The 22 Immutable Laws of Marketing: Violate Them at Your
    Own Risk!* (London: Profile Books, 1994).

2   John McNerney and David Walsh, *Wealth of Persons: Economics with a Human Face*
    (Eugene, OR: Cascade Books, 2016).

3   Clayton L. Mathile, Echo Montgomery Garrett, and Mary Beth Crain, *Dream No
    Little Dreams* (Bethel Township, OH: DNLD Pub., 2007).

4   John Haugh and Mike Shaughnessy, *Living in Color* (John Haugh and Michael
    Shaughnessy, 2014). https://issuu.com/thebraungroup/docs/livingincolor.

5   G. Bernarda, Y. Pigneur, T. Papadakos, A. Osterwalder, and A. Smith. *Value Proposition Design: How to Create Products and Services Customers Want* (Germany: Wiley, 2015).

6   Andreas Widmer, *The Pope & the CEO: John Paul II's Leadership Lessons to a Young Swiss Guard* (Steubenville, OH: Emmaus Road Publishing, 2011).

7   Matthew B. Crawford, *Shop Class as Soulcraft: An Inquiry Into the Value of Work* (Penguin, 2010).

8   Marcus Buckingham and D. O. Clifton, *Now, Discover Your Strengths* (Pocket Books, 2005).

9   Jay W. Richards, *The Human Advantage: The Future of American Work in an Age of Smart Machines* (New York: Crown Publishing Group, 2018).

10 Michael J. Naughton, *Getting Work Right: Labor and Leisure in a Fragmented World* (Steubenville, OH: Emmaus Road Publishing, 2019).

11 Steven Pressfield, *The War of Art* (London: Orion, 2003).

12 François Michelin, Ivan Levaï, and Yves Messarovitch, *And Why Not?: Morality and Business* (Lanham: Lexington Books, 2003).

13 Koch, *Good Profit.*

14 Paul J. Zak, *Trust Factor: The Science of Creating High-Performance Companies* (New York: American Management Association, 2017).

15 Dino Cortopassi, *Getting Ahead: A Family's Journey from Italian Serfdom to American Success* (Stockton, CA: Black Hole Press, 2014).

16 Patrick Lencioni and Charles Stransky, *The Five Dysfunctions of a Team: A Leadership Fable* (New York: Random House, 2002).

17 Chris Guillebeau, *The $100 Startup: Reinvent the Way You Make a Living, Do What You Love, and Create a New Future* (New York: Crown Business, 2016).

18 Luke Burgis, *Wanting: The Power of Mimetic Desire in Everyday Life* (New York: St. Martin's Press, 2021).

19 Arthur C. Brooks, *Love Your Enemies: How Decent People Can Save America from Our Culture of Contempt* (HarperLuxe, an imprint of HarperCollins Publishers, 2019).

20 Angela Duckworth, *Grit: The Power of Passion and Perseverance* (United States: Paula Wiseman Books, 2020).

21 Peter H. Diamandis and Steven Kotler, *Abundance: The Future Is Better Than You Think* (New York: Simon & Schuster, 2015).

22 Tyler Cowen, *The Complacent Class: The Self-Defeating Quest for the American Dream* (New York: Picador, 2018).

23 Walker Deibel, *Buy Then Build: How Acquisition Entrepreneurs Outsmart the Startup Game* (United States: Lioncrest Publishing, 2018).

24 Carl J. Schramm, *Burn the Business Plan: What Great Entrepreneurs Really Do* (John Murray, 2019).

25 Israel M. Kirzner, Peter J. Boettke, and Sautet Frédéric, *Competition and Entrepreneurship* (Indianapolis: Liberty Fund, 2013).

26 James Dyson, *Invention: A Life* (New York: Simon & Schuster, 2021).

Bibliography

"10 Stainless Steel Spring Loaded Things You Should Know About Swiss Army Knife." ger.myvadesigns.com. Accessed August 1, 2021. https://ger.myvadesigns .com/10-stainless-steel-spring-loaded-things-you-should-know-about-swiss-army -knife-706595.

2021 Edelman Trust Barometer Team. Rep. *The 2021 Edelman Trust Barometer*. Daniel J. Edelman Holdings, Inc., 2021.

"A Quote by Dalai Lama Xiv." Goodreads.com. Goodreads. Accessed August 6, 2021. https://www.goodreads.com/quotes/885801-the-dalai-lama-when-asked-what -surprised-him-most-about.

Amabile, T.M. "How to Kill Creativity." *Harvard Business Review*, 1998. https://hbr.org /1998/09/how-to-kill-creativity.

Argyris, Chris. "Teaching Smart People How to Learn." *Harvard Business Review*, 1991. https://hbr.org/1991/05/teaching-smart-people-how-to-learn.

Aschwanden, Pino. "Reporter—DAS Glück Der Arbeit—Warum Man Bei Victorinox So Gerne Angestellt Ist." Play SRF. Play SRF, 2007. https://www.srf.ch/play/tv /reporter/video/das-glueck-der-arbeit-warum-man-bei-victorinox-so-gerne-angestellt -ist?urn=urn%3Asrf%3Avideo%3A6c4a63ce-7a76-4ecb-8c60-696b68e1aad6.

Associated Press. "Americans Are the Unhappiest They've Been in 50 Years, Poll Finds." NBCNews.com. NBCUniversal News Group, June 16, 2020. https://www .nbcnews.com/politics/politics-news/americans-are-unhappiest-they-ve-been-50 -years-poll-finds-n1231153.

Barker, Eric. "Sun Tzu's Art of War: How Ancient Strategy Can Lead to Modern Success." *Time*, June 2, 2014. https://time.com/2801517/sun-tzus-art-of-war-how -ancient-strategy-can-lead-to-modern-success/.

Barsade, Sigal, and Olivia A. O'Neill. "Employees Who Feel Love Perform Better." *Harvard Business Review*, January 13, 2014. https://hbr.org/2014/01/employees-who -feel-love-perform-better.

Bhandari, Avishek, and David Javakhadze. "Corporate Social Responsibility and Capital Allocation Efficiency." *Journal of Corporate Finance*. Elsevier, April 2017. https://www.sciencedirect.com/science/article/abs/pii/S0929119917300652.

Bitzan, John, and Clay Routledge. "College Kids Don't Understand Socialism—or Capitalism. Our Research Proves It: Opinion." *Newsweek*, July 12, 2021. https://www.newsweek.com/college-kids-dont-understand-socialism-capitalism-our-research-proves-it-opinion-1608876?fbclid=IwAR0IHrKPJv8P4djFoRchwTy14QJv-BsZjArFZuWTW0c9qWe-Qm5TScPL0d0.

Blitzer, Carol. "Franchise Owners Weather Turbulent Economic Times." Palo Alto Online, December 11, 2011. https://www.paloaltoonline.com/news/2011/12/11/small-franchise-owners-weather-turbulent-economic-times.

Brooks, Arthur C. "Love Your Enemies: How Decent People Can Save America from Our Culture of Contempt." Amazon. HarperLuxe, an imprint of HarperCollins Publishers, 2019. https://www.amazon.com/Love-Your-Enemies-America-Contempt/dp/0062883755.

Buckingham, Marcus, and D.O. Clifton. *Now, Discover Your Strengths*. Pocket Books, 2005.

Burgis, Luke. *Wanting: The Power of Mimetic Desire in Everyday Life*. New York: St. Martin's Press, 2021.

Burns, Posted by Jim. "To Understand Content Strategy, Start with What Is Strategy?" Avitage, November 9, 2017. https://avitage.com/understand-what-is-strategy-to-formulate-content-strategy/.

Burns, Stephanie. "6 Ways Being Selfish Can Make You Successful." *Forbes*, March 12, 2020. https://www.forbes.com/sites/stephanieburns/2020/03/12/6-ways-being-selfish-can-make-you-successful/?sh=77ef5beb5538.

Carucci, Ron. "How Corporate Values Get Hijacked and Misused." *Harvard Business Review*, May 29, 2017. https://hbr.org/2017/05/how-corporate-values-get-hijacked-and-misused.

Chamorro-Premuzic, Tomas. "Does Money Really Affect Motivation? A Review of the Research." *Harvard Business Review*, April 10, 2013. https://hbr.org/2013/04/does-money-really-affect-motiv.

Colagrossi, Mike. "Can Creativity Be Taught?" Big Think, October 12, 2018. https://bigthink.com/personal-growth/can-creativity-be-taught?rebelltitem=4#rebelltitem4.

Cortopassi, Dino. *Getting Ahead: A Family's Journey from Italian Serfdom to American Success*. Stockton, CA: Black Hole Press, 2014.

Covey, Stephen R., James C. Collins, and Sean Covey. *The 7 Habits of Highly Effective People: Powerful Lessons in Personal Change*. New York: Simon & Schuster, 2020.

Cowen, Tyler. *The Complacent Class: The Self-Defeating Quest for the American Dream*. New York: Picador, 2018.

Cranston, Emma. "These Are the 30 Most Popular Wine Brands in America." VinePair, December 18, 2020. https://vinepair.com/booze-news/30-most-popular-wine-brands-in-america/.

Creative Comons. "First Swiss Army Knife from 1891, Produced by Wester & Co Solingen/Germany." Wikipedia. Wikimedia Foundation, June 6, 2009. https:// en.wikipedia.org/wiki/Victorinox#/media/File:Wester_&_Co_2.JPG.

Currier, James. "Your Life Is Driven by Network Effects." nfx.com, July 12, 2021. https://www.nfx.com/post/your-life-network-effects/.

Deibel, Walker. *Buy Then Build: How Acquisition Entrepreneurs Outsmart the Startup Game.* United States: Lioncrest Publishing, 2018.

Dewar, Carolyn, Martin Hirt, and Scott Keller. "The Mindsets and Practices of Excellent CEOs." McKinsey & Company, October 25, 2019. https://www.mckinsey .com/business-functions/strategy-and-corporate-finance/our-insights/the-mindsets -and-practices-of-excellent-ceos#.

Diamandis, Peter H., and Steven Kotler. *Abundance: The Future Is Better Than You Think.* New York: Simon & Schuster, 2015.

Duckworth, Angela. *Grit: The Power of Passion and Perseverance.* United States: Paula Wiseman Books, 2020.

"Entrepreneurship." entrepreneurship noun—Definition, pictures, pronunciation and usage notes | Oxford Advanced Learner's Dictionary at OxfordLearnersDictionaries .com. Accessed August 9, 2021. https://www.oxfordlearnersdictionaries.com/us /definition/english/entrepreneurship.

"Facts & Data on Small Business and Entrepreneurship." SBE Council.org. Small Business & Entrepreneurship Council, 2018. https://sbecouncil.org/about-us/facts -and-data/.

Fairlie, Robert, Sameeksha Desai, and A.J. Herrmann. Rep. *2018 National Report on Early-Stage Entrepreneurship.* September. Ewing Marion Kauffman Foundation, 2019.

Fernando, Jason. "Corporate Social Responsibility (CSR)." Investopedia. Dotdash Publishing, February 2, 2021. https://www.investopedia.com/terms/c/corp-social -responsibility.asp.

Ferriss, Timothy. *4-Hour Work Week.* Ebury Publishing, 2020.

Foroohar, Rana. "American Capitalism's Great Crisis and How to Fix It." Time, May 12, 2016. https://time.com/4327419/american-capitalisms-great-crisis/.

Friedman, Milton. "A Friedman Doctrine—the Social Responsibility of Business Is to Increase Its Profits." *New York Times,* September 13, 1970. https://www.nytimes.com /1970/09/13/archives/a-friedman-doctrine-the-social-responsibility-of-business-is-to .html.

Glaeser, Edward L. "How to Fix American Capitalism." City Journal. Manhattan Institute for Policy Research, 2020. https://www.city-journal.org/end-insider -privileges-of-socialism-to-fix-american-capitalism.

Glaeser, Edward L. "How to Fix American Capitalism." City Journal. Manhattan Institute, 2020. https://www.city-journal.org/end-insider-privileges-of-socialism-to -fix-american-capitalism.

Guillebeau, Chris. *The $100 Startup: Reinvent the Way You Make a Living, Do What You Love, and Create a New Future: Summary.* New York: Crown Business, 2016.

Gustaf, Katherine. "What Percentage of Businesses Fail and How to Improve Your Chances of Success." Edited by Allison Williams. Lending Tree, August 7, 2020. https://www.lendingtree.com/business/small/failure-rate/.

Haltiwanger, John. "John Haltiwanger: American Entrepreneurs During the Pandemic." AEI. American Enterprise Institute, July 29, 2021. https://www.aei.org/podcast/john-haltiwanger-american-entrepreneurs-during-the-pandemic/.

Hamel, Gary, and Michele Zanini. "A Few Unicorns Are No Substitute for a Competitive, Innovative Economy." *Harvard Business Review*, February 8, 2017. https://hbr.org/2017/02/a-few-unicorns-are-no-substitute-for-a-competitive-innovative-economy.

Harter, Jim. "4 Factors Driving Record-High Employee Engagement in U.S." Gallup, February 4, 2020. https://www.gallup.com/workplace/284180/factors-driving-record-high-employee-engagement.aspx.

Haugh, John, and Mike Shaughnessy. *Living in Color*. John Haugh and Michael Shaughnessy, 2014.

Heim, Michael. "Victorinox Kämpft Gegen Das SCHWEIZERKREUZ Aus China: HZ." handelszeitung.ch. Handelszeitung, February 7, 2017. https://www.handelszeitung.ch/unternehmen/victorinox-kaempft-gegen-das-schweizerkreuz-aus-china-1336469.

Henderson, Bruce D. "The Origin of Strategy." *Harvard Business Review*—Ideas and Advice for Leaders. Harvard Business Publishing, 1989. https://hbr.org/.

Hoover, Gary. "Entrepreneurial Thinking Made Easy." Hoovers World. Gary Hoover, January 4, 2021. https://hooversworld.com/entrepreneurial-thinking-made-easy/.

Hoover, Gary. "The Ten Myths about Profits." medium.com. Archbridge Notes, December 3, 2020. https://medium.com/archbridge-notes/the-ten-myths-about-profits-6b864c6963c5.

Hunter, Brittany. "Millennials Love Free Markets, but Don't Understand Them: Brittany Hunter." Mises.org. Mises Institute, August 24, 2016. https://mises.org/wire/millennials-love-free-markets-dont-understand-them.

Hwang, Victor W. "Entrepreneurship Should Be a Priority for Covid-19 Recovery." Inc.com. Mansueto Ventures, September 23, 2020. https://www.inc.com/victor-w-hwang/entrepreneurship-should-be-prioritized-amid-covid-19.html.

Hyatt, Michael. "How a Shift in Your Vocabulary Can Instantly Change Your Attitude." Michael Hyatt & Co., February 26, 2016. https://michaelhyatt.com/how-a-shift-in-your-vocabulary-can-instantly-change-your-attitude/.

Ingraham, Christopher. "Analysis | Not Only Are Americans Becoming Less Happy—We're Experiencing More Pain Too." *Washington Post*, December 6, 2017. https://www.washingtonpost.com/news/wonk/wp/2017/12/06/not-only-are-americans-becoming-less-happy-were-experiencing-more-pain-too/.

Institute, Archbridge. "Ten Myths About Profits, Part 2." Medium. Archbridge Notes, December 9, 2020. https://medium.com/archbridge-notes/ten-myths-about-profits-part-2-27869f0f7b3a.

James, William. "The Will to Believe." The Project Gutenberg E-text of The Will to Believe, by William James, May 8, 2009. https://www.gutenberg.org/files/26659/26659-h/26659-h.htm.

Kirzner, Israel M., Peter J. Boettke, and Sautet Frédéric. *Competition and Entrepreneurship.* Indianapolis: Liberty Fund, 2013.

Koch, Charles G. *Good Profit: How Creating Value for Others Built One of the World's Most Successful Companies.* PIATKUS Books, 2018.

Koch, Sarah. "Immigrants, We Create Jobs." The Case Foundation, August 18, 2017. https://casefoundation.org/blog/immigrants-we-create-jobs/ ?gclid=CjwKCAiA25v _BRBNEiwAZb4-ZXicpFMU9pGHJoWUVzjZ7kCOKesDGkk3aipdldU _gj4WzZbq4Lm3pxoCxB8QAvD_BwE.

Komsa, Stephanie, Kaatherine H. Wheeler, and Tanja Atanasova. "2011 Development Impact Report." Small Enterprise Assistance Funds, 2012. https:// www.seaf.com/wp-content/uploads/2011/03/2011-Development-Impact-Report -Impact-Beyond-Investment.pdf.

Land, George. "The Failure of Success." YouTube. TEDx Tucson, February 16, 2011. https://www.youtube.com/watch?v=ZfKMq-rYtnc.

Lencioni, Patrick, and Charles Stransky. *The Five Dysfunctions of a Team.* New York: Random House, 2002.

Lowrey, Annie. "The Underemployment Crisis." *Atlantic,* August 6, 2020. https:// www.theatlantic.com/ideas/archive/2020/08/underemployment-crisis/614989/.

Malesic, Jonathan. "How to Save Americans from the Hell of Work." *New Republic,* March 4, 2019. https://newrepublic.com/article/153205/save-americans-hell-work.

Marlar, Jenny. "The Emotional Cost of Underemployment." Gallup, March 9, 2010. https://news.gallup.com/poll/126518/emotional-cost-underemployment.aspx.

Martin, William (Marty). "Entrepreneurship at Any Age." IntechOpen, December 22, 2020. https://www.intechopen.com/chapters/73987.

Mathile, Clayton L., Echo Montgomery Garrett, and Mary Beth Crain. *Dream No Little Dreams.* Bethel Township, OH: DNLD Pub., 2007.

McNerny, John. "Heart Speaks to Heart: Saint John Henry Newman's Educational Ideals." The Institute for Human Ecology, December 2020. https://ihe.catholic.edu /heart-speaks-to-heart-st-john-henry-newmans-educational-ideals/.

McNerney, John, and David Walsh. *Wealth of Persons: Economics with a Human Face.* Eugene, OR: Cascade Books, 2016.

Meyers, Kerby. "Entrepreneurs of a Certain Age, in This Uncertain Time." Ewing Marion Kauffman Foundation, August 5, 2020. https://www.kauffman.org/currents /entrepreneurs-of-a-certain-age-uncertain-time/.

Michelin, François, Ivan Levaï, and Yves Messarovitch. *And Why Not?: Morality and Business.* Lanham: Lexington Books, 2003.

Michelini, Michael. "Buy Then Build: Book Review." *Mike's Blog,* July 29, 2020. https://mikesblog.com/buythenbuild/.

Moore, Karl. "The Great Power of Connecting Passion with Purpose." *Forbes*, January 19, 2015. https://www.forbes.com/sites/karlmoore/2015/01/19/the-great-power-of-connecting-passion-with-purpose/?sh=53e871298784.

Mullen O'Keefe, Shannon. "How Do You Say 'Success' in Strengths?" Gallup, September 20, 2020. https://www.gallup.com/cliftonstrengths/en/320447/say-success-strengths.aspx.

Naughton, Michael J. *Getting Work Right: Labor and Leisure in a Fragmented World.* Steubenville, OH: Emmaus Road Publishing, 2019.

Nesvisky, Matt. "Who Gains from Innovation?" National Bureau of Economic Research, October 2004. https://www.nber.org/digest/oct04/who-gains-innovation.

Novak, Michael. *The Spirit of Democratic Capitalism.* New York: Simon and Schuster, 1983.

Parrales, Luis, and Gil Guerra. "Episode # 6 Transcript: Gonzalo Schwarz on Markets, Inequality, and Economic Opportunity." *Panorama Podcast*, October 18, 2020. https://www.panoramapodcast.org/transcripts/gonzalo-schwarz.

Perry, Mark J. "The General Public Thinks the Average Company Makes a 36% Profit Margin, Which Is About 5X Too High, Part II." American Enterprise Institute, January 15, 2018. https://www.aei.org/carpe-diem/the-public-thinks-the-average-company-makes-a-36-profit-margin-which-is-about-5x-too-high-part-ii/.

Pethokoukis, James. "Creative Destruction Works Unless Undermined by Crony Capitalism." American Enterprise Institute, October 5, 2020. https://www.aei.org/economics/creative-destruction-works-unless-undermined-by-crony-capitalism/.

Pilon, Mary. "Monopoly Was Designed to Teach the 99% About Income Inequality." Smithsonian Institution, January 2015. https://www.smithsonianmag.com/arts-culture/monopoly-was-designed-teach-99-about-income-inequality-180953630/.

———. "The Secret History of Monopoly: The Capitalist Board Game's Leftwing Origins." *Guardian*, April 11, 2015. https://www.theguardian.com/lifeandstyle/2015/apr/11/secret-history-monopoly-capitalist-game-leftwing-origins.

Porter, Michael E. "Clusters and the New Economics of Competition." *Harvard Business Review*, 1998. https://hbr.org/1998/11/clusters-and-the-new-economics-of-competition.

Porter, Michael E., and Victor E. Millar. "How Information Gives You Competitive Advantage." *Harvard Business Review*, July 1985. https://hbr.org/1985/07/how-information-gives-you-competitive-advantage.

Pressfield, Steven. *The War of Art.* London: Orion, 2003.

Putz, Paul. Summer Book List: Henry George (and George Norris) and the Crisis of Inequality, July 2, 2015. http://peputz.blogspot.com/2015/07/henry-george-and-george-norris-and.html.

Rahn, Richard W. "Loux XIV, John Rockefeller Had Harder Life Than Common Man Today." *Washington Times*, December 22, 2014. https://www.washingtontimes.com/news/2014/dec/22/richard-rahn-loux-xiv-john-rockefeller-had-harder-/.

Rey, Carlos, Miquel Bastons, and Phil Sotok. Essay. In *Purpose-Driven Organizations: Management Ideas for a Better World*, 131. Cham: Springer International Publishing, 2019.

Richards, Jay W. "What Economists Know, Believe, and Debate." *Journal of Markets & Morality*. Acton Institute for the Study of Religion & Liberty. Accessed July 31, 2021. https://www.marketsandmorality.com/index.php/mandm/article/view/1490.

Richards, Jay W. *The Human Advantage: The Future of American Work in an Age of Smart Machines*. New York: Crown Publishing Group, 2018.

Ricketts, Joe. "Opinion | in Praise of Today's Entrepreneurs." *Wall Street Journal*, November 4, 2019. https://www.wsj.com/articles/in-praise-of-todays-entrepreneurs -11572909118.

Ries, Al, and Jack Trout. *The 22 Immutable Laws of Marketing*. London: Profile Books, 1994.

Roser, Max. "Democracy." Our World in Data. Global Change Data Lab, June 2019. https://ourworldindata.org/democracy.

Roser, Max, Esteban Ortiz-Ospina, and Hannah Ritchie. "Life Expectancy." Our World in Data, October 2019. https://ourworldindata.org/life-expectancy.

Schramm, Carl J. *Burn the Business Plan: What Great Entrepreneurs Really Do*. John Murray, 2019.

Schwarz, Gonzalo. "American Dream 2020 Snapshot." archbridgeinstitute.org. Archbridge Institute, October 19, 2020. https://www.archbridgeinstitute.org/wp -content/uploads/2020/10/AI-AmericanDream2020Snapshot.pdf.

"Selfish Definition & Meaning." Dictionary.com. Dictionary.com. Accessed August 9, 2021. https://www.dictionary.com/browse/selfishness.

"Small Businesses Are the Backbone of the Economy." Better Accounting, August 11, 2020. https://betteraccounting.com/small-businesses-are-the-backbone-of-the -economy/.

"Small Businesses Have a Big Impact on the US Economy." American National University, November 28, 2015. https://an.edu/blog/small-businesses-have-a-big -impact-on-the-us-economy/.

Smith, Adam. "An Inquiry into the Nature and Causes of the Wealth of Nations." *The Glasgow Edition of the Works and Correspondence of Adam Smith, Vol. 2: An Inquiry into the Nature and Causes of the Wealth of Nations, Vol. 1*, 1776. https://doi.org/10.1093 /oseo/instance.00043218.

Somers, Meredith. "Intrapreneurship, Explained." MIT Sloan School of Management, June 21, 2018. https://mitsloan.mit.edu/ideas-made-to-matter/intrapreneurship -explained.

Studio71, ed. "Das Beste Unternehmen Der Welt! Warum Ist Es Bei Mitarbeitern so Beliebt?" YouTube.com. Galileo, March 6, 2020. https://www.youtube.com/watch ?v=5PDOMsQ0ZUA.

Tabrizi, Behnam. "The Key to Change Is Middle Management." *Harvard Business Review*, October 27, 2014. https://hbr.org/2014/10/the-key-to-change-is-middle -management.

Thompson, Derek. "The Religion of Workism Is Making Americans Miserable." https:// www.theatlantic.com/ideas/archive/2019/02/religion-workism-making-americans -miserable/583441/. The Atlantic, February 24, 2019. https://www.theatlantic.com/ ideas/archive/2019/02/religion-workism-making-americans-miserable/583441/.

Turak, August. "Can Creativity Be Taught?" *Forbes*, May 22, 2011. https://www.forbes .com/sites/augustturak/2011/05/22/can-creativity-be-taught/?sh=5e2b28b61abb.

Unstuck. "Empathy: The Single Best Way to Get Unstuck." Medium, November 5, 2015. https://medium.com/@unstuck/empathy-the-single-best-way-to-get-unstuck -fba35f5ffb85.

"US Wine Consumption." Wine Institute, 2021. https://wineinstitute.org/our-industry/ statistics/us-wine-consumption/.

Vaidyanathan, Brandon. "What Creates Unhealthy Organizational Cultures?" The Catholic University of America. Accessed August 7, 2021. https://www.catholic.edu /research/big-questions/what-creates-unhealthy-organizational-cultures.html.

Villiger, Kaspar. "Moderner Staat: Nicht TURBOKAPITALISMUS—Eher Semi-Sozialismus!" Neue Zürcher Zeitung, February 4, 2021. https://www.nzz.ch /feuilleton/moderner-staat-nicht-turbokapitalismus-eher-semi-sozialismus-ld .1599621?kid=_2021-2-5&trco=&mktcid=&ga=&mktcval=&reduced=true.

Vozza, Stephanie. "How to Spot a Potentially Toxic Hire During a Job Interview." *Fast Company*, October 22, 2020. https://www.fastcompany.com/90566299/how-to -spot-a-toxic-person-during-a-job-interview.

Wagorn, Paul. "Burn the Ships." IdeaConnection, April 11, 2014. https://www .ideaconnection.com/blog/open+innovation/open-innovation-commitment.html.

Watters, Audrey. "The Invented History of 'The Factory Model of Education.'" Hack Education, April 25, 2015. http://hackeducation.com/2015/04/25/factory-model #:˜:text=Here%20he%20is%20in%202012,system%20in%20the%20late%201700s.

Weber, Max. *Protestant Ethic and the Spirit of Capitalism*. Wilder Publications, 2018.

"What Business Are You In?: Classic Advice from Theodore Levitt." *Harvard Business Review*, October 2006. https://hbr.org/2006/10/what-business-are-you-in-classic -advice-from-theodore-levitt.

Whelan, Robbie. "Why Goldman Sachs Is Interested in a Small Bike Shop in Mexico." *Wall Street Journal*, March 14, 2019. https://www.wsj.com/articles/why -goldman-sachs-is-interested-in-a-small-bike-shop-in-mexico-11552555801.

Widmer, Andreas. *The Pope & the CEO John Paul II'S Leadership Lessons to a Young Swiss Guard*. Steubenville, OH: Emmaus Road Publishing, 2011.

Wood, Meredith. "Raising Capital for Startups: 8 Statistics That Will Surprise You." Fundera, February 3, 2020. https://www.fundera.com/resources/startup-funding -statistics.

Zak, Paul J. "Paul J. Zak." pauljzak.com. Accessed August 9, 2021. https://pauljzak.
com/about/.

———. *The Moral Molecule: The Source of Love and Prosperity.* New York: Dutton, 2013.

———. *The Trust Factor: The Science of Creating High-Performance Companies.* New York:
American Management Association, 2017.

Index

A

abundance mindset, 132–133, 143
accountability, 22, 62, 160, 189
"acquisition" entrepreneurs, 30, 157
acquisitions, 91, 112
Alessi, Dick, 115
Allard, Bob, 1, 4
always think like an entrepreneur (Pillar 5)
  about, 7, 14–16, 22, 145–147
  challenges as opportunities, 155–159
  and core values, 108
  creator mindset, 108, 153–154, 158
  creators versus harvesters, 146–149
  decision making, 149–151
  deferred gratification, 108
  employees, 30, 32, 158
  implementing, 159–161
  ownership attitude, 29
  planning, 152–153
  solidarity, 108
  succession planning, 90, 152–155, 159–160
  sustainability, 108, 149. *See also* sustainability
American Dream
  Author's experience, 3, 28, 68

and business education, 163
competition, role of, 12
and creativity, 28, 67–68
and decline of entrepreneurship, 28, 156
economic success, benefits of, 104
entrepreneur, always thinking like, 22. *See also* always think like an entrepreneur (Pillar 5)
and entrepreneurship, 17–22, 28, 156–158
and flourishing, 3, 18, 53
and founding of United States, 21
and free market economy, 9
opportunity, 19, 21, 28, 53, 68, 191–192
and personal potential, 192
and Principled Entrepreneurship, 6–7, 17–19, 21–22, 191–192
and property rights, 125
and purpose of economy, 53–54
revitalization of, 157–158
social mobility, 3, 17, 22, 28, 53, 68, 192
And Why Not (Michelin), 60
anti-competitive regulations, 24
Apple, 147
Aquinas, St. Thomas, 173

Aristotle, 73, 171, 173
Art & Carlyse Ciocca Center for
    Principled Entrepreneurship.
    See Ciocca Center for Principled
    Entrepreneurship
art versus science, 6, 16, 77, 102

B
backward integration, 40, 42
Bangladesh, 120–123, 139–140
Bates, Lynn, 114
Baumol, William, 174
bKash, 123
board of advisors, 185–186
both/and solutions, 14, 129–130, 132,
    139, 182, 188–189
Burgis, Luke, 74
Burn the Business Plan (Schramm), 167
business
    charity distinguished, 86
    culture, 10–11
    decision making as art versus
        science, 6, 16, 102
    as force for good, 3–5
    hobby distinguished, 86
    internet, impact of, 26–27
    large companies, 23, 25, 85, 138,
        156–157
    movies about, 13
    objectives of, 9–10, 57–58, 63,
        65–92, 107–108
    perceptions of, 8, 13, 125, 130, 133
    person-centered approach, 7–9
    small- and medium-sized
        companies (SMEs), 18, 22–27,
        87, 156
    startups. *See* startups
    teaching. *See* Ciocca Center for
        Principled Entrepreneurship
    as war, 13. *See also* zero-sum game
    work as creative endeavor, 8–10

C
capitalism, 12, 62, 67, 126–127. *See also*
    crony capitalism
CarMax, 143
Carucci, Ron, 108–109
The Catholic University of America,
    5, 45, 163–164, 179. *See also*
    Ciocca Center for Principled
    Entrepreneurship
CellBazaar, 122
challenges, as opportunities, 155–159
Chamorro-Premuzic, Tomas, 65
character
    and business education, 168
    and core virtues, 103, 109, 177
    hiring for, 75, 102, 109, 153,
        170–171
    Principled Entrepreneurs, 147, 151
charity versus business, 86
Christensen, Clayton, 158, 182–183
Ciocca, Art. *See also* The Wine Group
    advice on starting or managing
        business as Principled
        Entrepreneur, 101–102
    as an "employee" entrepreneur, 32
    business education, involvement in,
        4–5, 163
    and California wine industry, 2
    career in wine industry, 2, 35–38,
        184
    childhood, 34–35
    consumer, focus on, 36–38, 46
    creators and harvesters, views on,
        146–147
    economic return versus excellence
        and creating value, 79–80
    employment history, 2, 32, 54
    excellence, pursuit of, 70–71, 191
    and Franzia. *See* Franzia
    labor relations, approach to,
        130–131

leadership, 1, 37, 71, 96, 113–116,
152–153
long-term thinking, 103–104
management buyout of The Wine
Group, 2, 37, 96–97, 101, 184
military service, 2, 146
motivation, 79–80
office politics, views on, 113–114,
116–117
ownership attitude, 29
as Principled Entrepreneur, 1–3,
6, 149
Principled Entrepreneurship,
teaching, 164–165
Principled Entrepreneurship
mindset, 158, 190–192
principles and values, 110, 191
stewardship as corporate value,
80–83
students, message to, 155–156
succession planning, 152–155
value creation for customers, 36–
37, 39, 48, 80
Ciocca, Carlyse, 41
Ciocca Center for Principled
Entrepreneurship
about, 163–165
aptitudes, creativity, and strengths,
discovering, 178–179
attitude, teaching, 167–171
components to teaching, 176–183
entrepreneurship, teaching,
165–168
experiential learning, 171, 179–180
feedback, invitation for, 165
free will, teaching students to
exercise, 167, 169–170
knowledge, teaching, 168, 171–174
role models and mentors, 183–186
skill, teaching, 168, 171
Small Business Lab, 179

trading game as gauge of
happiness, 174–176
"Vocation of Business" class,
176–179
cluster theory, 137–138
Coca-Cola Bottling Company of New
York (Coke New York), 2, 37, 39, 54,
80, 97–98, 113, 184
collaboration
and company culture, 112–113
flourishing as a result of, 9, 129,
174
and personal excellence, 54, 128,
151, 189
win-win solutions, 129–130
competition, 12–14, 24, 129, 135–140
competitive advantage
company culture as, 96, 100–101,
113
employees as, 15, 52, 58, 69–77
Franzia, 43–44
team, market-focused, 47
value, 48–49
complementary relationships, 14, 69–73,
77, 93, 120, 129–132, 150, 189
Constitution, United States, 21
consumers. See customers
contribution mentality, 64
co-opetition, 14, 135–139
corporate culture
building, 106–112
collaboration, 112–113
as competitive advantage, 96,
100–101, 113
core virtues, modeling, 108–112
cultural values, 10–11, 80, 85,
97–104, 111, 113, 117
flourishing, opportunities for,
107–108
impact of, 112–117
importance of, 102

leadership, 10–11, 95, 101–102,
105–109, 112–114, 147. *See also*
culture eats strategy for breakfast
(Pillar 3)
management, 100
at Michelin, 59–60
positive culture, elements of,
104–112
startups, 109, 129
sustainable business as purpose of,
112
and trust, 76, 105, 112–113
at The Wine Group, 83, 96–104,
110, 113–117
Corporate Social Responsibility (CSR),
8, 58
Cortés, Hernán, 154, 159
COVID-19, 26, 127, 156–157, 189–190
Create, Support, Reward (CSR). *See* to
work is to create; to create is to be
human (Pillar 2)
creation of goods and services. *See also*
to work is to create; to create is to be
human (Pillar 2)
as team effort, 64
work, nature of, 8–10, 57
creative destruction, 15, 190
creativity. *See also* to work is to create; to
create is to be human (Pillar 2)
and American Dream, 28, 67–69
and business objectives, 10
and crony capitalism, 13. *See also*
crony capitalism
as cultural value, 85, 105, 108
and education, 178–179, 181–183
and human flourishing, 107
and innovation, 13, 91
mindset of versus harvesters,
14–16, 92
and self-knowledge, 176
and thinking like an entrepreneur,
149–150, 157

creator mindset, 108, 153–155, 158
creators versus harvesters, 146–149
crony capitalism, 12–13, 67, 139, 142,
158
cultural values. *See* corporate culture
culture eats strategy for breakfast (Pillar
3). *See also* corporate culture
about, 7, 10–11, 95–99, 117
CEO, role of, 112
impact of company culture,
112–117
implementing positive culture,
95–96, 117–118
positive culture, 104–112
values, establishing, 99–104
customers. *See also* economy exists for
people, not people for the economy
(Pillar 1)
creating value for, 33–38, 47–48,
83, 133, 147, 160, 188
focus on, 34–39, 44–45, 48, 50–51,
129, 188
love for, 63–64, 94
needs, 9, 37, 39, 44–46, 53, 66
new market segments, 45
satisfaction, 9, 37, 45, 66, 88, 119,
125, 135, 139, 147

D

Dalai Lama, 88
D'Ambrosio, Lou, 114–115
Darrow, Charles, 124
decision making, 30, 84–85, 90, 148–
155, 171
Declaration of Independence, 21
deferred gratification, 11, 108
democracy, 22, 169
D'Eredita, Mike, 167
Di Giacinto, Guarino, 34–35, 191–192
dignity. *See* human dignity
Dragon Systems, 49–50
Drucker, Peter, 33, 68

Dyer, Jeff, 182

E

E. & J. Gallo Winery, 37. *See also* Gallo
  Wine Company
economic development, 19–20, 33
economy exists for people, not people for
  the economy (Pillar 1)
  about, 7–8
  and core values, 107–108
  customer need, finding profitable
    solutions for, 37–46
  customer-centered value, 49–51
  customers, focus on, 34–39, 44–45,
    48–51
  employee-centered culture,
    importance of, 51–53
  employees, focus on, 51–53
  excellence, importance of, 47–51
  implementing principles of, 54–55
  investors, 53–54
  purpose of economy, 33, 53–54
  value creation, 34, 36–40, 47–50,
    53
  The Wine Group example, 36–37,
    39–45
  and work, 57, 59. *See also* to work
    is to create; to create is to be
    human (Pillar 2)
either/or choices, 14, 129–130, 139
Elsener, Carl, 51
Elsener, Carl, IV, 51–52
employees. *See also* economy exists for
  people, not people for the economy
  (Pillar 1)
  and cultural values, 11, 51–53,
    108–109
  employee entrepreneurs, 30, 32,
    158
  empowerment, 10, 102
  feedback, 71
  flourishing of, 69, 118

hiring for character, 75, 102, 109,
    153, 170–171
  job changes, 106
  job dissatisfaction, 11, 105–107,
    190
  labor relations, 130–131
  love for, 64
  rewarding, 52, 58, 63, 78–92,
    107–108
  support of, 58, 63, 69–77
  and top-down management, 72,
    149, 173, 15071
  work as creation. *See* to work is to
    create; to create is to be human
    (Pillar 2)
empowerment, xi, 7, 10, 70, 102, 122,
  140–142
entrepreneurs and entrepreneurship.
  See also Principled Entrepreneurs;
  Principled Entrepreneurship
  about, 17–18
  age of entrepreneurs, 31–32
  and American Dream, 17–22,
    28, 156–158. *See also* American
    Dream
  creators versus harvesters, 146–149
  decline of entrepreneurship, 28,
    156
  deterrents, 156
  entrepreneurship defined, 166–167
  job creation, 23
  mindset, 145, 150–151
  motivation, 4–5, 146–147
  and opportunity, 166
  ownership attitude, 29
  risk and risk aversion, 25, 31, 103,
    111, 151, 156–159, 166
  and startups, decline in, 24–26. *See
    also* startups
  types of entrepreneurs, 30–31
  value creation, 23, 133
  wealth, 23

equality, 18, 129, 169
ergon, 73–77, 90, 93
eudaimonia. *See* flourishing
excellence
    and corporate culture, 102–108,
      110, 112–118
    and creativity, 68–69, 88
    and flourishing, 72, 93, 113
    and free market economy, 59
    as goal of Principled Entrepreneurs,
      29, 34, 47–48, 53, 57, 60, 74, 92,
      150–151, 189
    leadership, 70–71
    and office politics, 116–117
    in others, enabling, 9, 58, 63, 69–
      74, 93, 105, 115, 151, 189
    personal excellence, pursuit of, 9,
      29, 54, 63, 70–74, 77, 89, 151,
      189
    and teaching entrepreneurship,
      164, 167, 169–170, 179–181
    The Wine Group values, 80–81,
      102–103, 105, 110, 114–115
    as work objective, 9, 68, 79
exit value, 89

F
failure, 105, 111–112, 115, 118, 159,
    177, 179–181, 189
Federalist Papers, 21
Feriss, Tim, 66–67
financial market, 24–25, 27, 66, 82–83,
    157
financial performance, 53, 79–84, 86–89
financial reward. *See* reward
financial risk, 166. *See also* risk
financialization, 59, 66–68
fingerspitzengefühl, 6
flat organization, 73
flourishing
    and American Dream, 3, 18, 53
    and competition, 139–140
    and creativity, 107
    of employees, 69, 118
    entrepreneurship, role of, 151
    eudaimonia, 174, 188
    and excellence, pursuit of, 72, 93,
      113
    opportunities for and corporate
      culture, 107–108
    as a result of work, 8–9, 66, 107–
      108, 128
    as reward, 9, 63
    and win-win solutions, 141–142
    and working together, 174
The 4-Hour Workweek (Feriss), 66
franchise entrepreneur, 31
franchises, 31
Frankl, Viktor, 106, 173
Franzia, 2, 37, 42–45, 131
free market. *See* market economy
free will, 72, 141, 167, 169–170, 177
freedom, 3, 18, 21–22, 140–142, 169
Friedman, Milton, 58, 68

G
Gallo Wine Company, 2, 32, 36–37, 40,
    42–43, 54
Gates, Bill, 184
George, Henry, 123, 124
Geyser Peak winery, 40–41
Gore-Tex, 72–73
Grameenphone, 120–122
greed, 13, 125
Gregersen, Hal, 158, 182–183

H
Haltiwanger, John, 190
happiness
    and creative work, 157
    human excellence as, 164
    and Principled Entrepreneurship,
      189
    pursuit of, 22, 149–150

sources of, 66
trading game as gauge of, 174–176
trust and collaboration, effect of,
    112–113
Harvard, Alexandre, 59
harvesters, 14–16, 92, 145–149, 160
Hawking, Stephen, 57
hobby versus business, 86
Hoover, Gary, 183
human anthropology, 172–173
human dignity, 19–20, 65, 72, 79, 89,
    129, 140, 168

I
immigrants, 21, 34
informed population, 22
innovation
    creative destruction, 15
    and crony capitalism, 13
    entrepreneurs, 23, 25, 157–158
    incentives for, 18, 91
    management theory, 99–100
    opportunities for, 157
    in person-centered business, 8, 59
    as response to customer needs or
        problems, 39, 65, 122, 188
    and tech boom, 25
    through human excellence, 60
    The Wine Group's packaging
        problem, 45
The Innovator's DNA (Christensen,
    Gregersen and Dyer), 158, 182
internet, impact of on businesses, 26–27
internet of things, 157
investors, 9, 54, 63, 91–92, 94, 126, 139,
    149, 159, 188. *See also* shareholders

J
Jesse, Bill, 80
job creation and growth, 23
job descriptions, 76, 90, 93
job dissatisfaction, 11, 105–107, 190

Jobs, Steve, 147, 184
John Paul II, Pope, 63, 173

K
Kessler, Andy, 24
Keynes, John Maynard, 66
King, Martin Luther, Jr., 173
Kirzner, Israel, 174
KNY. *See* Coca-Cola Bottling Company
    of New York (Coke New York)
Koch, Charles, xi, xii
Koch Industries, xi

L
labor and capital, relationship between,
    14, 129
"The Landlord's Game" (Monopoly),
    124–125
large companies, 23, 25, 85, 138,
    156–157
leadership
    Ciocca, Art, 1, 37, 71, 96, 113–116,
        152–153
    corporate culture, 10–11, 95,
        101–102, 105–109, 112–114,
        147. *See also* culture eats strategy
        for breakfast (Pillar 3)
    excellence, 70–71
    and spontaneous order, 73
    succession planning, 90, 152–155,
        159–160
Levitt, Theodore, 38
long-term decision making, 84–85, 90,
    148–155
long-term success, 10–11, 15, 80, 85, 92,
    98, 186–187
long-term value creation, 11, 14–15,
    80–84, 89, 92, 149

M
Mackey, John, 147
Magie, Elizabeth (Lizzie), 123–125

management theory, 99–100
market economy
 and American Dream, 9, 28
 benefits of, 3–4, 126–128
 capitalism, 12, 62, 67, 126–127
 defending, 4–5
 economic freedom, importance of,
  3, 18
 and entrepreneurship, 18–19
 and human dignity, 19–20, 140. *See*
  also human dignity
 and Monopoly game, 123–126
 negative image of, 13–14
 and opportunity, 28, 132
 profit, 134
 prosperity, 132
 self-interest versus selfishness,
  133–135
 and socialism, 67
 teaching about, 167–168, 172, 174,
  176
 win-win nature of, 3, 130, 134–135.
  See also principled entrepreneurs
  always seek to create win-win
  solutions (Pillar 4)
 zero-sum game fallacy, 124–126,
  130
Market-Based Management (MBM),
 xi, xii
Marxism, 14, 129
materialist myth, 125
McNerney, John, 68–69
MCODE, 177
MCORE test, 94
McShane, Lynn, 114
mentors, 31–32, 160, 183–184
Michelin, Édouard, 59–61, 64
Michelin, François, 59–63, 70
Michelin Tires, 59–64
Mignol, Marius, 60–61, 63–64, 93
mission statements, 11, 177

mistakes, learning from, 62, 72, 115,
 180. *See also* failure
Mogen David, 113–115
Monopoly (game), 123–125
The Moral Molecule (Zak), 112
Multinational Corporations (MNCs),
 23, 25
Myers–Briggs test, 76

N
Newman, John Henry, 142
Nordhaus, William D., 23
Novak, Michael, 173

O
opportunity
 and age, 31–32
 and American Dream, 19, 21, 28,
  53, 68, 191–192
 challenges as, 155–159
 COVID-19, impact of, 26, 156–
  157, 189–190
 and entrepreneurship, 166
 equal access to, 3, 28, 150
 failure as, 189
 and market economy, 28, 132
 problems as, 15
ownership mentality, 29, 99, 189
oxytocin, 112–113

P
personal responsibility, 3, 15, 92
personal virtue, 141
personalities, 75, 147
person-centered economy, 8–9, 20,
 34, 108. *See also* economy exists for
 people, not people for the economy
 (Pillar 1)
pillars of Principled Entrepreneurship
 about, 6–7
 always think like an entrepreneur
  (Pillar 5), 7, 14–16, 22. *See also*

always think like an entrepreneur (Pillar 5) culture eats strategy for breakfast (Pillar 3), 7, 10–11. *See also* culture eats strategy for breakfast (Pillar 3)

economy exists for people, not people for the economy (Pillar 1), 7–8. *See also* economy exists for people, not people for the economy (Pillar 1)

principled entrepreneurs always seek to create win-win solutions (Pillar 4), 7, 11–14. *See also* principled entrepreneurs always seek to create win-win solutions (Pillar 4)

to work is to create; to create is to be human (Pillar 2), 7–10, 57–59. *See also* to work is to create; to create is to be human (Pillar 2)

Plato, 171–173

Pollard, Bill, 147

The Pope & the CEO (Widmer), 4–5

Porter, Michael, 100, 136–138

Positioning (Ries and Trout), 100

potential, personal, 60, 63–64, 66, 70, 107, 116–117, 140–141, 192

poverty, 12, 19, 27, 124, 126–127, 140, 174

Prial, Frank, 43–44

Principled Entrepreneurs
  as creative problem solvers, 29
  learning opportunities, 31–32
  mindset, 145, 150–151, 189
  motivation, 28
  starting or managing a company, advice for, 101–102
  types of, 29–31

principled entrepreneurs always seek to create win-win solutions (Pillar 4)
  about, 3, 5, 7, 11–14, 119

Bangladesh business solutions example, 120–123, 139–140
  benefits of principled entrepreneurship, 126–127
  and competition, 135–139
  complementary relationships, 14, 69–73, 77, 93, 120, 129–132, 150, 189
  and core values, 108
  implementation of, 142–144
  labor relations, 130–131
  selfishness and self-interest distinguished, 133–135
  virtuous behavior, 139–142
  The Wine Group examples, 41–44, 130–132
  winning defined, 127–133
  zero-sum game fallacy, 123–126

Principled Entrepreneurship
  about, 188
  and American Dream, 6–7, 17–19, 21–22, 191–192
  defined, xi, xii
  pillars of. *See* pillars of Principled Entrepreneurship
  teaching. *See* Ciocca Center for Principled Entrepreneurship

profit
  "bad" profit, 88
  benefits of, 9, 86–88
  as goal of business, 5, 33
  and market economy, 134
  negative perception of, 86–87
  and rewards, 78–79, 87–89
  short-term, 107, 160
  through addressing customer needs, 38–40, 88, 112, 128
  through creating value for customers, 7–9, 33–34, 37, 53, 57, 88, 107, 112, 134, 188
  and win-win solutions, 5

property rights, 20–21, 125, 141

prosperity, 12, 17–24, 32, 34, 66, 88,
119–120, 127–128, 130, 132–133,
140–141, 149, 157–158
"pure" startup entrepreneur, 31

Q
Quadir, Iqbal, 120–123, 139–140, 142
Quadir, Kamal, 122–123, 139–140, 142

R
recitals, The Wine Group, 81–84, 110–
111, 153–154
regulations, 13, 24, 156
reward
    for contributions other than
        productivity, 79, 89
    and corporate culture, 104, 113
    for creators versus harvesters, 147,
        160
    for excellence, 113
    financial, 9–10, 86–89
    flourishing as, 9, 63
    implementing, 90–94
    incentive plans, 80, 110
    for long-term decision making,
        84–85, 90
    as objective of business, 9–10,
        57–58, 63, 78–92, 107–108
    profit, 78–79, 87–89
    types of, 87
    The Wine Group's long-term
        reward system, 80–81, 84–85,
        89–90, 110
Ries, Al, 100
risk and risk aversion, 25, 31, 103, 111,
151, 156–159, 166
role models, 70, 183–184. *See also*
    mentors

S
scale, economies of, 23, 25, 41, 48, 131
scarcity mindset, 125, 132–133, 143

Schramm, Carl, 167
Schumpeter, Joseph, 174
self-determination, 20, 103, 140–141
self-interest, 71, 85, 133–135, 138, 180
selfishness, 58, 125, 130, 133–135, 180
self-knowledge, 171–174
ServiceMaster, 147
shareholders, 58, 62, 82, 110
small- and medium-sized companies
    (SMEs), 18, 22–27, 87, 156. *See also*
    startups
Smith, Adam, 133, 135, 173
"so what" game, 50
social mobility
    and American Dream, 3, 17, 22,
        28, 53, 68, 192
    and entrepreneurship, 27–28, 157
    generational change, 157, 192
    and property rights, 125
    and wealth redistribution, 67, 133
    work as element of, 67
social responsibility, 8, 58–59, 106, 111
socialism, 67. *See also* Marxism
solidarity, 108, 140
spontaneous order, 71–73, 94, 138
startups. *See also* small- and medium-
    sized companies (SMEs)
    company culture, 109, 129
    creator mindset, 15
    decline in, 24–28, 156
    high-tech, 17
    pandemic startups, 26, 189–190
    as part of cluster of businesses, 138.
        See also cluster theory
    "pure" startup entrepreneurs, 31
    small- and medium-size companies,
        18, 22–24
    success rate, 31
stewardship, 80–81, 85, 103, 110,
    153–154
strategy, 10–11. *See also* culture eats
    strategy for breakfast (Pillar 3)

succession planning, 90, 152–155,
  159–160
sustainability, 10, 15, 18, 46, 69, 77,
  85–86, 90–92, 108, 112, 134, 149
Swiss Army knives, 51–52

T
taxes, 23–24, 67
technology companies, 17, 21, 25, 46,
  135–136, 157
Telenor, 121–122
thinking like an entrepreneur. *See* always
  think like an entrepreneur (Pillar 5)
Thomas Aquinas, Saint, 173
Tirone, Henry, 40–41
to work is to create; to create is to be
  human (Pillar 2)
    about, 7–10, 57–59
    assessment questions, 93–94
    and core values, 107–108
    creation as first objective of
      business, 58, 65–69
    creation as team effort, 64
    implementation of business
      objectives, 89–92
    Michelin example, 59–63
    reward as third objective of
      business, 9–10, 57–58, 63, 78–
      92, 107–108. *See also* reward
    support as second objective of
      business, 58, 69–77
top-down management approach, 71–
  72, 149–150, 173
Tribuno Vermouth, 96–99, 110, 148
Trout, Jack, 100
trust and company culture, 76, 105,
  112–113

U
United States history and
  entrepreneurship, 20–22

V
value
    creating, 7–8, 11, 14–15, 23–24,
      30, 32, 34, 80–85, 89, 91–92,
      133, 148–149. *See also* economy
      exists for people, not people for
      the economy (Pillar 1)
    customer-centered value, 49–51
    demonstrable and perceived, 48–49
    exit value, 89
    long-term, 11, 14–15, 81–82, 84,
      89, 149
    money as measure of, 67, 133
    quality and price, 47–48
    taxes and regulation, impact of, 24
values
    core, 106–109
    corporate values of The Wine
      Group, 80, 98, 102–104, 110–
      112
    personal, 106–112
Victorinox, 51–53
virtues, 103, 108–112, 139–142, 177
vision statements, 11

W
Walls, Jim, 99
wealth. *See also* prosperity
    creation of, 19–20, 125, 133, 140
    redistribution of, 67, 91, 133
    without creation of value, 59,
      67–68, 125
Whole Foods, 147
The Wine Group
    company culture, 83, 96–104, 110,
      113–117
    company politics disallowed, 116
    consumer, focus on, 36–38, 48, 83
    consumer value, 98, 103
    as creator company, 153–154

distributors and wholesalers, win-win relationships with, 41–44, 131–132
excellence, focus on, 80–81, 102–103, 105, 110, 114–115
executive stock redemptions, 155
Franzia, 2, 37, 42–45, 131
labor relations, 130–131
long-term decision making, rewarding, 84–85
management buyout of, 2, 37, 96–97, 101, 110, 184
Mogen David acquisition, 113–115
Principled Entrepreneurship, 149
Principled Entrepreneurship, 191
as private company, 81–83
recitals (investor agreement), 81–84, 110–111, 153–154
reward system (incentive program), 80–81, 84–85, 89–90, 110
stewardship goals, 80–83, 153–154
succession planning, 152–155
talent, attracting, 113–116
teamwork, 71–72
values, 80–83, 99–104, 110–112
vermouth quality problem, 96–99, 110, 148
wine packaging problem, 39–45
wine industry
branded wines, 36–37, 43–44
in California, 2
cluster theory, 137–139
competitiveness, 12, 43–44
growth of in US, 35–37, 44
as metaphor for business and entrepreneurship, 187–188
WineTap, 2, 42–45. *See also* Franzia
win-lose mentality, 13, 130–131, 133–134, 141–143. *See also* zero-sum game
win-win solutions. *See* principled entrepreneurs always seek to create win-win solutions (Pillar 4)
work
creation. *See* to work is to create; to create is to be human (Pillar 2)
flourishing as a result of, 8–9, 66, 107–108, 128
and human anthropology, 173
nature of, 8–10, 57, 107
purpose of, 65–67, 79, 157
reward. *See* reward
trend toward less work, 66–67
workaholism, 107

Z

Zak, Paul, 112
zero-sum game, 13, 67–68, 123–127, 129–131, 133–134, 140–144. *See also* principled entrepreneurs always seek to create win-win solutions (Pillar 4)

About the Author

Photo credit: Michelle Widmer-Schultz

Andreas Widmer is the founder and director of the Art & Carlyse Ciocca Center for Principled Entrepreneurship at The Catholic University of America's Busch School of Business where he loves to teach and mentor students to find their true calling. Previously, Andreas helped lead high-tech companies, bringing more than one hundred leading-edge technology products to market and also led several organizations focused on enterprise solutions to poverty. He is a former member of the Swiss Guard serving under Pope John Paul II and author of the book *The Pope and the CEO*, which describes the ten lessons he learned from the late pope about leadership and the centrality of the human person in work. Andreas's biggest accomplishment in life is building a great marriage together with his wife, Michelle, and his biggest joy is seeing the character of their teenage son, Eli, develop and grow.

Andreas has a passion for helping professionals of all ages to find deeper meaning in their work and sustainable success in Principled Entrepreneurship. One way he does this is to discover and share the stories of successful Principled Entrepreneurs like Art Ciocca who overcame great challenges and built wonderful companies by never losing sight of their humanity. If you are interested to learn more about Andreas's work, or would like to engage him to speak, coach, write, or simply to share your own Principled Entrepreneurship story, he would love to hear from you at andreas-widmer.com.